Praise

"This book is a necessary remedy for any couple wanting to stay together and feel even more connected after a betrayal. It gives purposeful advice without shaming the betrayed or the betrayer. Its careful use of ideas around trust and forgiveness are unique in the contemporary world of affair repair. I would recommend this book to anyone experiencing infidelity."

TAMMY NELSON, PhD, AUTHOR OF *THE NEW MONOGAMY* AND *OPEN MONOGAMY*, HOST OF THE PODCAST *THE TROUBLE WITH SEX*

"To heal and rebuild a better, stronger partnership after an affair is a daunting task. In *Affair Repair*, Amanda shows you exactly how. This is truly a comprehensive step by step guide that normalizes complex emotions and charts the journey of growth and repair. You could not find a better guide!"

ELLYN BADER, PhD, CO-FOUNDER OF THE COUPLES INSTITUTE, CO-CREATOR OF THE DEVELOPMENTAL MODEL OF COUPLES THERAPY

AFFAIR REPAIR

Proven Strategies to Heal, Forgive,
and Rebuild LOVE after Infidelity

Amanda Deverich, LMFT

ISBN 979-8-9920715-0-4

For the couples who transformed, those who tried, and above all,
those who journey now.
With all my heart,
Amanda

Contents

Introduction

I am grateful you are reading this book. If you are reading *Affair Repair*, likely an affair has affected your life, and you are not sure what to do. This book can help. I wrote this guide for both partners: the one who was hurt by the affair, and the one who had the affair. You are going to need support individually and as a couple in a relationship. When an affair is discovered, two people are scared and unsure. I intend to help each of you overcome the hurt you have experienced and achieve what you may not believe possible. I have helped hundreds of couples and want to share my experience of what works with you.

I have been married, widowed, and professionally trained in nurturing relationships. I have worked with couples for weeks, sometimes years, to support them through the repair process, and witnessed turnarounds I never thought could happen.

This book is more of a step-by-step coaching tool than an emotional validation of what you already know. What you have in your hands is the culmination of lessons learned over more than a decade in private practice helping hundreds of couples overcome an affair and transform their marriage. There is no suggestion in this book that I have not tried and seen work. I hope your experience will be among them.

The current broken, standard course of couples counseling focuses on making the person who cheated express nothing but complete remorse, expose every action or thought of betrayal, and provide a never-ending expression of regret for the affair. This approach works for some, but not for all.

Affairs are remarkably common for an act that is considered the worst possible thing a person could do in a marriage. I am not saying affairs are okay because they are common, but if we continue to try to address affairs with black-and-white judgment and scarlet letter shame, our paths to healing and overcoming will be limited. We will be so brittle, we will break.

Some affairs are just another scar acquired on the front line of marriage. Some end the relationship with a fatal blow or are the end note of a long, slow death that has been dragging on for years. Some affairs, however, can be the catalyst to a whole new relationship. It is likely far too soon and painful to offer that promise of hope right now. Despite the initial instinct to divorce, *the reality is that many people stay together and overcome the affair.* This book is no guarantee, but can be a helpful guide to get through the crisis and transform your marriage.

The depth of pain due to an affair is known only to those who have been betrayed. A freshly betrayed client once shared, "I understood my ex was hurt when I cheated, but I had no idea the pain until I came home and caught my spouse in bed with her running partner." No truer words have been said. Some knowledge you cannot have until you have experienced it yourself.

Good people have affairs. A person who broke their vows has made a bad choice, but rarely have I encountered someone who had an affair *specifically* to hurt their partner. People who have affairs are not bad people. In fact, the partner involved in the affair is usually not thinking of their spouse in the moment at all. This is a painful, near unimaginable truth for the betrayed.

If you don't have a therapist, I would encourage you to find one. Find one who is pro-marriage but open minded. Shaming or issuing demands to either partner will not work in the long run. Find a counselor who does not try to tell you to end the marriage, or questions your decision to stay, but helps you be physically, emotionally, and financially safe as you decide what to do. Finding an experienced *couples* counselor is important. Individual counselors focus on personal fulfillment. Couples counselors know how to revive and sustain relationships so that both individuals thrive. Ask a potential therapist how long they have been working with couples. What is the focus of their work? Under what circumstances would they encourage divorce?

Find a counselor who will help you mend your relationship with a compassionate eye toward the experience of the person who was betrayed, the person who had the affair, and the relationship. The decision to have an affair is a failure in judgment; it is not necessarily a permanent character flaw. The repair process should help repair the relationship as well as support the person who had the affair to be authentic, not just repentant. If you feel the therapist isn't helping, get another therapist. Don't waste time going and then decide that therapy isn't for you. This book can help you navigate your experience.

In these pages I share every pattern, tip, trick, and strategy I have learned in helping couples overcome the devastating effects of an affair. Here you will find the affair repair process well described to help keep yourself safe, reestablish trust, and build toward a relationship you really desire.

I want your copy of this book to have so many highlights, underlinings, and notes in the margin that it looks like a worn-out workbook at the end of a middle school year. Here each of you will find guidance and encouragement on what to do next.

Chapter 1
Expect the Unexpected

I wrote this book for two people: the person who was hurt by the affair, and the person who had the affair. Your affair repair and marriage transformation journey will be shared and, at times, solo. Consider this book as your guide to your individual and relationship experience. Overcoming an affair and transforming your marriage is an intuitive dance of trust and hope. No two experiences are the same, but a way is known.

You two begin the journey as the **betrayed** and **betrayer**, who over the course of affair repair evolve into the **wounded** and **responsible partner**, then the **healing** and **repairing** partner, until ultimately, you both become **transformed** partners. A wounded partner can heal. A responsible partner can repair damage. Both of you can evolve and transform, whether you stay together or not. Be prepared for growth and healing. You can repair your relationship and yourself.

Ellie and Aaron's Bubble Bath Miracle

> Mark had found his soul mate in Ellie. It was not just her beautiful eyes, long brown hair and body he had come to know so well. It was her open heart, thoughtful attention, and awakened mind that had made him fall completely in love with her. Together they mapped out their five-year dream plan to travel the world.

They created an itinerary of exotic Airbnbs, hole-in-the-wall live music venues, and award-winning local cuisine. They envisioned spending late nights talking about his assignments as a journalist that would send him abroad, some of which she would accompany.

Ellie lit up when she talked about their future but darkened when she talked about her best friend, Aaron, her husband. Aaron and she had known each other since high school. They had been best friends for thirty years and married for eighteen. Throughout the first twenty years of their relationship Aaron and Ellie just enjoyed being in each other's company. They played games at the kitchen table, went for Sunday walks, and read to each other. Taking bubble baths together was one of their favorite rituals.

Aaron discovered the emails between Ellie and Mark, their neighbor. It was like a bomb blast in Aaron's heart, sending shockwaves of pain ripping him apart and bringing to rubble what was once a safe reality. Aaron had taken for granted that Ellie would always be there, as she had been through hours and hours of work and several seasons of baseball where she had been benched in another room while he decompressed in front of the TV. The friendship-turned-marriage had been abandoned. For five years or more, Ellie had felt as Aaron did now: ignored, alone, and wondering how their solid foundation had dissolved to empty nothingness.

Aaron had ignored her pleas for attention and connection. He admitted he had muted her requests for emotional and physical intimacy. He gave everything to work and came home exhausted, collapsing in front of the TV for evening- and weekend-long baseball and beer binges. For a while, Ellie entertained herself. Then she met Mark. The newness and attention were like water in a desert. The novelty and energy of someone interested in her awakened her indifferent heart.

Aaron was energized now, no longer interested in baseball games or naps on the couch. He loved Ellie. He knew she was his best friend and his soul mate, but now she was disconnected. The pain of the separation was devastating. Ellie was only moderately sad for that pain. She had suffered too much time in neglect, yearning for him, that her heart had sealed where the pain had been. The past several years showed her what she could have expected in the next ten, twenty … fifty years with Aaron.

Ellie could not imagine staying with him now. All thoughts of the future were filled with Mark. Ellie dreaded going to bed each night, fearing Aaron would reach out for her. Each night, Aaron fought the battle deep within his body not to touch her, to plead with her, and to promise things would change. (He had learned through our work together that this would not work.) It was excruciating. Everything in Aaron yearned to reconnect, but the door was closed. Aaron was devastated without Ellie and would do anything to repair. To his credit, he did.

Ellie needed space and time to think about what she wanted and what she would do. She valued the history of their relationship, Aaron's good character, and the family of four they had created together. She wanted to do the right thing, but she wasn't sure what that was. True to her own good character, Ellie did the hard work to understand the balance between "doing the right thing" and never going back to the emptiness she had escaped. Doing the right thing is not resigning yourself to a life of unhappiness.

Friends gave mixed advice. Some, including her mother, told her to "Do what makes you happy." Others, whom she respected more, counseled her to think harder but could offer no real hope on how or if things could really get better. "Sometimes the grass isn't greener" is not exactly encouragement when you are in a worn-down brown patch.

Ellie came to therapy. She was honest with herself and me that she was struggling. She acknowledged Aaron had been her best friend her entire life. They had gone to prom and graduated high school together. They went straight to work, saving money to buy a home. They built a home and had two great kids. They used to have long talks and take bubble baths together. More than half of her life had already been grafted with his. They were one.

Ellie acknowledged Aaron was awake now. He was doing everything she asked, including giving her space and not smothering her or making her feel more guilty. She knew he was suffering and saw how he took ownership of how he had neglected her, but she could not just make her emotions turn around. She had detached from Aaron and was now attached to Mark. The risk of returning to a new change from what had been bad for so long versus something that had never been bad seemed too great.

Aaron resisted the urge to smother Ellie; he took effective action. He gave her space and assumed full responsibility for how he had pushed her away. Still, she was not drawn back to the relationship. (She was not pushed away either.) Aaron made the hard changes she had asked for, but she no longer wanted them from him, nor did she trust they would last. Ellie was completely consumed by Mark, who had not ever let her down, and disconnected from Aaron, who had a long history of not nurturing the relationship. Her heart was looking the other way. Aaron persisted with everything he had. The magnetism of her lover and the unattractive memory of what the marriage had become were compounding forces pulling and pushing Ellie away from her marriage.

Still, she was there in my room, doing the difficult task of self-reflection and evaluation. Aaron followed all the strategies we discussed and continued to tweak his efforts, doing only the ones that worked and none of the ones that didn't. Love is worth fighting for, and underneath the rubble of their relationship, there was some very good foundation in their character and the history they had shared. Over the next eight months, the couple went through the greatest trial of their married life. Ellie maintained distance and they fought, having intense arguments long into the night. At one point, Ellie lost her wedding ring. It seemed like a sign. They were both devastated and exhausted.

Ellie went on a business trip and insisted Aaron not call her but agreed that once each night for just ten minutes they could talk to say good night. Aaron suffered wild imaginings as he struggled not to call her more often than agreed. He knew if he called her too much, she would turn away. He struggled with pain, doubt, anger, fear, and a longing of a magnitude you can only understand if you have been through it yourself. Ellie forced herself to be available for the phone call. She dreaded but answered the calls. She engaged in the conversation, despite her own desire to avoid discomfort, guilt, and forced feelings. The stilted, painful interaction pattern continued for months, each making some accommodation to give the marriage a chance. Aaron desperately wanted it to succeed; Ellie was doing it out of duty. Their talks continued, and trust began to be rebuilt. There was a tentative trust that Aaron would put Ellie's needs first and a tentative trust that Ellie was reexperiencing the good relationship they once had.

Then one day Ellie found her lost wedding ring at the bottom of the laundry hamper. She came to therapy with a cautious smile. She was still not ready to give up her dream of traveling the world with an attentive partner, but maybe Aaron really had changed. He had been spending more time with her and not in front of the TV. He was not pressuring her but was consistently present. Aaron knew his wife; he could see her slowly and cautiously turning toward him, which was what he deeply wanted more than anything else. He did not pressure.

Slowly Ellie was considering, but nowhere was she near recommitted. Agonizingly, Aaron waited, yearning for her to return to him, all the while resisting his desire to punish or plead. At that time, I had no idea what was happening, but now I can clearly identify the process. If in the beginning we had demanded Ellie apologize and spend more time with Aaron as traditional affair repair advice suggests, Ellie would have shut down. If Ellie had not taken responsibility for her betrayal or ignored her needs out of guilt, they would not have succeeded. I have learned through Ellie and Aaron and other couples what treatment is needed at what time. Like a bone that has been broken, a medical professional knows what to do but does not actually control how the cells activate and repair. Sometimes complications arise. Not all bones can repair; some are too compromised, but the healing process can be supported and influenced. No two couples are alike, but there are patterns and responses that work. I know that process and want to share it with you.

The foundational love Ellie and Aaron had, survived the bomb blast of the affair. They did not stop at overcoming the pain and rebuilding trust. They transformed their marriage with purposeful action. They claimed what they wanted. They listened, learned, and acted on that knowledge. Ellie would not be left alone. Aaron wanted a partner who wanted him. Neither compromised. Aaron was sure to make time for Ellie, and Ellie was sure to tell him how much he meant to her. Sexually they were a match, and once they were emotionally reattached, their sex life came back with a flourish. Each got what they wanted and more.

According to their own report, their marriage is better than ever. They spend time, accomplish goals, and enjoy their family as best friends. Above all, they still take bubble baths together to this day.

Chapter 2
Stop! Do Not Divorce.

Some of you reading this may be thinking, "What? Do not divorce?" Others of you may be relieved because divorcing is not what you want to do right now anyway. Regardless of which way you are leaning, if you are reading this book, you are unsure. An affair sends marriages to the therapist's emergency room, like a couple involved in a life-threatening car crash. I don't know what will happen, but I know what can happen. I have treated many affairs and know that all cases are unique in their own way. However, as in medicine, there is a general course of action with useful interventions to speed up recovery and prevent total loss in the event of a setback. Unless you are in imminent danger, take a moment to assess what can be done to repair your relationship. There is a path to healing.

Any reason is a good reason to hesitate in divorcing. I am adamant in taking advantage of an opportunity to put a pause between stimulus (affair) and response (divorce), so that a more thoughtful decision can be made. Sometimes divorce is the answer, but there may be other answers, and I hope to help you get there. Noble motives such as guilt, staying together for the children, or proving you have tried everything are great reasons to try to repair the relationship. Less noble goals such as avoiding financial loss, maintaining social standing, or having no place else to go are just as good—provided no abuse is happening. (If you are unsure if your relationship is abusive or need help getting out, don't wait. Seek professional individual counseling and get help now.) Other acceptable reasons for staying and working on the relationship are fear of failure or fear of what happens next. These reasons should not be considered traps, but the backstop from which you move forward.

Stephanie and Chuck Part 1

Stephanie and I had been working together for almost two years to help her move past the midlife crisis affair her husband had with a staff member of his political campaign. Stephanie was vibrant, athletic, active, and a loyal supporter of his career. He was her first lover, and they had been married for more than thirty-five years. Their two adult children were married and starting families of their own. Stephanie and Chuck had invested in their family, his career, and each other. They were one, until Stephanie discovered the affair.

She demanded it end and threatened to ruin him. He agreed. Chuck's betrayal devasted her. She had invested completely in what she thought was their shared life. She had held up her end to what she understood to be the bargain of complete sacrifice for family and a happily ever after together. She had been all-in, going for the gold. Chuck's step outside the relationship left her feeling used and less-than worthy. It felt like a punch to the gut. She had been taken for everything she had—emotionally, physically, and energetically. Her entire life force of time, youth, and efforts had been invested in their life together. And now, she had been rewarded with a hollow second place finish.

Stephanie was working to overcome the emotional devastation of his affair. A true fighter, she wanted to regain the rewards of their hard work and see their retirement dreams come true. She had always said she would leave if Chuck ever cheated, but now there was too much on the table, and in truth, she still loved him. She was willing to try but was going to keep herself safe and hold him accountable.

Once Chuck ended the affair, Stephanie agreed to stay but had the photo evidence locked in a safe, should she ever have to sue for divorce. She wanted her investment to pay off, if nothing else, financially. But what she really wanted was his love again. She wanted the attention he had given another woman. His love was the real goal, but if she could not have that, she would at least keep the material gains they had made together over the years. She made me promise that if he cheated again, I would hold her accountable for leaving.

I have been working with couples for more than a decade, coaching them through communication gridlock, emotional outbursts, parenting failures, addiction, debilitating depression, crushing anxiety, and invasive in-laws, but there is no challenge so great to the life of a relationship as an affair—especially when the transgression repeats.

One day I was surprised and happy to see Chuck come into my office with Stephanie. This was an opportunity to further support the couple in their healing journey! They had a long history, new grandkids, and the pay-off of a successful career to enjoy. He had been her first love, and they had accomplished so much. Chuck sat down on the couch, frozen like a deer in the headlights of an oncoming pickup truck. "He did it again," Stephanie said.

He had cheated. The love between them had been betrayed again. I felt his visceral, frozen panic of impending doom as he shut down, accepting his well-earned fate of losing everything, including Stephanie.

If you have been betrayed by an affair, your first instinct will likely be to divorce. Not one person I have met stepped up to the altar and thought to themselves, *I will stay with this person if they break this sacred vow.* Most people, when they learn of an affair, think *I would never put up with that*—until they find themselves in that exact situation. Affairs are not the norm but are common.

- Fewer than half of marriages will suffer an affair. (Approximately 30–40 percent.)
- Half of the affairs that occur will never be known.
- Of the affairs that are known, most will be discovered, some will be disclosed.
- Of the affairs that are disclosed, most will be within one week to a month—unless you are married. Being married delays disclosure due to the painful risk of divorce.

You might think avoiding disclosing the affair is self-serving, but in my experience, not wanting to lose a marriage is a sign of placing high value on the marriage and not wanting to hurt the betrayed partner. The marriage is in some way more important than the affair. The affair may be exciting and energizing, but the marriage is a foundation not easily discarded. The cheating partner has placed a value on the marriage, though if you are the betrayed, you will wonder where that "value" was when they were having an affair. Unless you are married to a true narcissist (which in fact is fewer than approximately five percent of the population), your partner has made a mistake. If you find yourself in this rare category of being married to a narcissist, seek treatment with a specialized therapist. Most cheating partners are not narcissists but people making bad decisions for a variety of reasons.

I knew Stephanie truly loved Chuck and that their marriage was fundamentally compatible, despite his current midlife crisis. I could see he was frozen in fear. Generally, Chuck was not a fan of therapy, and if he had not wanted to come, he would not have. Stephanie could hold sway, but if this man had truly been without moral character or indifferent to her, he would not have bothered to come to meet his fate. He was there to take accountability, though he was scared and conflicted. That demonstration of character, their long-shared history of a good life together, and the care for her in showing up was something to work with. Professionally, I could see a way to mend, but it would be a lot of work.

Most Affairs Do Not Last

Most affairs end, even if the marriage dissolves. Only a small percentage of men marry their affair partners, and of those who do, approximately 75 percent get divorced. Most affairs last a year or two. Some only days or less than a month. Very few last longer than four years. Affairs do not solve the underlying issue. Unhappiness is not always the cause of an affair. Sometimes the marriage—and the sex life—are just fine.

Staying committed to one partner is not easy. Human beings always want more. There is a concept known as *hedonic adaptation*, where we achieve some pleasure then adapt to that new level of enjoyment. Soon that level will be the baseline, and we seek more. Sometimes an affair is a distraction from the baseline of life. Now is the opportunity to work on what makes a person seek an affair and resolve the root issues.

Once a Cheat, Always a Cheat?

This is sometimes true, but not always. Most often, another affair happens because the core issue has not been worked out. That core issue lies first in the betrayer, who must work to identify what needs are not being met and learn how to fulfill them without compromise. Fulfilling those needs might include divorce or ongoing demand for change in productive ways.

Stephanie and Chuck Part 2

I did not tell Stephanie to leave Chuck. She loved him, did not want to be hurt again, and did not want to lose everything she had dedicated her life to building. Chuck was present, conflicted, unsure, but willing. He was unsure if he wanted to stay in his marriage, unsure if he wanted to leave. Both were unsure if Stephanie was willing to forgive him. He was willing to take responsibility. He was willing to do the work.

As a couples counselor, my client is the marriage. I work to make relationships healthy for both parties. If there is a willingness to work on the marriage, there is hope. Stephanie was conflicted. Chuck was conflicted. Both were hurting and in my room for a reason and for guidance.

This was Chuck's second breach of trust, so in one way, some of the work on how to handle the crisis was already done, and in another, the setback was all the greater and more damaging. The work of knowing how to check his whereabouts and his intentions was already established. She knew how to put a tracker on his car, and he knew how to share the passcodes to the phone and computer.

Chuck knew he needed to rededicate to being communicative about his whereabouts and that honesty was the fastest way to trust. He knew he was struggling with a midlife crisis and that Stephanie was the right choice for him. The burden of being under constant scrutiny was the weight he was willing to bear to recover his marriage and keep himself true to who he really wanted to be.

Stephanie knew how to keep herself safe—but that did not mean she felt safe. She kept the evidence in a vault in the event of a messy divorce, planned a financial exit, and worked to gain further insight into her own emotions and needs. The work they had done in the first attempt at affair repair significantly sped up the second.

Stephanie and Chuck had not done so well the first time due to limited emotional insight and expression which hampered their ability to be intimate with each other. Stephanie had spent a lifetime detaching from her feelings in service to their mutual career and family goals. Chuck, too, followed the script, succeeding without really being emotionally connected to himself, let alone Stephanie.

The couple committed to emotional honesty and many difficult discussions. Stephanie extracted the contrition she needed to know Chuck was all in. She needed to feel that he felt her pain and that he was reconnecting to her completely. This was more than a surface level pact; this was a deep dive in connection. This process took months, not sentences to accomplish.

More than ten years later, I happened to see the couple walking hand in hand, sunglasses and smiles, with the light shining behind them. I saw them, they did not see me. I could only witness the glow they were living, but in some way I could feel the warmth from afar. If Stephanie (and I as her therapist) had given up on the relationship, and Chuck failed in his ability to rise to be the man of integrity he could be, they would have lost everything: their retirement, world traveling, shared celebrations with their grandchildren, and most of all an abiding love and friendship of more than forty years.

Key Concepts

- **Don't divorce yet.** The pain of an affair is overwhelming, and Western society says divorcing is what you should do, but in fact, many people work through the affair.
- **Any reason, short of being trapped by abuse, is a good reason** to give the relationship a chance. Staying for the kids, out of guilt, or in fear of what will happen is as good as any backstop to give yourself a moment to reflect and work on repair.
- **Most affairs do not last** according to research. Do not overvalue the importance of the affair relationship.
- **You never know what either of you will do or what will happen.** Even the seemingly most hopeless cases can repair.

Chapter 3
Can't We Just Move On?

Once the affair has ended you both may be tempted to just move on. If you have been betrayed, you may want to forgive and forget, rushing to return to life as you knew it. This is not possible. Life as you knew it is no longer. For the person who ended the affair, the problem is in the past. However, the hurt for your partner lingers on. Work must be done.

Size Doesn't Matter

A one-night stand can hurt as long as a five-year love affair. For couples trying to work through a betrayal of any size, it is better not to try to scale the affair as "not that bad." It is not possible to establish a grading scale where a one-night stand can be measured against an on-again/off-again office relationship four years ago. For some, sexting with an anonymous person is the same as hooking up. The incremental increase in pain in discovering an illegitimate child versus a longstanding love affair over decades is impossible to measure. Don't argue over definition; it's abstract and pointless. Focus on meaning. Whether the affair involved pictures or penises, you would not be the first to separate—or stay together—upon discovery and you will not be the last.

Affairs of the Past

Joan and Walter: An Affair of the Past

Joan fell in love with the neighbor, Roger. Their affair was passionate and intense. The scandal of the town in the 1970s, Joan left her husband, Walter, and their three children. For two years, Roger promised to leave his wife and join her, but he could never bring himself to do it. Joan returned to Walter, who forgave her. It was difficult, but the couple renewed their wedding vows and remained married for sixty-one years, the last three of which were devasting for Joan. As Walter succumbed to ever deepening stages of dementia, he became more and more aggressive toward her.

Joan and Walter had not attended counseling after the affair; they fought their way back together through perseverance, character, and a foundation of commitment. Walter loved Joan. Joan loved Walter, though her path had led her to stray. Their marriage, like a broken leg, had been reset without professional intervention, and now the imperfect repair was giving way.

The long-ago betrayal rose to the surface as Walter's faculties diminished. Joan was devastated. He would not let her care for him. She was being rejected with no recourse. Years of good memories, loyalty, and caring since they renewed their vows were discarded. Now with dementia, there was no way to do the repair work they had skipped so many decades ago.

Sometimes time is the healer, but the original wound can fester or be reinjured years later. I have worked with couples who were decades into their marriage and the affair of fifty-two years ago is coming up today. Past circumstances may have prevented couples from addressing the wound of betrayal. Affairs may have been normalized. Society may have stigmatized therapy. Some partners may have had no other means of support, or their moral code prevented them from considering divorce. Too many couples bury the hatchet and move on, acting as if forward functioning is complete healing. The partners move forward as very good but sad and wounded actors. Moving past the affair is a sign of dedication and strength but healing should be complete for both partners.

There is no time limit for addressing the pain of an affair, but there is a limit to the amount of punishment. Endless punishing does nobody good. The punishment may be a temporary relief for the betrayed and sometimes the betrayer, but over time it becomes empty and detrimental. The goal is healing, not punishment or an ongoing experience of pain. Being stuck unable to process the pain of an affair because it happened in the past is punishment.

Expressing suppressed hurt and anger is not a punishment; it is an act of healing. Addressing an affair of the past will not keep you stuck revisiting old wounds over and over again but will help you properly process so you can move forward and know what to do when the old wound begins to throb again. This book can help a couple do the work that wasn't done then.

Forget Forgiveness for Now

If the affair has been recently discovered or remains excruciatingly painful, forget forgiveness for now. Asking someone to forgive an affair too soon is like asking someone who just had their legs broken to run a marathon and hand you the finisher medal. Don't rush to forgiveness too soon. If the driving force is to focus on forgiveness, it is likely out of the betrayed partner's fear of further abandonment, the betrayer's impatience to get past this, and discomfort for everyone. People naturally want to feel safe, and forgiveness is one of the keys, but it cannot be forced.

Too often I hear therapists rush the process, pushing forgiveness before the betrayed has really felt heard. The therapist and the betrayer are likely tired of hearing the complaining. I am sure the betrayed is tired of the pain. I am not encouraging ongoing wallowing or punishing but facilitating healing. Allow the pain to be voiced before suggesting forgiveness.

You cannot forgive if you have not fully understood what has happened. What would you be forgiving? Often the person who was betrayed wants to know everything. In some cases, the betrayed does not want the gory details of the truth; they just want to know it will never happen again and move forward. This is rare, and it is up to the betrayed—not the betrayer, family members, or therapists—if that is the path they would like to take.

Do not withhold forgiveness if you feel it. Withholding forgiveness, like giving it too quickly, is done out of fear. Betrayed partners may manage fear with control. Withholding forgiveness maintains control. Withholding can look like ongoing punishment of the betrayer for the affair. Withholding can also look like complete cutoff. Punishing or cutting off keeps the betrayed emotionally safe by not having to deal with the fear and pain, but thwarts healing.

Some betrayed partners will move quickly to forgiveness because they already know they love their betraying partner more than anything. They want to forgive, to help the betraying partner overcome resistance to reconnecting. Forgiveness can happen in steps and takes time.

Like the healing of that broken leg, we don't know exactly how the cells repair the bones, but we know that they do, and it takes time. We know some things to do and some things not to do. You cannot rush healing from an affair; you can support it. Forgiveness comes at its own pace.

Mara and Greg Forget Forgiveness for Now

Mara threw her wedding rings in the trash. This was the third affair of her husband Greg's she had discovered in 17 years. He picked the rings out of the rotting leftovers, stopped his philandering, and begged her to stay. Mara did not put her wedding rings back on but unleashed her wrath nonstop for the next four years. She was in agony but could not bring herself to go. A previous therapist had worked with her for over a year, trying to help her to leave. Her fury was unrelenting. Both were struggling. I wondered if her punishing was insatiable and unhealthy for both Mara and Greg.

Despite the atmosphere of negativity, they both wanted to remain in the relationship. Greg forgot forgiveness for now and focused on self-understanding and personal growth as he attended to the pain he had caused his wife. He felt he deserved her rage; he had not lived to the standard of the person he wanted to be and willingly endured her passionate anger until she was able to trust the relationship once again.

Greg received no support from Mara in confessing to his self-discovered shortcomings. She would not forgive him for now. Personal growth and accountability were Greg's struggle. Mara's struggle was to regain a sense of safety with him and to overcome her shame and anger with herself loving him despite it all.

Greg did not waiver in his commitment. One day on their way out to dinner with friends, Mara risked putting her rings back on—with no promises. Greg was encouraged but guarded. Soon thereafter Greg had a battle with prostate cancer which drew out the nurturing commitment deep within Mara. Ultimately, after much pain and punishment for both, Mara forgave herself and allowed her heart to love him again.

Forgiveness comes when the betrayed partner fully understands what happened, what caused it, and how things have changed. The betrayed partner must know they are safe, and the pain will not happen again. This may mean leaving the relationship if necessary. Like Mara, the betrayed must also come to the final acceptance that the affair cannot be undone and be ready to move forward. When the betrayed partner feels safe enough and confident enough, they will be in a place to offer forgiveness.

Forgiveness is given. True forgiveness cannot be taken, demanded, or expected. In forgiving, both partners must overcome a wounding of pride. The pride of the betrayed has been wounded by the undeserved cheating and the choice to stay despite it. The pride of the betrayer is wounded, in that they must acknowledge their failure and accept what cannot be undone. Forgiveness is a shared, humble experience.

Confessing an Affair

Confessing an affair is not a bad idea. First, carefully consider the purpose and value of disclosure. Many betrayed partners would like to know if an affair has happened, but not all. If you are disclosing an affair, it should be for the benefit of the relationship. Do not use an affair to force the hand of your partner. Hurting your partner so badly they want to leave is basically forcing them to do the hard work you were unable to do. If you want out and an affair has happened, please exit with dignity. Ask for divorce first. Divorce is painful, betrayal worse.

If you are considering confessing your affair to absolve the guilt you feel, please think twice. Your partner is not your confessor. If you are more concerned about relieving your guilt than healing the wound to your partner, you are rolling the dice for a self-centered motive. You will forever change your partner, and you may lose your marriage. Your partner is not your priest or therapist. Your partner is betrayed and may respond unpredictably. I cannot promise what your partner will do, but I can help you prepare for best outcomes to move toward repair and transformation should you decide you want to disclose the affair.

If you are unsure of your motive or whether your partner would want to know, consider writing a long letter that can be dated with electronic verification or a sealed, stamped envelope. Give yourself time to think about the disclosure but take advantage of these days to document your thoughts and actions. Your memory will fade especially over time and under duress. Your thinking ahead will demonstrate your sincerity in wanting to repair the relationship, not to avoid responsibility. Your writing should express but not focus on your remorse. Be sure your letter includes your love for your partner, the reasons why you chose not to disclose the affair (including lack of courage if that is applicable), the reasons why you ended the affair, and every detail of the affair you can remember. Include how, when, and where you met. Document dates, times, and money spent.

The purpose of your writing is to be prepared for the affair repair journey you will go on once the affair is revealed. Your forgetting of even the littlest detail will be painful, infuriating, and disorienting to your partner once the questioning begins. Small details are critical datapoints that will help your partner heal as they begin to piece things together. What your partner thought was real was not. They cannot trust your words. The document demonstrates what was real. Absent data, what your partner imagines, is often worse than what was reality. Data is a truth that can be trusted. Be prepared if you are going to confess an affair. Truth and verifiable facts provide a more stable foundation and advance your chances of repair.

If an affair has happened and you want to confess the relationship because your partner is the type of person who would want to know, you are the type of person who wants to take responsibility at all costs, or the affair will certainly be discovered, take courage! Though difficult, there is a path to repair and transform the relationship, which includes a new you and a new partner. The greatest pain in the process will be sustained by your betrayed partner, and you will play a critical, challenging role in the healing. You will need all the strength, patience, and love you have. Though I am encouraging you to have heart, I am warning you, it will be painful.

The first step is to tell your partner you cheated. It is best to tell your partner in person. Your partner will be able to pick up on your sincerity by your words, tone, body language, and energetic presence. Pick a time and place that is safe and unhurried. A weekend walk or therapist's office are good examples. Avoid birthdays, holidays, right before bed or going to work. Be succinct and clear that you betrayed your partner and that you want to repair it. "Honey, I have something difficult to tell you.

I have had an affair, and I want to repair our relationship." Too often we say things at the wrong time out of our inability to hold the pain or guilt, not because it is the best timing for our partner.

Be open and defenseless, but do not accept abuse. Affirm your desire to repair and be as honest as possible in response to any questions asked. Be prepared for a long discussion. The key is honesty and presence. Read ahead in this book so you will know what to expect and how to engage in the healing process. The path to healing is challenging but known. Transformation is possible.

Key Concepts

- **Size doesn't matter** when it comes to affairs. Rather than argue it is not as bad as it could have been, focus on the pain that exists.
- **Affairs of the past** are emotional wounds that were not completely healed but shoved down, moved past, or ignored. These wounds can fester and burst when touched. Do the work now that was not done then.
- **Forget forgiveness for now.** Some partners will rush to forgiveness, seeking a return to normalcy and immediate repair. Allow the time for amends to be made, trust to be established, and the relationship to be rebuilt.
- **Confessing an affair** should be considered carefully. Confess an affair if you are seeking the best interests of the betrayed partner, not for forgiveness to remove your sense of guilt. Be succinct and sincere in your confession. Remain dedicated to the healing process.

Chapter 4
Two Paths, One Journey

Like a bomb, the discovery of an affair sends everyone running. Both partners find themselves without a plan. The person involved in the affair, who had been trying to prevent detonation, is caught in the explosion. The person who was betrayed is shocked with no control over what is happening. Both people are scared, trying to save themselves, and unsure if they want to run toward their partner or away. Most people want to return to the last safe place they knew which was the peace that came before. Even the normal bad days that came before were better than the chaos they are experiencing now.

As the dust of destruction floats in the air, the couple begins to make amends. Early repair attempts often look like the person involved in the affair taking 100 percent responsibility for everything out of guilt and ignoring their own emotional needs. Or the betrayed partner may rush to forgiveness, shoving down their own hurt and fear to put things back together. Neither scenario will lead to a secure relationship. The betrayed and betrayer must be guided to safety.

Both partners need help in the aftermath. Generally, the overwhelming pain of the betrayed partner takes priority, but without support the betrayer may not be able to be part of the healing process. Helping the person involved in the affair maintain calm, be authentic, and find courage is crucial to affair repair. The person who was betrayed needs the full presence of their partner. It is not easy to be calm, authentic and courageous in the face of so much pain and destruction. Nor is it easy to put your world back together when your life just blew up out of your control. The betrayed and the betrayer have unique intertwined paths on the healing journey.

The Path for the Betrayed

As the betrayed partner, the world you knew just ended. You are flooded with love and hate upon discovery of the affair. You may have only love or only hate that overwhelms you. Your first thought is self-protection. Then you begin to weigh the cost and benefit of ending the relationship. Do you leave even though you have children? Do you leave even though you have built an entire life together? Do you leave out of self-respect even though you love them? Do you leave even though you have no means to support yourself?

You go between confusion and clarity with each painful trigger or peaceful moment. Your rage may be so great you cannot breathe. You may want nothing—or everything—to do with affair repair. You may want to confront the affair partner and smear their reputation. Or you may just want to emotionally shut down and leave. You may want to show your partner you can be what they need. These are examples of fight, flight, freeze, or fawn survival responses. (Fawning is people pleasing to prevent further harm. It is a survival strategy.) These fight, flight, freeze or fawn responses are in your body, which is messing up your mind. You literally cannot think straight.

You may feel shame, not wanting anyone to know. You may discover that others knew all along, making the humiliation worse. You wonder if they are laughing at or pitying you; neither feels comfortable, and you had no chance to protect yourself. Many people wonder how someone could stay with a partner who cheated. *How weak!* they may think. *I would never tolerate that.* You yourself may have thought that once. Now that you are in the situation, you understand more. You understand conflicting, paralyzing emotions. It's not so cut and dry.

You can shut everything down and leave, or you try to heal.

If you think of your partnered friends, the famous, and the not-so-famous, many have stayed despite betrayal. Very likely, friends you know have survived affairs that you do not know about. There is a path to overcoming the trauma of an affair. Your path has two parts: one is to heal from the pain of betrayal and regain a sense of safety (whether you stay with your partner or not). The other is to define and work toward a marriage you want.

You will need guidelines for:

- dealing with the discovery of each new bit of information.
- managing the body's ongoing response to the trauma and its effect on your ability to relate.
- navigating difficult and authentic conversations with your partner.
- establishing a sense of trust in the relationship without feeling a need to control.
- transforming your relationship into something you desire.

The Path for the Betrayer

Your affair has been discovered. You may feel relieved or be grieving at the possible loss of the affair, marriage, or both. You may feel frozen. You are not sure what to do. You do not want to hurt your partner further, but you also do not want to hurt your affair partner. You feel guilty and conflicted.

Something about the affair was attractive or it would not have happened in the first place. You may have grown emotionally, intellectually, or physically apart from your partner. The affair may have happened in a moment of weakness or something you had been trying to avoid. You may feel so dried up or resentful inside that you are clear the affair was something you needed and wanted. The affair partner may have met some or all of those needs.

Now that the affair has been revealed and things have blown up, you must sort through the rubble. What do you keep? What do you let go of? What do you rebuild? Who do you rescue? Who do you protect? What about you? Likely a part of you just wants to run away.

Normal human beings caught in an affair are influenced by a sense of guilt and doing the right thing. Sometimes there is a self-protective mechanism that deflects the guilt. This is normal, too. You will wrestle within yourself wondering how you betrayed your own inner ideal, yet you understand what feelings motivated you to engage in the affair. It is possible to feel incredibly sad about the pain you caused and still have a need for happiness.

You may have thought you just wanted out of your marriage after years of struggling within it. Now, in the aftermath of discovery, you are questioning your motivations and thought processes. You likely don't know what you really want. The stress is overwhelming. Now is the time for you to do the hard inner work of understanding yourself and honoring in the end what you really want. Your old marriage is gone. You are not going back.

If you want a healthy marriage with your partner, it can happen. If you are unsure about your marriage, but know you want to heal the hurt you caused, the journey begins the same. The path has two parts. One is to show up for the partner you betrayed and the other is to discern your needs. Healing will require courage to make it happen for yourself and your partner.

You will need guidelines for:

- knowing how to address the pain you caused your partner.
- assessing your own motives and actions.
- authentically communicating your needs and desires.
- establishing a sense of trust in the relationship without feeling controlled.
- transforming your relationship into something you desire.

Key Concepts

Once an affair is discovered, both partners are scared. The couple is launched upon an unknown journey. The experiences of each partner are separate and unique but intertwined and mutually affecting.

- In the beginning **both of you are in survival** mode.

- There is **not only a psychological, but a** *physiological* **response** to betrayal, pair-bonding, and reconnecting.
- **If you are the betrayed partner, you will need guidelines** to keep yourself safe as you re-engage in relationship and learn to trust.
- **If you are the betrayer,** the person who was involved with the affair, **you will need guidelines** to manage the intensity of emotions and work toward the relationship you really want.

Chapter 5
A Map for the Journey

Many couples have made the journey of healing. The trails are known and charted with shortcuts and pitfalls. Knowing what to expect and how to handle the challenges will increase your chances of success. **The map of affair repair and marriage transformation provides guidance for the person hurt by the affair, the person involved in the affair, and the couple as a unit.**

There are two parts to the map: affair repair and marriage transformation. Affair repair is the initial road you two will take to address the pain of discovery, repair the wound, and establish trust. Should you decide, you two will venture on to the mountains of marriage transformation where your relationship will evolve into one that is vibrant, mutually satisfying, and evergreen thanks to the new skills you have learned along the way.

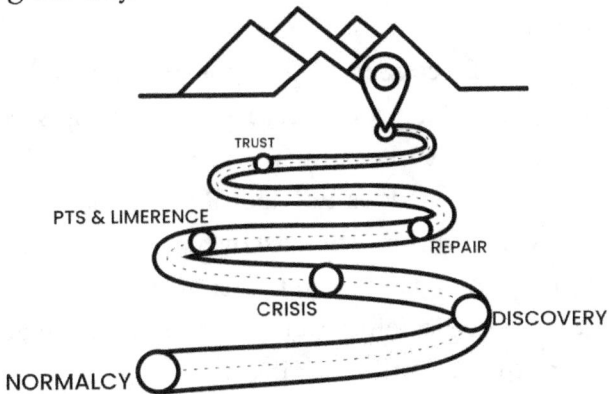

Road of Affair Repair Overview

Affair repair is a journey through six known phases plotted on the map of the road of affair repair:

1. Normalcy
2. Discovery
3. Crisis
4. Affair Post-traumatic Stress (PTS)/Affair Limerence
5. Affair Repair
6. Establishing Trust

The first phase of affair repair is called **normalcy**. Normalcy is the state of your relationship before the affair. If you are reading this book, normalcy is likely long gone. Your marriage may have been storybook perfect straight out of a romantic movie. Your relationship may have been volatile with poor communication, or, like Ellie and Aaron in the Bubble Bath Miracle story, you may have been best friends who drifted apart.

The quality of your relationship before the affair will influence, but not determine, your healing journey. Affairs happen in good marriages. Ellie and Aaron had a history of friendship that shored them up through the affair repair process. If normalcy in your marriage included angry outbursts, you will need to focus on managing emotions as you journey forward together. If normalcy was an atmosphere of cool distance, you will be challenged to be vulnerable and present to reconnect. A good marriage and a poor one can improve.

The second phase, **discovery**, begins the moment the affair comes to light. Discovery is your proof positive, the texting screenshot, the walking in on the act, or the admission. Sometimes there is a **pre-discovery** experience that does not feel like normalcy. Pre-discovery is the foreshadowing within the discovery phase when suspicions arise and something seems amiss. Yet, there is no conclusive evidence. Sometimes the evidence is being overridden because the betrayed can't imagine or accept that an affair is going on.

Chelsea asked Farouk about the women's cotton underwear she found while unpacking his suitcase. "I don't want to come home exhausted from working overseas to be grilled by my wife!" he snapped and glared at her. She left the room and nothing more was said. There is an element of shock in discovery that prevents some people from processing the full meaning of what is happening.

As the shock of discovery wears off and more information is revealed, the pain of the third phase, **crisis,** begins. Crisis is when the body and mind begin to take in the meaning of the evidence before them. Crisis affects each of you for different reasons. If you are the person who was betrayed, you were caught by surprise and things are out of control. The relationship you thought would last forever is suddenly not what you thought. If you were the person involved in the affair, everything has changed with no safe harbor in sight.

The discovery and crisis phase rarely reveal all the truth. If you have been betrayed, you cannot get enough information. You must know how this happened and how to stop it from happening again. If you are the one caught in the affair, you don't know what to do to minimize further damage and get through the healing process as quickly as possible. The betrayed is so upset they cannot get enough information, nor can they take it all in. The betrayer is overwhelmed with everyone's out-of-control emotions and doesn't know what to do that would be effective. Both fear what comes next. The crisis phase is so physically and emotionally intense it cannot last. Your body will exhaust itself from the constant state of high alert and ultimately move to the next phase.

The fourth phase of affair repair is characterized by intense feelings of fight or flight that come and go uncontrollably. An affair is a trauma. Affair posttraumatic stress (**affair PTS**) is the trauma being reexperienced intermittently versus the constant flood of crisis. The person involved with the affair may feel they are well beyond the trauma now that discovery is over and the intensity seems to have calmed, but the betrayed person is still experiencing the trauma repeatedly and uncontrollably. The body and mind sound the alarm at the slightest trigger regarding the affair—and even every now and again just to be sure it is safe. This alarm will continue going off at real or perceived threats and occasionally as a drill to protect from further betrayal. This will continue until the trauma can be completely processed by the body and the brain. While both partners will be working together to address affair PTS, the person involved in the affair will be dealing with affair **limerence** (and disenfranchised grief.) Affair limerence is the longing that lingers for the affair partner and disenfranchised grief is the socially unacceptable feelings of loss over the affair.

Progression along the road of affair repair is in a general direction but not a straight line. Phases overlap, and sometimes you will move two steps forward and one back. Affair PTS can pop up in any phase post-discovery. *If you are aware of what you are experiencing, you can more efficiently address the challenge.* Affair PTS is difficult to defuse without knowledge and awareness. This book will help you.

You as a couple must learn to handle the affair PTS symptoms before you can move to the next phase, **affair repair**. In the affair repair phase, couples sort through the wreckage of the aftermath and work to put things back together. The affair repair process is not neat and clean. Sometimes the affair continues while things are sorted out, like Aaron and Ellie in the Bubble Bath Miracle story. Aaron had to hold back his own pain while he waited for Ellie to sort out what she wanted. If you are the one caught in the affair, you may be sorry, but that is rarely the only feeling you have. Likely you have mixed emotions or are unsure if you want to repair the relationship. You may even feel forced. If you are the partner who has been betrayed, you may want to leave but feel stuck financially or because of the kids. Or you may want to forgive but are too fearful to risk further hurt.

In affair repair you will have long talks, examine every detail, exhaust yourselves in truth-telling, and above all, experience authentic emotional connection. It will not be easy. In the affair repair phase, you as a couple begin to work together to understand what happened, what needs to mended, and what is needed to go forward. The joint effort of sorting and making sense is the shared history that lays a new foundation for going forward. In the affair repair phase, things begin to settle but neither partner is secure.

The last phase, **establishing trust**, is when you reinforce your new hard-earned, understanding of reality and keep it safe. In this phase you will test and retest your relationship. Establishing trust is a phase where you each demonstrate skill in handling affair PTS, difficult truths, and emotions. Establishing trust is proving with consistency that the relationship will be different going forward for both partners. Together you will identify and practice concrete, trust-but-verify strategies. You will show each other consistent behaviors of communication, mutual nurturing, and change. The betrayed must be able to trust they will not be hurt again. The betrayer must be able to trust hope is possible for a better future.

An affair is a **transformative experience**, one that changes who you are, what you think about the world and how you approach it. Surviving cancer is a transformative experience. In surviving cancer, you gain insight and strength you did not anticipate. You no longer see the world as you did before. Once the discovery of an affair occurs, the fundamental perspective for both of you changes. The world shifts. You may have cheated and had thought you would never cheat. You may have thought you would be caught but were not sure what that would look like. The reality of discovery is more intense and unknown than imagined. If you were the betrayed partner, you may have thought you would never stay if you were cheated upon. Yet here we are. Now faced with the reality, it is more complicated. Be kind and patient with your process as an individual and a couple. Whatever your response to the transformative experience, may it be brave, healthy, and creative.

Marriage transformation is the ongoing work of living happily ever after. Marriage transformation has been happening all along in the earlier phases of affair repair. You learned to improve communication, deepen your understanding of each other, and strengthen your ability for behavior change. Without awareness you have taken steps toward transformation. If you are doing the work of affair repair now, take heart. The journey is hard, very hard, but you can reach your destination.

Mountains of Marriage Transformation Overview

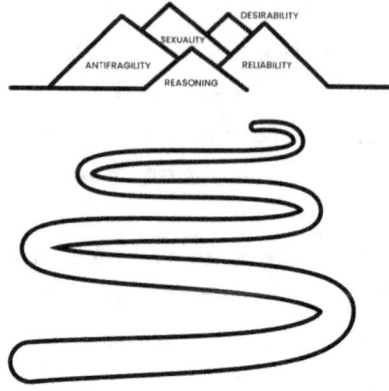

Upon arrival at marriage transformation, you will understand your own **transformation of reasoning**. You will become aware your way of reasoning has changed in unexpected ways based upon this experience. You have done things out of love, fear, panic, guilt, loyalty, and a host of other emotions you had not anticipated. You will come to know why the affair happened, why you stayed, or why you chose to leave.

Our couple from the Bubble Bath Miracle story made decisions they never thought they would. Ellie never thought she was going back. Aaron knew he loved Ellie despite the pain of the betrayal. He realized he could never again neglect Ellie while he tuned out on the sofa. He took responsibility for what he really wanted. Aaron had to counter his every instinct, which was to pursue and pressure Ellie to get her back. Ellie didn't think she was going back. However, through the affair repair process she saw she didn't have to leave. Her life could be better with Aaron. She could be forgiven, voice her needs, and trust Aaron to stay engaged. The affair repair process transforms reasoning in ways you could not have imagined. Now you know what you want and how to get it.

Marriage transformation brings new levels of emotional and physical intimacy through **transformation of reliability** *and* **desirability**. Ellie and Aaron's relationship became more reliable because they gained the skills to grow together. They learned how to handle affair PTS, have an affair repair conversation, and establish ongoing trust. Ellie and Aaron learned to communicate their wants and needs. Ellie did not want a partner who neglected her. Aaron did not want a partner who did not want him. The affair repair process helped transform their marriage into one they both desired.

Couples actively engaged in marriage transformation may also experience **transformation of sexuality**. Ellie and Aaron were sexually compatible, but the affair process deepened their partnership which only heightened their sexual intimacy. Some couples may capitalize on their newfound trust and communication skills to improve their sexuality.

> *Tonya and Brent had reestablished trust. Their marriage was reliable and desirable, but sex was routine. Tonya had always wanted something spicier, but she resented Brent's affair. Brent had discovered something new in himself and wanted to share it with Tonya, but for Tonya, it was hard to overcome the thought of the other woman. Tonya wondered why Brent had not discovered that side of himself with her. That wound had to be addressed. The affair repair process paved the way for safe, authentic communication and responding to each other's fears that broke open a new sex life for both.*

Successful completion of the healing journey leads to a **transformation of antifragility** in the relationship. Antifragility is not resilience, which is the ability to return to a previous state. Antifragility is the ability to grow. Antifragile couples confidently confront challenges together knowing it will only make them stronger. Confronting with confidence takes a history of success, which is what affair repair begins to build. When Brent and Tonya began exploring their sex life, Tonya was able to convert her insecurity to empowerment in the bedroom, releasing her own, true desire for great sex. The couple was not just resilient, helping Tonya feel better about herself. Together they transformed their relationship, creating more excitement.

When all areas of marriage transformation become your new normalcy, you have achieved **transcendent transformation**. In transcendent transformation you both experience wholeness, security, and adventure. You are confident in yourself, your partner, and your relationship to make any journey together. As an individual or a couple, if you have mastered the necessary skills of communication and authenticity you will transcend. Transcendent transformation is a lifetime goal. There is no end point. There is no summit where you can plant your flag and stop. Transcendent transformation goes with you as the next valley or vista on the map appears. Your arrival is a new level of being.

Affair Repair versus Marriage Transformation

Your efforts at affair repair and marriage transformation complement each other, but serve different purposes. Affair repair is a known path of general progression. You can't enter the establishing trust phase if your body is responding in crisis. Together you must come out of crisis to move forward. Marriage transformation is growth that occurs after discovery, bringing unforeseen insights and gifts to the relationship. Tonya needed to know she was the one Brent desired before she could unleash her inner tiger. The couple needed to work on affair repair before they could begin taking their sexuality to the next level. Ellie needed to know their marriage had transformed and she was no longer at risk of being abandoned for the TV before they could experience the marriage Aaron was ready for.

Knowing which challenge you are facing at any given moment can move your relationship faster along the map. Affair repair focuses on healing the affair wound. Marriage transformation focuses on developing a marriage worth having. Both must be achieved for your relationship to be reliable and desirable. Affair repair involves fact-finding, addressing the gut pain of the emotional wound, and finding a way to trust again. Marriage transformation deals with addressing what (if anything) was wrong in the marriage and how it can be better going forward. If Brent had not tended to Tonya's insecurity in affair repair and Aaron had not focused on marriage transformation with his consistent change in attentiveness, neither would have succeeded.

Affair repair and marriage transformation are two separate processes that can occur one before the other or at the same time. Most couples intuit what challenge they are working on. Things go off track when competing needs clash. Brent wanted better sex as soon as possible. Ellie wanted to know she was never going to be abandoned again. *Generally, the partner in the most pain will dictate which healing process is happening at any given time.* Most often the person in the most pain is the betrayed, which is why couples usually work first on affair repair and then marriage transformation.

> *Mara was in so much pain after discovering yet another of Greg's affairs she could not think. She was heartbroken and angry. All she could experience was anger, though deep down she still loved Greg. This made her angrier. For four years her rage protected her. He knew he loved her, too, and worked through affair repair, helping her release her anger. He also took the time to understand himself and the choices he had made, which was helpful to the process. The couple waited to begin focusing on marriage transformation.*

In the beginning of the healing process, most efforts are focused on affair repair, with occasional steps toward marriage transformation. Most likely you will begin with affair repair, then move back and forth between affair repair and marriage transformation, until the majority of your relationship is spent in marriage transformation. Affair repair can be a matter of months or years before moving to a marriage transformation discussion. It is important to know what you are working on at any given moment.

Out of Phase

Out of phase means you as a couple are working out of order on the map of affair repair and marriage transformation. The most common route is affair repair then marriage transformation. However, there is no *the* way, there is only *your* way. Like Ellie was, your partner may not be willing to work on affair repair without some hope that the marriage will transform to be reliable and desirable.

Some people who have been cheated on just cannot work out of phase. They feel it is an unjustifiable request; after all, they were the one who was betrayed! The rules of fairness say the person who had the affair is the one who should do the work of proving the relationship is worth the effort before making desirable changes. Reality is rarely ideal. Working out of phase is not ideal, but it happens often and can be successful.

If you would like, it is okay to move forward to prove your marriage can be better, as Aaron did. This work can take months or years. Ellie dragged her feet before giving Mark up and turning back toward Aaron. She needed to know the marriage would be different. She had to trust that he would pay attention to her and not just when baseball season was over. It took nearly a year before she believed Aaron had changed. Then she could give herself back to him.

I would not recommend a betrayed partner take the extreme risk of offering love unless they know they are all in, can survive potential failure, and that the changes they are about to make are something they want in their life. It is a bad idea to pretend you like working out, having more sex, or some other stretch beyond uncomfortable into uncharacteristic. You are better off not making changes that sacrifice the real you in the end. Working out of phase within limits can be very successful.

Affairs of the Past

Affairs of the past should be repaired and benefit from any out of phase work already done. Affairs of the past have been buried in an unmarked grave over time. Beneath the years of child rearing, career building, or stoic silence, the bones lie. Many couples did not go to counseling due to generational norms, stigma, personal prejudice, lack of education, or availability.

Farouk achieved his ambitious goals and evolved to be a present, involved partner. Farouk respected and cherished Chelsea, his partner, wife, and mother of their children. He and Chelsea found their way, accepting and appreciating each other. After the wedding vows of their youngest child were exchanged, Chelsea regained her voice and confronted Farouk about the under- wear she had found in the suitcase. At first Farouk bristled and brushed it off. This time Chelsea was persistent. Farouk did not want to revisit the immaturity of their early years. He wanted to shove down those missteps they had overcome and focus on how their marriage was now. It was true, their marriage had transformed, but the wound remained and the pain in Chelsea's eyes moved him. Not all couples who skip affair repair transform their marriage like Farouk and Chelsea. Some couples remain in a traumatized state with ongoing fights seemingly about other frustrations or cool detachment that makes everything seem fine, but no one is really connecting.

Affairs of the past can be buried, but as with Joan and Walter, the skeletons rise. When Walter aged into his nineties, his declining mental condition prevented the couple from being able to do the work neces- sary to repair his broken heart. He and Joan were left devastated despite both wanting to be connected. Couples can't skip any phase completely. The wound that scarred over or the pain that went numb will be seen or felt. Couples do best when they go back and complete the healing journey of affair repair and marriage transformation.

Key Concepts

The *map of affair repair and marriage transformation* is a helpful guide in the healing journey that **serves both the betrayed and betrayer.**
- **Part one of the map is affair repair** which focuses on the shock of discovery and overcoming the wound of betrayal.

- Affair repair has **six phases**:
  - **Normalcy**, which is life before the affair
  - **Discovery**, which is the moment the affair is confirmed
  - **Crisis**, which is when the pain and realization sets in
  - **Affair PTS**, which involves uncontrollable, intrusive thoughts
  - **Affair Repair**, which focuses on healing the wound
  - **Establishing Trust**, which establishes trust in the head and heart
- **Part two is marriage transformation** which focuses on making the marriage better by transformation of:
  - **Reasoning**, which deepens understanding and logic
  - **Reliability**, which enables confidence
  - **Desirability**, which stokes desire
  - **Sexuality**, which improves sexual functioning
  - **Antifragility,** which empowers the couple to face any challenge
  - **Transcendent Transformation**, which is the ultimate goal
- Generally, couples address affair repair first, then marriage transformation.
- **Many couples will go back and forth** between the two parts of the map as they heal.
- Some couples will work **out of phase**, which means focusing on marriage transformation before affair repair.
- Healing **affairs of the past** is important and involves out of phase work.

Part One
Affair Repair

*"Our capacity to destroy one another is matched
by our capacity to heal one another."*
Bessel Van der Kolk

Chapter 6
Normalcy

you are here:
NORMALCY

*The challenge of the normalcy phase
is to understand how you behave in relationships.*

Normalcy is the baseline state of the marriage before an affair is discovered. Normalcy may have been good, bad, acceptable, or barely surviving. Life during the normalcy phase was experienced as stable and predictable. Key components of normalcy that will influence your journey through affair repair include your **attachment** to one another, your relationship **patterns**, and **preexisting conditions**.

Attachment

Attachment is the deep and enduring emotional bond between two people in an intimate relationship. Attachment is physiological as well as psychological. The bond begins with the physical. *Am I physically safe with you?* And deepens emotionally. *Am I psychologically safe with you?* (Some people override physical safety looking for emotional connection. This is unhealthy. Abusive relationships are not safe.)

As relationships form, we begin with definite boundaries of "you" and "me." "Us" develops over time and with more interactions. There is an understanding of who "us" is when attachment is formed. This "us" is an island of safety in a world of billions of individuals that can feel like an empty, isolating space. When people are attached, they feel secure and cared for. This sense of safety and care goes beyond the knowing and feeling of mind and emotion, but into the subconscious and the body. In a state of secure normalcy, you have your person. Survival of the fittest is not the strongest, but the most attached. **Attachment is a physiological and psychological survival impulse like eating and sleeping.**

Human beings are hardwired for connection. When we want to punish someone, we put them in prison. When we really want to punish them, we put them in isolation. Attachment is survival, and there are three basic attachment strategies: **secure**, **avoidant**, and **anxious**. These attachment strategies are considered organized because they are consistent and reliable patterns for connection.

Attachment strategies develop in childhood via the interactions with caregivers. Attachment strategies can change based on the experiences with other relationships throughout our lives. They can improve or they can change to cope with threat. Understanding each partner's attachment strategy before the affair will help couples understand their actions and reactions in their affair repair journey.

Secure attachment is warm and loving. There is a sense of trust. A foundation of trust allows securely attached partners to share vulnerabilities and be resilient in the face of uncomfortable feelings. When couples with secure attachment argue, they do not fear saying something that cannot be taken back or that their partner is going to leave them. Securely attached individuals do not panic that things cannot be resolved. Sometimes affairs happen in marriages where the attachment was once secure, but the state of normalcy has deteriorated.

Ellie and Aaron, mentioned earlier in the Bubble Bath Miracle story, had been best friends until emotional distance set in. What was once a securely attached, loving, and mutually fulfilling relationship had become an atmosphere of distance and neglect. Aaron fell into a routine of work, evenings checked out in front of the TV, and baseball on the weekends. Normalcy was a state of detachment. Their road back together was anchored by Aaron's enduring pledge to change, and waiting for Ellie's willingness to return to the intimacy they had once shared.

Aaron and Ellie benefited from the preexisting condition of secure attachment they had experienced for years. Knowing how to securely attach enabled them to risk trusting that real change had occurred.

Avoidant attachment is characterized by a shutting off, unwillingness, or inability to risk deep emotional connection. People using an avoidant attachment strategy in normalcy tend to be kind and helpful but will not risk intimate vulnerability. Sometimes partners are unaware one of them is actually avoidant because there is so little conflict. One of the conveniences of being with a person using an avoidant strategy is you rarely have to deal with their feelings. They don't trust you to handle them anyway. They can be very warm and loving, pleasing partners as they seek love, but not fully exposing themselves emotionally. Partners using avoidant strategies tend to accommodate or ignore rather than risk being hurt. In stressful circumstances, partners may shut all the way down. Some, under pressure, will take a risk to share their feelings, but if the sharing experience is nonproductive, the partner will revert to avoidance.

William was clear: Sheila had done nothing wrong that would justify his betrayal. She had been a good wife, handling things at home, managing the finances, raising the kids, and staying fit and healthy while he was traveling for work 80 percent of the time. He had always relied on her to take care of the hard stuff in life, such as packing up the house and moving when he was transferred, caring for the kids when they were sick, and organizing family celebrations. He would participate when he was home, but he was not the point person. Sheila had been independent all her life and was capable of these tasks. She enjoyed freedom and control, but she wanted intimacy.

When Sheila was diagnosed with breast cancer, William did not know how to respond. He let his independent wife take charge of her own health journey. She felt abandoned, but neither knew how to cross the great divide. As usual, Sheila bore down and muscled through. The couple lived parallel lives in their avoidant attachment strategies.

Their ultimate marriage transformation involved Sheila exposing some vulnerability, which took great risk, as William had assumed so little responsibility in the past. William held himself accountable and took ownership of his actions. He began working on himself, dedicated to transparency in actions, and responded to Sheila's vulnerability. It took some time, but ultimately Sheila learned to rely on the new William to show up.

An **anxious attachment** strategy involves a desire for attachment, but a deep mistrust. It is ambivalent, a combination of "I want you!" and" Get away from me!" messages. People with anxious attachment can be very warm and loving, then have emotional outbursts or withdrawals. They approach and then they flee. They did not trust their caregivers as children and/or their partners. Experience has taught them that caregivers or partners will hurt them. They are in constant conflict between approach and withdraw, between a desperate need for love and fear for their life. Repair after an affair with an anxious attachment can be challenging but is possible.

Thea was an emotionally volatile person. She was a good woman, caring, and providing, but she was sensitive and subject to outbursts and negativity. Angela was good at reading her moods and soothing her. She walked on eggshells to keep the relationship connected and at peace. Normalcy was a state of Angela managing Thea's anger.

Thea's attachment strategy was anxious, and Angela strove to secure her. Angela was avoidant. She managed her feelings by keeping them locked down, unexposed, and invulnerable. Angela's escape was work and the camaraderie she found there, particularly with her director. Angela's director became her emotional affair partner. Thea sensed Angela pulling away. Angela no longer tried to engage and soothe her moods. Angela did not fight, but she left her emotionally.

Thea worked very hard to better manage her emotions and draw her partner back into relationship. She was successful, but as of this writing, Angela was unable to risk her newfound sense of peace and freedom to return to an unproven marriage. Thea will need to continue to build a history of emotional regulation and authenticity to rebuild Angela's trust and transform the relationship.

The journey on the map of affair repair and marriage transformation requires vulnerability to repair the attachment. All couples will need to be able to work through problematic attachment strategies and build a foundation of secure attachment. Sheila and William were both avoidant, which kept things calm but disconnected. Ellie and Aaron had been securely attached, which helped them repair. Angela was avoidantly attached, but Thea anxiously so. Thea and Angela had a lot of work to address their emotions so they could begin to securely attach.

Avoidant and anxious attachment pairings are common. The avoidant person shuts down their feelings and needs so there is room to deal with their partner's. The anxiously attached person has a sense of security because the avoidant strategy does not trigger a threat, is calm through storms, and never overwhelms with their own needs. When the avoidant person begins to express their needs, the game changes and is difficult for everyone. The goal is not to negate the needs of the person using the anxious strategy, but to improve the strategies of both people.

Anxious and anxious attachment pairings can be challenging. There will be great moments of connection when you are in sync, both feeling vulnerable and open to one another. But both partners can be very volatile when you are out of sync trying to connect. As the disconnection grows, tactics will escalate. An example would be crying with anger "I can't believe you did this to me! I hate you for it!" and hoping for a hug. Or asking for a hug and then crying out.

Conflicting feelings are normal, but it is difficult for the person who wants to repair to know if you really want that hug or want to be left alone until you can receive that hug. If you have been betrayed and are anxiously attached, you may not know yourself if you want the hug or not. You want it, but you don't.

If the person who wants to repair is also anxious, they may want to force that hug upon you, never wanting to lose you. Or they may want to run away in the face of your pain. Anxiously attached people are seeking to soothe the pain by clinging or hiding. When the needs of the moment are out of sync for anxiously attached people, chaos can happen. Healing will have to begin with each person becoming aware of their strategy and working with it to evolve to a more secure attachment.

Attachment strategies can change under pressure and can evolve to a secure form. In fact, it is likely your attachment strategy will change for maximum self-protection when you are scared. The goal is not to label and lock a person into an attachment strategy paradigm. Rather, it is to *understand what strategy is being employed* so that both partners can move to a more secure strategy. Both partners should strive for vulnerability, emotional self-regulation, and an ability to listen (which requires an ability to tolerate your partner's different experiences).

Attachment Strategy Survey

Don't know your attachment strategy? Here is a short survey to help give you some insight. You may keep two scores, one that reflects how you may have attached before discovery and another how you feel now after discovery. This can highlight the preexisting attachment strategy that may or may not have contributed to the quality of the relationship and the effect the affair has had.

Instructions:

Rate how true each statement feels for you in close relationships, using the scale below:
1 – Not at all true
2 – Slightly true
3 – Somewhat true
4 – Mostly true
5 – Completely true

Survey Questions:

I feel comfortable relying on my partner and letting them rely on me.

1 2 3 4 5

I often worry that my partner may stop loving me or leave me.

1 2 3 4 5

I prefer to handle problems on my own rather than depending on my partner.

1 2 3 4 5

I trust that my partner will be there for me when I really need them.

1 2 3 4 5

I feel uneasy when my partner wants to get too emotionally close.

1 2 3 4 5

I often feel afraid of being rejected or abandoned by my partner.

1 2 3 4 5

I feel safe sharing my true thoughts and feelings with my partner.

1 2 3 4 5

I try to maintain some emotional distance from my partner.

1 2 3 4 5

I frequently need reassurance from my partner about our relationship.

1 2 3 4 5

I feel confident in our ability to work through relationship challenges together.

1 2 3 4 5

I feel more in control when I keep emotional space between me and my partner.

1 2 3 4 5

I get anxious if I don't hear from my partner for a while.

1 2 3 4 5

I feel secure and satisfied in my relationship.

1 2 3 4 5

I tend to pull away when my partner seems too dependent on me.

1 2 3 4 5

I fear that I might come across as too needy in my relationship.

1 2 3 4 5

Scoring

Group the questions and total the scores for each attachment style.

Secure Attachment

Questions: 1, 4, 7, 10, 13
Total: _____ / 25

Anxious Attachment

Questions: 2, 6, 9, 12, 15
Total: _____ / 25

Avoidant Attachment

Questions: 3, 5, 8, 11, 14
Total: _____ / 25

Interpretation Guide

21–25: Strong tendencies toward this attachment style
16–20: Moderate tendencies
11–15: Mild tendencies
5–10: Unlikely this is your dominant style

High scores in more than one category may suggest a mixed attachment pattern (e.g., anxious-avoidant).

Individuals who rely upon **secure attachment** strategies generally have positive views of themselves and others. They are comfortable with intimacy and independence in relationships.

Those who use **avoidant attachment** strategies often prefer independence over intimacy. They may have difficulty trusting others and may feel uncomfortable with emotional closeness.

Individuals using **anxious attachment** strategies may worry about rejection and abandonment in relationships. They often seek reassurance and validation from others and may fear being alone.

The score range provides a *general* guideline for interpreting attachment strategies, but it's important to remember that attachment strategies are complex and can vary based on individual experiences and contexts. Attachment strategies can and do change.

If you kept two scores, compare your attachment strategies before and after discovery. Consider how the way you attached affected your relationship before discovery and how the strategy will affect your work on the map of affair repair and marriage transformation. You may want to take this survey one or two more times over the course of your healing journey to see if you are moving toward a more secure attachment, and if not, consider what might be holding you back.

Patterns

Relationship patterns have sometimes been referred to as the "dance" you two do. When your partner takes step A, you do step B. We fall into certain roles, and each follows the other's lead. This dance occurs in workload distribution all the way through to who initiates sex and how we fight. If one escalates, what does the other do? The relationship patterns that existed in normalcy will arise as you journey along the road of affair repair and can sometimes be exaggerated under stress. It is a good idea to reflect on and identify any unhelpful patterns that endured in normalcy.

Sean and Sarah came together over common values and shared work ethics. He worked swing shifts while she managed the kids and the 4,500-square-foot home. He was exhausted, and Sarah was overwhelmed with the responsibility.

Many times, Sean would come home, the house a mess, homework not done, and food barely on the table. So, he would jump in to assist with dinner and the kids. Sarah felt like a failure because she needed help. What she really needed was a little more attention than Sean could muster after long hours of work and interrupted sleep patterns.

Sarah was not as strong as Sean in detaching from her emotional needs. Sean, overworked and frustrated, had shut down. He could find no relief when he came home. Sarah felt Sean was controlling the relationship, from hugging and touching to finances and functioning. Both were right.

Normalcy for Sean and Sarah was a state of neglect and never living up to expectations. Sean needed the proverbial "acts of service" kind of love, and Sarah some "quality time." Sarah succumbed to the attention of another man. Sean was devastated by her betrayal. She was deeply remorseful and rededicated herself to her portion of the work of their life, maintaining the family and home. Sean continued the controlling pattern to keep himself safe. He confessed he loved her, though it was killing him. He stayed for the kids.

Sarah worked hard and improved her ability to maintain her share of the workload. Soon, in the comfort of things running smoothly in their familiar pattern of normalcy, Sean fell off on spending time with her. The scar tissue from the wound was preventing him from healing. He did not change. The more she failed, the more he entrenched in his expectations and focused on her shortcomings.

Their road to recovery was long, as Sean held out expectations of how she should apologize and what to do to fix things. She strove to meet those expectations, but just as in normalcy, it was never quite enough to make Sean feel secure again. Their patterns couldn't be broken.

There are many common patterns couples fall into. One of the most difficult patterns to break out of is conflict avoidance. "The marriage died in silence," a client once told me. Throughout their twelve-year marriage, she had sensed a distance. She had accepted, respected, and worked to bridge the disconnect. Her husband would not spend quality time with her, share what was bothering him, or respond to her overtures for connection. This couple was dealing with a *shut down and shut out* pattern grounded in an avoidant attachment strategy.

Another silent but deadly relationship pattern is two individuals who take care of their own concerns and focus on contributing to the common good. In one such case, each partner came from a healthy, secure home. They shared common values and work ethics. Rather than burden their partner, they would *self-soothe and solve* (avoidant attachment strategy) the problems on their own. The challenge came when this couple had to work through the healing process. The incredible skill of handling things internally and on one's own became an obstacle to sharing pain and rebuilding trust.

Another common pattern is where *one partner explodes and the other soothes* (anxious attachment strategy.) One partner may explode in anger or tears while the other gets small and seeks to soothe the emotion that now dominates the room. Dysregulation derails and detours the healing process. Or in other cases, each may be hair-trigger sensitive to the other blocking communication as they seek to avoid upset or upsetting. Walking on eggshells or just waiting for the next painful flesh wound freezes everyone in place.

Though there are common patterns of relating, each couple is unique. Consider your relationship pattern and become aware of how that pattern might interfere with your healing as an individual and as a couple.

Preexisting Conditions

Preexisting conditions will affect how the betrayed and betrayer travel together on the road of affair repair. Positive preexisting conditions such as a good sex life, clear communication, or deep friendship all help in healing. Challenging preexisting conditions such as financial strain, cultural differences, chronic illness, or disability must be accounted for as the couple embarks on their healing journey. Common negative preexisting conditions include addictions or trauma history.

Addictions

Addictions may be in the form of substances or processes. Addictive substances may be alcohol or drugs. Addictive processes may be sex, work, exercise, disordered eating, or gambling. Addictions are often used to cope with uncomfortable feelings. Rather than do the hard work of addressing what is wrong in life or in a relationship, people turn to their addictions for a sense of soothing or control. It is much easier to go to work or to a porn site than deal with the kids or your partner's depression at home. Those in relationship with a person struggling with addictions may not be aware the substance or process is an addiction. Lots of people enjoy sex without it being an addiction. Work is affirmed as a productive and beneficial activity.

Affairs can be very like a process addiction. Process addictions involve process, emotion, neuroscience, and reinforcement. Like a gambling addiction, the behavior is reinforced with intermittent reward. Often the partner of someone battling addiction knows in their body something is wrong before the information comes out. It is not uncommon for the partner of a gambling-addicted person to experience gastrointestinal issues or headaches as money begins to go missing or new credit cards are showing up. Affairs are not dissimilar.

The Sex Addiction Story

Lisa woke up one day with sores she had never had before. Her doctor confirmed it was herpes. Lisa then discovered multiple cash withdrawals and massage parlor visits on the joint credit card statement. George had been soliciting while on business trips. According to George, it was common and acceptable among his peers (though he overlooked the point that "common" was less than 10 percent of them, and he had to hide his "acceptable" activities in general). He minimized the fact that he could lose his job if caught. This is addictive thinking. The addicted brain overlooks obvious facts to keep its source of pleasure.

The affair, in many ways, is just another symptom of addiction, but that is hard for a betrayed person to grasp. An addicted person may have an affair because they are more attached to the substance than to any relationship. They are not thinking of their partner as a person with feelings; their loyalty is to the substance. Addiction has moved from a conscious choice to an automatic response to the brain's constant cuing for reward.

Addictions, in the context of relationships, can be understood from an attachment perspective. The addicted person is more attached to their addiction (alcohol or sex, for instance) than they are to their partner. Addictions are reliable; they can make a person feel "secure." An addicted person will choose their addiction over their partner every time.

The addicted person must put a pause between stimulus and response (or remove the stimulus) to make a choice. The betrayed is powerless in this process, and it feels personal. The only person with the power to overcome addiction is the addict. Of note, a partner of an addicted person may end up having an affair because they feel very alone. The addicted partner is more attached to their drug of choice than to them. Addiction is the compounding condition, the first betrayal, and the root problem.

When George and Lisa met, they were highly passionate and madly in love. Each presented their best selves and admired what they saw. Each was attached to an image of the other, not the real person. Over time, reality rubbed away at some of the image. George could be critical and Lisa competitive. The real human version of their partner was failing to meet their needs.

Normalcy for Lisa and George was at its core an emotionally detached state. They were only partially attached from the very beginning and had not done hard personal growth along the way to come together. The sex outside the relationship met George's desire for attention and adoration, but it did not address any need for deep attachment. The affairs were simply another manifestation of false attachment. They felt good, but they weren't real. It was addictive coping in life. Like all addictions, they take you down in the end. George's life was beginning to unravel.

Addiction sneaks in the back door of a relationship and is sometimes the grease that keeps the relationship together. For example, it is much easier to stay with a functioning alcoholic who goes to their high-paying job every day than to go through the pain and difficulty of getting sober, reducing your lifestyle, or getting divorced. Lisa came to understand the function of addiction but did not want to acknowledge it to George, for fear of "letting him off the hook." **Addiction is not an excuse; it is an explanation.**

Addictions can be overcome, but they are difficult, and there is rarely the option to just quit. George did "just quit." He did not return to massage parlors or other women as far as Lisa knew, but he did not do the work to really understand himself, his needs, and what needed to change in the relationship. He did the outward work, but not the inward. Both could feel the chasm between them. Lisa could not forgive him because of her competitive nature, and intuitively she could not trust him. George replaced his addiction to sex to competing in triathlons. He chased endorphins by working out all the time and traveling to various races across the country. George was avoiding real relationships with his family and his wife.

Trauma

Trauma often comes with addictions. If your partner has a trauma in their past, normalcy has a unique element that must be understood and considered as you move forward on the map of affair repair and marriage transformation. Combat, extreme poverty, assault, a mass shooting, a major accident, or any life-threating event are examples of trauma. Other possible traumas, such as childhood sexual or physical abuse, can leave a hidden attachment wound, which may make it difficult for a partner to attach from the beginning of the relationship. Prior experience of an affair in your current or previous relationship would also be considered underlying trauma. Smaller, little "t," traumas that people have soothed with an affair include infertility, having a baby, loss of job, or moving to live in another culture.

Individuals who have survived trauma may compartmentalize relationships because relationships have been unsafe. Shutting off your heart to the world keeps you safe. Traumatized people are often themselves unaware they are doing this. Just as a fish doesn't know it's wet, they don't realize what they are doing is not "normal." People who have not experienced trauma will not intuitively understand this compartmentalization because their traumatized partner seems so normal. A person who has never experienced trauma has been relating to their partner as if they were just like themselves. A traumatized person may be able to talk about their trauma and engage in what seems like a well-attached relationship, however, under stress or if the trauma is not truly resolved, the attachment may be impaired.

A person with a traumatic past may have an affair and not feel it is such a serious breach of the relationship because it is generally hard for them to connect and trust at the heart level. They understand what they did was wrong, but they keep their heart safe and may assume you do, too. Therefore, it is logically not possible to be hurt *that bad*. For one person to be empathetic to another's pain they first must access their own.

If the partner with trauma in their past is the one who is betrayed, the betrayal may be doubly wounding. They have risked trusting someone with the safety of their heart and been hurt again. A traumatized person will not respond like a non-traumatized person when dealing with an affair. Coping strategies will appear, and they likely will look like any unhealed trauma coping strategies from the past. If in the past your partner coped with the trauma by shutting down, self-harming, running away, reacting violently, or binging on substances that is likely what they will do in dealing with the affair whether they are the betrayed or the betrayer.

Often people who have experienced trauma will seek relationships in which they can reenact the trauma so that they can resolve it. This person is not seeking to reexperience trauma; they are seeking to resolve it. The goal of the healing journey on the map of affair repair and marriage transformation is to resolve the trauma of the affair. Preexisting trauma may be healed along the way, but individual therapy may be helpful. As a couple is critical to understand how the reactions of a traumatized person are affecting the process. The reactions are legitimate, not simply to be shoved aside as rooted in a "trauma experience in the past," but as an understandable response to what is happening now. Previously traumatized people can heal from their prior trauma and work through the affair recovery process. This is very difficult work, but it can be done.

Understanding the strengths and weaknesses of your relationship normalcy will empower you in affair repair. Rather than focusing on the past, incorporate any changes you would like to make in your relationship as you heal from the affair. Know that these changes take time and you will be doing it under difficult circumstances, but this situation may bring out the motivation you have always needed to create a healthy or improved normalcy.

Key Concepts

Normalcy is the way you behaved in your relationship before the affair was discovered.

- **Attachment strategies** are the ways you seek to connect with your partner.
  - **Secure strategies** are non-attacking and approach your partner with the belief they want to help you. Securely attached people do not feel unsafe or offended when their partner fails to meet their needs, they are self-confident and can re-engage to make the relationship better.
  - **Avoidant strategies** hold back. When you use an avoidant strategy, you engage from a distance to keep yourself and the relationship stable. Avoidant strategies keep the peace but eliminate close connection via emotional and physical distance.
  - **Anxious strategies** can be confusing for each of you as you move in and out of closeness depending upon how confident and safe you feel. When you feel confident, you can be charming. When you feel threatened or rejected, you can be volatile or manipulative.

- **Patterns** are the habitual ways you use to behave in normalcy. Patterns are unspoken agreements like the roles you automatically assumed in housekeeping, financial providing, and holiday planning. Patterns also refer to your usual ways of responding to each other, for example, when one person is sad, the other rescues. Or one person gets angry, the other gets angrier. Become aware of your patterns and work to improve or build upon them.
- **Attachment strategies** and **patterns** that were part of normalcy in your relationship will exaggerate on your journey along the map of affair repair.
- Addiction and trauma will affect your attachment strategies and patterns.
- **Pre-existing conditions** are strengths or challenges that existed in your marriage before discovery and will be present on your healing journey. A good friendship, sex life, or shared faith would be a strength. Addiction, trauma, or financial strain would be a challenge.
- **Duration:** Normalcy includes all time before discovery.
- **Goal:** The goal of thinking about your normalcy is to come to understand how you behave in relationships. Identify attachment strategies, patterns and pre-existing conditions that were part of your relationship for information purposes only; **the past is not the destination**. Use the information to guide you as you go forward.
- **Do:**
  - Allow yourself to grieve what was good that is no more
  - Identify your attachment strategies
  - Identify your patterns
  - Identify pre-existing conditions
  - Prepare for your attachment strategies and relationship patterns to exaggerate
  - Prepare to capitalize on strengths or overcome challenges of pre-existing conditions

- **Don't:**
  - ○ Get stuck in wishing what you had would come back
  - ○ Ignore what was good about your normalcy
  - ○ Spend too much time reviewing normalcy or overvalue it
- **If you are the betrayed partner,** consider what attachment strategies and patterns you and your partner employed during normalcy. Think about what worked and what did not. Become aware of how these strategies and patterns might affect your journey along the map of affair repair.
- **If you are the betrayer**, consider what attachment strategies and patterns you and your partner employed during normalcy. Think about how these patterns and strategies played into your becoming involved in the affair. Become aware of how these strategies and patterns might affect your journey along the map of affair repair.

Chapter 7
Discovery

you are here:
DISCOVERY

*The challenge of the discovery phase
is to put a pause between stimulus and response.*

Discovery is the end of normalcy as you once knew it. Discovery, "D-Day," is the actual moment the affair is confirmed. The discovery phase does not reveal all the information that will ultimately be known about the affair, it is just the first moment the affair's existence is confirmed. The discovery phase lasts approximately two to three weeks. Discovery can take longer if there are multiple affairs, a long-term affair, a history of affairs, or truth is withheld that will result in ongoing discovery of more world-altering information.

> *Nia could feel Kayla's distance most at night. After coming home late from a busy day, Kayla would give her a peck on the lips, then roll over to sleep. She used to snuggle her and breathe in her*

hair before heading off to dreamland. She said she was tired, but something told Nia it wasn't quite true.

Pre-discovery is the time within the discovery phase that the affair was suspected. In pre-discovery, behavior changes, strange charges appear on credit cards, partners return home late, and suspicious texts are found. Cheating partners may be cold, distant, or irritable. Pre-discovery is the awareness that something is not quite right, but you can't be sure.

In pre-discovery, you may have been suspicious but afraid to make an accusation and be wrong. Maybe you did question what was going on but were gaslit with outrage and anger. Outright denial of facts would leave you feeling crazy or deciding to avoid future confrontation. Like when Chelsea confronted Farouk about the underwear she found while unpacking his suitcase. He yelled at her for starting an argument after a long trip overseas to support their family. Feeling guilty, she let it drop. Evidence may be overridden psychologically by the betrayed or the betrayer, not wanting to deal with the facts before them. Neither Farouk nor Chelsea ever thought about that underwear again until years later when she brought it up at their child's wedding.

Affairs involve secrecy, which is why if you were the person who was cheated on, you didn't know. Betrayal is not your fault. Your partner had been trustworthy for a time which is why you did trust them. We all must trust each other for efficiency's sake; we cannot move about the world constantly checking or worrying about our partner while trying to care for the children, go to work, or accomplish all the things we must do. Secrecy is part of the definition of an affair. Pre-discovery can feel like a fog because it is confusing and undefined. Things feel normal, but they are not.

Pre-discovery suspicions may make it more difficult for you further along the map of affair repair when things begin to feel "normal" again. Suspicions may pop up just because it feels like pre-discovery. Any time the betrayed partner feels things aren't safe or slightly off, they will be concerned they are missing a warning signal like they did last time and will go into fight-or-flight mode. Betrayed partners may re-experience trauma even if no affair activity is happening.

In pre-discovery, the person involved in the affair is living in two different worlds. Discovery is when those two worlds collide and mass destruction occurs. What was hidden in the dark has now crashed into the light of reality. Ignoring or letting go of even slightly irregular activity is no longer possible. Sometimes, there are no clues at all, which can make discovery even more traumatic. Discovery can be totally unpredicted and catch both of you by surprise.

Discovery is the smoking gun. The day you walked into the room and found your partner with another, or the time you picked up your partner's phone and found the intimate texts. Everything has changed. If you have just experienced discovery, give yourself time to consider all your options and do the work on the map of affair repair. Healing begins with truth.

The Discovery Story

Carla and Wayne had moved from the West Coast to the East. Wayne had sold his business, and they were preparing to enjoy the good life when Wayne retired. For the past ten years, Carla and Wayne had been regularly involved with their golf community, playing in tournaments as a team and individually. Carla had much more time to invest in the game, as Wayne spent many hours at the office, building up the business.

One evening Carla had gone to bed, leaving her phone downstairs in the kitchen. Turning off the TV and making the rounds while closing the home before going upstairs, Wayne found her phone on the counter. A message came up with a cheesy grin emoji from one of their mutual golf friends: Mike.

Wayne clicked on the message expecting a funny meme or friendly joke from Carla that invoked the cheesy grin. Instead, he read a message, "I miss washing your balls, but we must stop. I love

Wayne." This text was preceded by a string of messages reminiscing about rounds and rounds of golf followed by afternoons in bed and showers together. Wayne threw the phone against the wall, cracking the tile.

Upon discovery, normalcy is no more. Even if Wayne chose never to mention the texts to Carla, the secret would exist, forever a wedge between him and his wife. Though the affair was over, as confirmed in the text chain, the memories of what Carla and Mike had done remained. The impact of the affair meant something different to everyone involved.

Discovery results in near-instantaneous activation of the body's alarm system. Betrayed people may feel butterflies in the stomach, elevation of blood pressure, tension of muscles, and dry mouth. If a person gets stuck in this physiological state for too long or it becomes too intense, the betrayed may find it difficult to concentrate and cannot move forward.

The most common physiological response to discovery is rage. This is the body going into *fight* mode in response to the pain of betrayal. If you have been betrayed, you sense danger at the deepest level. The experience is preverbal, before thought, and not filtered. Betrayed partners often report rage at the sense of being taken advantage of. Love, the whole gift of self, has been taken and not appreciated or returned. If a betrayed person is not fighting, they might take *flight*, completely shutting down and leaving the relationship emotionally or physically. Shock is a *freeze* response to discovery. Some people do not know what to do in the moment they learn of the affair. There are too many overwhelming, conflicting emotions and too much at stake to fight or flee. *Fawn*, a lesser known but well-established response to physiological danger, is to try to please the aggressor. Betrayed people may experience and express their fear to the betrayer by doing anything to keep the relationship. The betrayed person who is fawning is desperately trying to return to the perceived safety of normalcy.

People who are caught cheating may have many responses to discovery. Some, like Chuck, who was caught a second time and brought to my office, will freeze. Chuck sat there like a deer in the headlights, waiting for me to take the lead in the discussion. He was ready to take the hit, to hear the bad news of his well-earned sentence. Some people will fight and become defensive to protect themselves in the explosion of the moment.

When Wayne discovered Carla's affair, he asked for full access to her phone. She resisted, asking, "How much of myself must I give up?" In Carla's mind, the affair was over, and she had already apologized.

Carla's question may have seemed insensitive, but in the discovery phase, people say many illogical things that give insight to their emotional experiences of fear, longing, pain, and hope. Carla desperately wanted to repair her marriage, but her attachment strategy was avoidant, and her pattern was defensive. She was deflecting pain with all energies dedicated to making everything right as fast as possible. Her pattern was to avoid hurt by not exposing her emotions and removing the burden of a real relationship for Wayne.

The healing journey of affair repair will require introspection and painful personal sharing. Carla will be challenged in the affair repair phase to share deeper levels of emotional intimacy, which may require giving up some of her comfortable walls of avoidance and outward perfection.

Preexisting conditions such as trauma or addiction can influence the response to discovery. Discovery may trigger a binge of addictive behavior in either partner. The person who was betrayed may experience an exaggerated physiological response. One betrayed client experienced uncontrollable body shakes upon discovery of the second affair. Another threw up in a plant. These are extreme but not uncommon cases of how the body reacts and what it experiences in response to the real wounding and threat to their well-being.

If you have experienced prior trauma, you may have more extreme fight-or-flight responses, escalating or shutting down in more extreme ways. An extreme example of fawning could be expressed as over-the-top love-bombing and desperate actions to keep the relationship together. The reactions of the betrayed and the betrayer to discovery set the stage for the crisis phase.

Confronting The Affair Partner

Do not confront the other man, woman, or person. Your issue is with your partner who chose to step out of the marriage. The affair partner is a scapegoat. Confrontation is a natural fight response, and if it goes too far, it can land you in jail. Confronting the affair partner may soothe a need to defend yourself by bringing justice, but it rarely resolves well. Most affair partners will shut you out or worse, they may attack back. A screaming match on someone's front lawn is a reality TV drama that neighbors find entertaining at best, but most find it annoying and think less of you. Others may understand your motive for lashing out at the affair partner but will perceive you as out of control. Even if you are successful in destroying the affair partner's life, you do harm to the potential repair of your marriage. Aggressive actions can also damage your relationship with your children and distance your close friends and family. Confronting the affair partner is a side battle that could cause you to lose the war.

Calling, emailing, or texting the affair partner is not recommended. However, if you are in the rare circumstance where the affair partner is willing, and you can maintain control, you may consider asking factual questions to get a timeline and understand of the scope of the affair. You could ask when they met, how often, and where. It may also be helpful to ask if contact continues and what the understanding of the relationship was. Keep your list short and your reactions level. Do not attack the affair partner, and do not contact them more than once.

Sometimes the affair partner will reach out to apologize. You may simply say, "Thank you. You don't need to contact me again." Engaging in an ongoing fact-finding or solidarity relationship is fraught with pitfalls. The motives of the affair partner may be sincere, but a relationship with you is also a way to maintain connection with your spouse. Speaking with you gives insight into the status of your marital relationship. Even if the motives of the affair partner may be to genuinely repent, you have already thanked them. Allow them to seek support elsewhere. You need to heal yourself and your relationship.

Telling Others

Upon discovery, you may want to sound the community alarm. This may be your first impulse to keep you and everyone else safe from the danger you just experienced. However, in the end, telling others is a vengeful move. Shaming is an attempt to kick your partner out of the community, to vote them off the island. Better to put a pause between stimulus and response.

The reality is that telling everyone backfires in the long run. Communities tend to not get involved. Posting pictures and stories on social media will get a few followers who enjoy the drama, but many will say nothing while wondering about your "crazy," and some will unfollow the whole mess. Very few followers jump into the fray. Allies who get involved are contributing unnecessary drama and causing emotional escalation that does not serve to establish true safety.

If you have been betrayed, you might seek someone with sympathetic anger, but that person may feel frustrated and used when you soften and begin to work on your marriage. The once-sympathetic friend you leaned on now becomes someone who will continue to stoke the pain of betrayal to move you out of the relationship.

If you are the person who had the affair, you may seek someone who validates your motives for having the affair in the first place and supports you in leaving the marriage to seek happiness. This validation is often temporarily soothing and can distract you from doing the hard work of taking responsibility and examining yourself to make a clear decision. Most friends don't want to confront you and don't want to see you unhappy. Validating is the easy way out.

Sometimes, whether you are the betrayed partner or the betrayer, the person you brought in as an ally upon discovery can become overly invested in your decision to stay or go. If either partner must discuss the discovery of an affair, seek a friend, family member, or therapist who cares about both of you.

Keep the Children Out of It

Do not discuss discovery with or in front of the children—even if they already know. The pain of discovery is between you and your partner; avoid handing it to your children. It is not for your children to help you heal the wound. They did not cause the pain, and it is not their burden to bear the healing. How you handle this life-changing experience throughout the map of affair repair and transformation will influence the healing of your children. It is the parent's responsibility to protect and provide for their children—even if one partner fails. Throughout your healing journey, assure your children their lives are secure and you are an emotionally stable and reliable parent.

Often children become proxies for processing adult pain. Most parents don't do this on purpose, many do it unaware. The pain you are experiencing is overwhelming, so the burden is transferred to your children via questioning, explaining, or comforting. Or you may be using your children as instruments to resolve your pain against your partner by subtly or openly criticizing your partner. Be aware of how you are handling your feelings. The betrayed partner may be trying to ally the children against the betrayer to solve their hurt. The betrayer who was involved in the affair may try to be extra nice to the children to absolve their guilt and prove they are not such a bad person.

Most children will be angry at the betraying spouse, which feels good to the betrayed partner, but over time, your children's anger will lessen, and in my experience, 90 percent return to a functioning, inclusive relationship with the parent who had the affair The hope of the betrayed partner that the betrayer would be held accountable by the loss of love and respect from their children for their wrongdoings is ultimately dashed, leaving the betrayed partner feeling lonelier and more hurt.

New Discovery About an Old Affair

New discovery about an old affair can be the discovery of *new information* about a known affair or the *discovery of a past affair that is now over*. Emotions are not time limited. They may fade, be suppressed, or detached from current experience, but as soon as that associated memory, object, or person comes close enough, the emotion will be released. Unprocessed pain of the past is felt in present-day reality; it knows no timeline.

New discoveries of information from an old affair can trigger affair PTS symptoms. New discoveries may be a photo, a fact about where the affair took place, a realization others knew, or a love child. Upon new discovery of information about an old affair, expect the betrayed partner to regress and rethink everything. Do not be discouraged, though it feels like you have gone back to the beginning, you can move quicker along the affair repair map.

New discovery is like the first discovery to the betrayed. The pain of new discovery is a fresh wound. Even though the affair is over or the knowledge of the affair is not new, the couple will need to do the work through the strategies on the map of affair repair to manage the response to the new discovery. Logic does not make the pain go away. Knowing that this is not a new affair does not override the fresh rupture of the bond between you. If you are processing new discovery regarding an affair from long ago, be patient with each other. The work is worth it.

Key Concepts

Discovery is the proof positive moment of the affair. (It is not all the information that will ultimately be disclosed.) Discovery will activate the fight-or-flight system in the betrayed and the betrayer.

- If you are the **betrayed partner**, you have encountered a world-altering and therefore life-threatening event. The pain is mentally, emotionally, and *physiologically* overwhelming.
- If you are the **betrayer**, you also are likely overwhelmed and experiencing an activation of the fight-or-flight system, but it is less life altering than the experience of your betrayed partner because the affair is not a surprise to you. Discovery may have been a surprise, but the affair was not.
- **Average Duration:** The discovery phase lasts two to three weeks. Discovery can take longer if there are multiple affairs, a long-term affair, a history of affairs, or truth is withheld that will result in ongoing discovery of more world-altering information.
- **Goal:** The goal of the discovery phase is to put a pause between stimulus and response. Give yourself time to think before you act on discovery. Your body needs time to calm as your mind begins to figure out what to do next.
- **Do:**
  - Accept and understand that your physiological response cannot be reasoned away with logic
  - Get professional help
- **Don't:**
  - Make rash decisions
  - Tell the kids, your family, and everyone
  - Blame yourself
  - Become so emotionally upset you cause more damage
- **If you are the betrayed partner,** allow time for your emotions to sort out before taking extreme action. Understand this is a real physiological crisis that will pass. You have a choice to leave or work through this. Gather information and know you will survive.
- **If you are the betrayer** who was involved in the affair, try to stay as present as possible. Be grounded as the information is discovered. Work to not overreact to the extreme emotions you and your partner may be having. Try not to defend, run away, or attack back. Do not panic. Commit to working through the process, regardless of outcome.

Chapter 8
Crisis

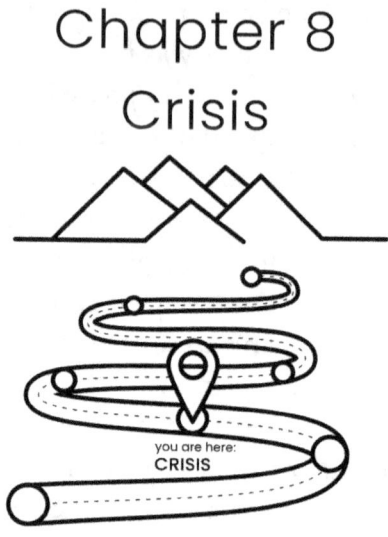

you are here:
CRISIS

The challenge of the crisis phase is to tell the truth.

If an affair were a car accident in which you were knocked out, discovery is the moment of impact. Crisis is when you are coming back into consciousness, trying to piece together what just happened, discerning what is still intact, and wondering if you will survive. Discovery is the sensation in the pit of your stomach when you find texts on the phone. Crisis is the thoughts and feelings that begin to flood. Pain begins to set in, and you can barely think due to overwhelm. You and your marriage are now in the emergency room, fighting for life. Crisis is the most painful phase and can last weeks or even months in some cases. The crisis phase does not go on forever.

The first step in a crisis is to be sure you are physically okay. Now is the time for you to get a test for sexually transmitted infections (STIs). I am grateful to the doctors who, upon learning about an affair, suggest their patients get an STI test. It saves having to make the embarrassing request. You will not be the first person who has disclosed an affair to your doctor. A good doctor, out of genuine care, kindness, and professionalism, will also recommend a therapist to help you through the crisis.

Most couples call me during the crisis phase when the pain and realization of what has happened begins to set in. Threats and screaming matches ensue. There are freeze-outs and throw-outs as the betrayed partner seeks safety. One or both partners may emotionally shut down. Couples may choose to move to separate bedrooms or in with family members or close friends.

In the crisis phase, the mid-part of the brain, called the amygdala, is fully activated. Life-threatening trauma is happening. Outwardly, there is no threat to the body, but inwardly, the body is now being told by the amygdala—which is responsible for processing emotion and is where a sense of safety, security, and attachment is assessed—that there is a threat! Someone close has surprise-attacked, and they may again at any moment. If the threat is great enough, processing in the amygdala will supersede any processing in the frontal lobes of the brain, where logical thought occurs.

Do your best to resist immediately seeking a divorce, attacking your partner, or confronting the affair partner before you have had time to process what has happened beyond the crisis phase. Give yourself some time to think.

Two Immediate Actions You Can Take

There are two immediate actions that can be taken to steady things in the crisis phase.

1. The first is for the person involved in the affair to let the affair partner know discovery has been made, the affair is over, and that you will be working on the marriage.
2. The second action is to spend as much time together with your spouse as possible.

Ideally, communication with the affair partner ending the relationship happens in a way that the betrayed partner can witness or verify. This can take place in a telephone call, text, or email involving all parties. Tell the affair partner the affair is over and you are going to work on the marriage. This is usually very difficult for the partner who is ending the affair. Even though it may be the right thing to do, the betrayer does not want to hurt the affair partner. Try to understand that though the action is clear, emotions are a mess. Clear action will put boundaries on the mess.

Once the affair has ended, you both must cut all contact with the affair partner. Neither of you should drive by the former affair partner's house or place of work. Strive to avoid all places where they might be encountered if possible. No matter how tempting, the partner who is hurt and angry by the betrayal must not contact the other person. The affair is over. If you are the person ending the affair, no contact will shorten your period of pain because even the littlest experience with the affair partner encourages a yearning for more.

Avoid "just friends" phone calls or interactions with the affair partner. If you can switch jobs, churches, softball teams, or other situations where the affair partner may be, do it. Often this is not possible, but if it is, consider it. Expect the affair partner to try to continue contact. Contact attempts could range from texts and phone calls, to coming to where you work, exercise, hang out, or live. If you happen to see your former affair partner, be diplomatic. You can apologize for any pain you have caused, but do not engage in conversation. You will best serve yourself and your former affair partner by being clear there is nothing to be pursued between you. False hope is painful.

Always be sure to let your betrayed partner know if the former affair partner has made contact. Do not wait for a "convenient time"; let them know as soon as possible. Contact with the affair partner includes texts, emails, calls, sightings, or mentions. Yes, sightings or even casual mentions are important. These small brushes with the existence of the ex-affair partner are rattling for your partner. Being in a state of unknowing was how your betrayed partner was hurt the last time. If things are known, they can be addressed and understood.

If you are the partner involved and do not want to end your affair, be honest. Give your betrayed partner the respect of choice so they can consider if they are able to tolerate the time it may take for you to decide if you want to work on the marriage. You might negotiate for a week to decide. There is no forcing the end of the affair. Forcing at best leads to resentment and at worst to more lying. Many people do work through a limbo of tolerating an affair as Aaron did in the Bubble Bath Miracle story. Not every partner, though, will be like Aaron.

If you are the betrayed partner with someone continuing an affair, you may decide to stay, go, or set a time-to-move-on date. You are not to be forced, either. You may decide you need a week to evaluate your options. While the betrayer is considering the other relationship, you should be considering what separating looks like just in case. Sometimes facing the reality of financial and family splits makes the decision a little more clear and less scary.

Pressuring a partner to end an affair or pressuring a partner to be patient will hasten the end of the primary relationship. Time is your best hope for healing. In cases where one person wants to walk away and the other wants to stay, I recommend the solution-focused, out-of-phase strategies presented here in *Affair Repair* and those in Michele Weiner Davis's books, *The Divorce Remedy* and *Healing from Infidelity: The Divorce Busting® Guide to Rebuilding Your Marriage After an Affair*.

The second action couples can take in the crisis phase is to spend productive, not destructive, time together. Time together may be intense or relaxed. In any case, be together in peace if possible. Time apart compounds the fear of what is happening while you are separate. Work on projects, take walks, go for coffee, or spend time together as a family. Time together is normalizing and calming, helping to turn off the alarm systems activated in crisis.

Gary and Desi Make Time

Gary was jealous of the time his wife, Desi, spent with their children, tending to their needs, shuttling them around, and listening to their stories. He felt abandoned as her role as mother overshad-

owed her role as wife. Desi found purpose as her children grew and took on more in life. Gary felt like a needy dependent versus a contributing or inspiring partner.

Desi avoided time with Gary in the guise of being with the children. She began spending long afternoons at the soccer field with their middle son. Desi found herself attracted to the capable and organized assistant coach, whose son was also on the team. Soon sexual encounters were arranged in the guise of "play dates." Desi maintained emotional distance from Gary as she hid herself in motherly duties and the affair.

Ultimately, the discovery was made when mom and coach were caught in a kiss by one of the boys. Both agreed to end the affair and return to their spouses. Desi was ambivalent but willing to spend more time with Gary. Gary felt guilty—and worse, needy—for wanting and taking their mother from the children. Mom was the center of their universe, Gary wanted her, too. Reprioritizing time together was a good first step toward healing their marriage and correcting unhealthy normalcy patterns. Desi showed up like a champ, but it was a while before Gary would really believe she wanted to be there. That took more work on the map of affair repair.

If you were involved in an affair that is now ended, you may want to avoid the extreme intensity of the emotions of your betrayed partner, but avoidance is a luxury only you can afford. You can escape the pain because *you know* what choices you are considering in the moment. In the crisis phase, your betrayed lives on a rumbling, shaking ground that has not quite settled. Desi was all in, never looking back. Gary was fresh in crisis. He just doesn't know—yet. Having Desi around in calm, real presence helped Gary's body *feel* safe. The feeling is deeper than words. If you can't take time off work, increase the contact you have throughout the day with phone calls, texts, and emails. Have lunch together, and when you come home, be present.

Crisis is the most painful phase, but it does not last. Our bodies cannot remain at peak activation on an ongoing basis. The body must take a break, then return to alert. The alarm will begin to go on and off intermittently marking the next phase, Affair PTS, which takes longer and is harder to overcome. Our bodies will continue to raise the alarm almost randomly as we investigate each potential threat before shutting it off. In crisis, expect a full five alarm fire. Nothing is intermittent.

Betrayed Crisis Phase Experience

If you are the betrayed partner, you may *fight, flee, freeze,* or *fawn* in crisis. Your partner caught in the affair will be overwhelmed by the fallout of discovery, but you are the victim of the explosion. Your fight, flight, freeze, or fawn default survival strategy will affect your healing journey. Your survival strategy may interfere as you seek to get payback, separate, shut down, or move too quickly to forgive. Your strategies may also help to keep you safe as you work to repair. You will benefit if you are aware when you are acting out of survival mode.

Fight

A fight response includes rage and understandable, yet irrational behavior. Your fight behavior is understandable because we can see why you would be so angry you might behave that way. Your behavior is irrational because what you do doesn't work or it backfires. Betrayed fight behavior includes public scenes, reaching out to the affair partner, telling everyone they know to gang up on the person who cheated, calling the boss, and posting on social media.

Another common, self-protective fight response is sleuthing. It is amazing how skilled betrayed people become at using technology to discover details. You can find texts and emails the government can't. Sleuthing is nearly unavoidable and done to discover facts without a filter. Stalking is also a fight response. Stalking can become obsessive and antagonistic.

As the betrayed partner in crisis, you may sleuth and stalk to take control of further discovery. No more surprises. No relying on disclosure from your partner who had the affair. Stalking, however, is illegal, anti-relational, and can be a setback to repair. There is a fine balance between stalking the truth and stalking a person. When you obsessively stalk and sleuth, you may find yourself deeper in relationship with the affair partner versus getting them out of your life. Your fight behavior may seem justified now when the anger is hot, but later, it will be seen by your children and others as out of control. Learn to recognize and avoid damaging fight behavior. Productive fight behaviors include setting boundaries, speaking your truth, and standing up for what you need.

Flight

A flight response can look like quiet withdrawal as you prepare to leave. You might seek escape into substances; this is leaving in a different way. If you are a betrayed person in flight mode you may move to the other bedroom, your parents' home, or a new place altogether. One client, upon learning about an affair, began assessing his finances versus turning toward his wife to try to work things out. An extreme flight looks like cut-off and immediate divorce. Flight responses are self-protective. Productive flight behaviors include focusing on your own safety and giving yourself space to think. Before you take full flight, stop. Complete your healing by staying the course on the map of affair repair.

Freeze

An extreme freeze looks like shutdown and numbness. If you are a betrayed person, you may be in such shock that you have no ability to move forward in or out of the relationship. You may fall into a deep depression, unable to get out of bed. A more moderate freeze response is a desire to tell no one and to check into the cold, lonely shameful prison of being betrayed. As a moderately frozen betrayed partner, you may dissociate or disconnect from your pain, avoid conflict, and go through the motions until things settle into a new illusion of normalcy.

If you are a betrayed person in freeze mode, you might avoid burdening your partner with any of your feelings. There is a sense of numbness and dumbness. The numbing and the dumbing—as in not speaking—stops you from feeling your own pain or bringing on more by learning more information. You may sit locked in a sense of shame, wondering, "How could I be so stupid? How could I let this happen to me? Why am I still with this person?" As a person in freeze mode you will be tempted to skip the important fact-finding you need to establish a true foundation for moving forward. Productive freeze behaviors include not saying the first thing that comes to mind or not heading straight to the divorce lawyer's office. Freezing does not provoke protective behaviors from your partner. Freezing gives you time to think, allow the information to begin to sink in, and puts a pause between stimulus and response.

Fawn

Almost the opposite of fight, flight, or freeze is a betrayed person in fawn mode. In fawn mode you will do anything to get your partner back into the relationship. As you fawn, you may use sex, helpfulness, people pleasing, an upbeat mood, and extra effort to win your partner back. A fawning person is acting out of a need for safety and security at the cost of giving too much of themselves. Productive fawning behavior opens you to repairing the relationship and seeing your partner as a person who made a mistake, not the enemy. A fawn response can be an advantage but is not a guarantee.

Betrayer Crisis Phase Experience

If you are the person who cheated, you may not be directly traumatized, but you are directly dealing with trauma and most likely are not trained. You likely don't know what to do. Sometimes even trained personnel are stunned, like Caleb, a fireman. Caleb came in with his wife, Minh. He sat on the sofa and looked at me for help like a dissociated, mute man in shock as his wife presented copies of the nude photos that he and their daughter's teacher had exchanged. It wasn't that he didn't want to repair; he didn't know where to begin. Here was a first responder, highly skilled in dealing with emergencies and trauma, but not this kind.

When caught in an affair you may also have an initial fight, flight, freeze, or fawn response as you try to deal with the intensity of the trauma. Caleb, the fireman froze. Terrence, the store manager fought when his betrayed wife confronted him, demanding to know if he wanted her or the other woman. He attacked back, saying, "Why do you think I am here in therapy?!" Terrence's trauma response was to fight. Though he felt guilty and was open to repair, in crisis he felt threatened and was unable to be vulnerable enough for self-examination or reconciliation.

There are four types of betrayer responses in crisis: regretful, uncertain, doubtful, or forced. Traditionally, the betrayed will want the betrayer to be regretful and will experience any hesitancy as uncaring. This is not necessarily the case. Nearly every person caught in an affair will feel guilty. All but very few partners will immediately want to end the affair.

In my experience, approximately 5 percent of the people caught in an affair are fully regretful, 60 percent are uncertain to varying degrees, a solid 30 percent are outright doubtful, and the remaining 5 percent are forced. Partners who have been betrayed will do better if they do not expect immediate and complete remorse. Unmet expectations only cause more pain and the feeling of being let down. A regretful betrayer helps but this is no guarantee for a secure and lasting repair. Such was the case with Ariel. She was regretful and would shed tears at the thought of how she had hurt Carl. He was angry but ultimately accepted her back into his heart. Three years later she was caught with another man. Complete regret is not a guarantee of marriage transformation.

Regretful

Regretful is the rarest type of betrayer response. **Regretful means to have an overwhelming feeling of sadness and remorse for what you have done.** There is little to no fear of consequences because when you are regretful, you accept them. More than anything else, a regretful betrayer wishes the affair had not happened. Above all they regret the pain they have caused their partner and their relationship. This does not mean other concerns about the relationship are ignored or forgotten as the couple moves forward, but the overriding sentiment is regret.

All people caught in an affair, to some degree, are regretful unless they are amoral, antisocial, pathological, or so wounded they are incapable of empathy. Your betrayed partner may think you are without regret, but most likely this is not the case. It is very, very rare to encounter a partner who has zero guilty feelings.

People are imperfect. Yes, people of good character cheat. And if you are the person who had the affair and are reading this book, you are at least curious about what you might do to help heal the hurt you caused. Let the map of affair repair be your guide.

Uncertain

To be uncertain is the most common type of betrayer response. **If you have been caught in an affair and are uncertain about repairing, this is normal and does not mean your marriage will fail in overcoming the affair.** You do not have to know what you want right now. You can repair the hurt and make your mind up along the way.

If you are uncertain, your guilt may be mixed with disenfranchised grief. **Disenfranchised grief** is the socially unacceptable sadness you may experience when the affair ends. You may regret hurting your partner and the choices you made, but you still miss the affair. You may still have feelings for the affair partner. Even if you are ashamed of those feelings and are successfully disowning them, those feelings don't go away, they go underground. Your attachment wound from ending the affair must be healed. *Your betrayed partner is not the one to soothe the disenfranchised grief that adds to your uncertainty.* Disenfranchised grief is part of your individual experience.

Most people who cheated feel guilty and want to help fix their partner's broken heart. Many betrayers feel so bad that they consider returning to the marriage even when it is not the marriage they want. You may feel conflicted in returning because you do not know how to resolve the problems that were masked by the affair. Now you must confront the problems without escape to the other relationship. It is common to be unsure. The map of affair repair can help you repair the damage from the affair and transform your marriage. You can take responsibility for repair and expect that both of you will work toward a better relationship. Your uncertainty will turn into resolve as you and your partner gain momentum along the journey.

Doubtful

Doubtful is the second most common type of betrayer response. **A doubtful betrayer doubts the affair can be overcome and that the marriage is worth repairing.** As a doubtful betrayer, you may resist revealing your feelings. You do not want to lie, but you also don't want to deal with the pain and trouble of fixing everything. The truth of your feelings may be ugly, uncomfortable, or hurtful to your partner.

If you are doubtful, you may be unsure how to ask for change. You may feel hopeless or unworthy. You may also be afraid you will be hurt again if you return to the unsatisfactory marriage you left. Unbelievable as it may seem to your partner who was betrayed, you have gone through a lot in breaking up your marriage. Now that the affair has been discovered, you may resist going back. You may worry that now you will have to work even harder to get the changes you need because of the betrayal. You doubt the effort will be worth it.

If you are doubtful, the process of repair seems too difficult, so you think, "Why bother?" Even if the relationship can be repaired, the relationship is not worth returning to anyway. You may have little desire to embark on the affair repair journey and have little hope for marriage transformation. If you are doubtful and your partner is willing, you might consider working out of phase at times. Making relationship changes while you repair can inspire hope in the face of your doubt.

Forced

This type of betrayer does not last long in the relationship. **If you feel like you have to repair, but really don't want to, you may feel forced.** The difference between an uncertain and forced betrayer is that a forced betrayer does not want to be in the marriage, and they know it. Most people will consider leaving the marriage. People will also consider repairing out of guilt, damage control, for the kids, or other reasons, but a person who is forced cares less about those things and just wants out. When you feel forced, you may be angry. You may resist or fake participation in counseling. You may avoid reading or discussing this book with your partner. You do not expect your marriage to evolve into anything good. If you find yourself in this category, give yourself some time to see if anything changes. Some people go between forced and doubtful or have sweeping swings between feeling forced and regretful. Out of phase work, which means focusing on marriage transformation versus affair repair, may help you feel less forced and possibly inspire you to work toward what you want versus what you do not.

Betrayers, Try to Be Calm

If you are the person who was caught in the affair, strive to be as calm as possible in the face of your partner's rollercoaster of emotions—short of abuse. Betrayed partners in pain can cross the line saying unproductive and emotionally abusive things with the intention to punish, hurt directly, or attack your worth as a human being. This creates a cycle of fear and power, rather than a path to healing and repair. Neither partner should accept abuse. You can set boundaries on the expression of pain. You can say, "I know I hurt you and I am willing to listen, but you cannot emotionally abuse me, yell in front of our children, throw things, or hit me."

Not overreacting to the pain and anger of your betrayed partner will help them feel safer. You are the person who can help. Being calm may feel impossible since you have likely been avoiding difficult interactions with your partner for some time. Now is the time to do something different to change the course of your future for the better.

How You Might Stay Calm

- One good way to stay present with pain is to **say nothing and listen**. Focus on calming your body by exhaling slightly longer than you inhale. You can count in for four and out for seven. This will help you ground your body as emotions escalate. *Your elevated partner may call you out on your seemingly fake and detached calm. Be authentic. Tell them you are trying to be calm, present, and not run away from this difficult moment.*

- **When you speak, use reflective listening**. Reflective listening is using descriptive words to show that you are listening and hear them. You can say things like "I hear that you are furious" or "You don't feel you can forgive me." Saying, "I understand" is *not* reflective listening. Saying, "I realize you feel you can never trust me again, your heart is broken because of it, and you don't know what to do now," is reflective listening. The key is to use more descriptive words.

- **Offer no defense.** Simply listening without interruption or defense is a healing presence. Offer no defense when your partner is in crisis. If your partner says, "You are a liar!" Do not respond with, "If we had been having sex, I wouldn't have had to lie." Just agree or nod. You will discuss the sex later. If the conversation escalates to ongoing yelling, attacking, or violence, the conversation must pause. It is unproductive. Take a break.

- **Offer reassurance** if you can. Do not over-promise. If it is true, you can say things like, "I love you." "I choose you." "We will find a way." Do not lie. State the things you intend to do to make things right. You might say, "I will be here as long as it takes to work through this," "I will be home early tonight," or "I will answer your texts right away."

Tell the Truth

A person in crisis is limited in their ability to think clearly. The biological alarm for both partners is so loud in crisis your thoughts are constantly interrupted. You cannot think. Feeling is taking over thinking as you instinctively and urgently seek safety. Both partners need facts to understand whether they are moving toward or away from further disaster. There is an intensity in fact-finding. The alarm system will not shut off easily.

Your betrayed partner is in a double bind of "I need you/get away from me," as they turn toward you for information in this crisis. The double bind for you is that telling the truth will not stop the pain and chaos quickly, which will make you want to run away. Taking in and telling the truth in crisis is difficult.

The truth will have to be told over and over on the map of affair repair. Your betrayed partner needs you to weather the storms along the way. Remember, the challenge of the crisis phase is to tell as much truth as possible to shorten your journey overall.

Crisis is the first opportunity to take steps toward healing. Telling the truth is an opportunity for change and the first request for a healing sacrifice. A **healing sacrifice** is when the person who cheated puts their partner's pain first. A healing sacrifice happens when you empathetically embrace your partner's pain at your own cost to repair the wound you caused. A healing sacrifice is not to be confused with abuse. There is no healing in payback or out of control emotional abuse. There is healing when you hold the pain of another and put them first. Your pain also will be addressed over the course of the map of affair repair.

Avoid Trickle-Down Truth

People who have cheated may feel they are protecting their partner from further pain by opting for **trickle-down truth**. Trickle-down truth is sharing a little bit at a time. Trickle-down truth only increases the fear and insecurity of your betrayed partner. The betrayed is always wondering, *"What else do I not know?"* Sometimes trickle-down truth comes from fear and avoidance. This is angering, abandoning, and disrespectful to the betrayed. Trickle-down truth provokes the betrayed partner because they cannot get to safety. You are always withholding some information that may hurt them. Get it out now.

Sometimes trickle-down truth is truth that was not shared but discovered by the betrayed partner. You may have forgotten that detail or even tried to avoid disclosure. Betrayed partners are skillful detectives. They are very good at getting copies of old messages, emails, and locations. They are experts at trapping cheating partners in inconsistencies. If your betrayed partner has discovered more truth, it is best that you be honest as to why you did not disclose the facts in the first place.

Old Ways and Patterns

The way you handled stress in the past may interfere with trusting or telling the truth in crisis. Past patterns may trap you and your partner into roles, making it difficult for either of you to believe the other could possibly change. As discussed in the chapter on normalcy, an old response pattern may cause a person who had the affair to default to fighting, fleeing, freezing, or fawning. Both the betrayed and the betrayer are experiencing unique physiological responses to the crisis that will exaggerate their response. Become aware of how your survival response is keeping you safe by thwarting reconnection.

Past Ways and Patterns in Crisis

Barbara and Bill, both in their early seventies, came to me to work through an affair of the past. Barbara had grown up in a critical, detached home. Her mother was judgmental, and her father absent, approving only when Barbara was behaving and well-groomed. Barbara learned to please, use her sexuality, avoid showing weakness, and never directly pursue what she wanted. She sneaked around, presenting herself as the good girl while she drank and committed petty shoplifting crimes. She married Bill and followed him across the country to law school. Barbara gave up finishing her PhD to please him and did not pursue her own desires. Bill absorbed himself in his career and came home to the "perfect wife" with "no needs."

Unfortunately, when Barbara began to express her needs, Bill did not know what to do with them. That was not part of the original relating pattern, so Barbara went back to sneaking drinks and began having affairs. Bill found out, the family moved, and nothing was said again for thirty years until Bill began assessing his life and legacy. He wanted to be with a partner he could trust. He wanted to take the journey on the map of affair repair.

Barbara began doing her personal growth work. She attended Alcoholics Anonymous meetings and regular weekly sessions with her therapist. Barbara acknowledged that as a young girl she had coped with the detached and contingent love from her parents by presenting herself as perfect while sneaking attention from others. She also acknowledged that she forgave herself this coping strategy even though it hurt Bill.

Barbara had a hard time staying present with Bill's pain. Bill had a hard time believing she was really trying. Bill struggled to understand, accept, and forgive her weakness despite her honesty and

*genuine desire to repair the relationship. Past patterns prolonged
their experience in the crisis phase.*

Crisis can trigger negative problem-solving strategies that include
lying, appeasing, fighting, or fleeing. The betrayed person may wonder
how the cheating partner cannot tell them the whole truth or why
they are now feeling like the victim. Past trauma prevents people from
behaving in more productive ways in crisis.

The stress and high emotion of discovery has also thrown the person
who cheated into survival mode. They too are afraid of losing their
whole world. Defenses will arise to protect the betrayer from flooding
with fear as they confront the fact that they may lose their primary
relationship, family, friends, self-respect, and more. The person who
was betrayed may not care about those fears, thinking those consequences should have been considered before the affair began. Regardless of what should or should not have been done, we are now in crisis.
Both people will need to manage their own activated system to bear
and hear the truth. Addiction, trauma, or poor patterns of relating that
were part of normalcy will affect how you manage the crisis phase.

Trauma and Coping in Crisis

*When Antoni discovered Clair's affair, he wanted to know all the
details. Clair did not want to disclose the identity of the women
who helped her set up the evening of anonymous kinky sex. Nor
did she want to share the email she had exchanged with her
affair partner in coordinating the meet-up. She claimed she did
not want to share the correspondence without the affair partner's
permission. This enraged Antoni further because she cared more
about protecting women he didn't know and another man than
addressing his hurt.*

*Protecting the affair partner is a very common knee-jerk reac-
tion in the crisis phase. Clair claimed she was frightened Antoni
would act irrationally and go after the affair partner. This was*

a reasonable fear, as Antoni was quite angry. However, her fear was exacerbated by a history of physical and sexual abuse prior to meeting Antoni. In her experience, men were unpredictable and abusive. Like many victims of sexual abuse, she felt Antoni's actions would be her fault and her responsibility. Not only did she feel responsible for Antoni's broken heart, but also for his actions.

Clair deleted the email exchange leading up to the encounter to make everything go away and prevent further provocation. Like the betrayal, this was yet another decision made without Antoni's input. Clair told herself Antoni wouldn't care about those details. However, no detail is too small for a betrayed person. Details are critical in making sense of what happened. The smallest piece of evidence can help piece together the reality that has been blown up. Clair's past trauma history was getting in the way of telling Antoni the most desperately needed truth.

If you are caught in an affair and are afraid your betrayed partner will act irrationally, you should be direct. Offer to share the requested information when your betrayed partner is calmer. Disclose the information in a therapist's office. Notify the affair partner or other targeted person and authorities if you suspect a threat to anyone's physical well-being. It is reasonable to try to prevent damage driven by uncontrolled emotions. Unnecessary damage includes physical harm, threatening someone, ruining careers, or endangering livelihoods. Beyond that, it is best that betrayers do not unnecessarily protect the affair partner.

Hyper-Healing

Occasionally a couple will experience **hyper-healing** in crisis. Hyper-healing is an intense emotional and physical coming together. This can be the best sex of the couple's life, fueled by a deep, psychological desire to reconnect. Hyper-healing can be an animal drive in the betrayed to mark their territory or prove they are a better lover. The person who was cheated on longs to experience the spark that was shared with the affair partner, to capture it and take it for their own. For some, jealousy is an aphrodisiac and an erotic revenge.

The hyper-healing couple is seeking to establish a connection they can feel. This connection is experienced in their heads after long talks, in their hearts through shared emotions, and in their bodies by physical sensing. The partner who was cheated on is processing every word, intonation, and gesture like a supercomputer, seeking safety and soothing from the betrayer. The partner who had the affair may feel such remorse that they seek deep intimacy with their partner. Hyper-healing can be the deepest sense of acceptance and reassurance that all might be forgiven. Regardless of motive, a physiological process of reconnecting is happening. Emotions are intense, talks are deep and intimate.

Do not hold back on hyper-healing if you feel it. The best thing a couple can do is to build upon the connecting experience. However, if you are not feeling it, *do not force hyper-healing*. Forcing hyper-healing can make you want to turn away from intimacy altogether. Not all couples experience hyper-healing, and that is okay. Absence of hyper-healing does not detract from your chances of success on the map of affair repair.

Forgiveness in Crisis

The betrayed partner may or may not be interested in offering forgiveness. The person who had the affair may or may not be interested in asking for it. Forgiveness in crisis will be influenced by each partner's trauma response to discovery and may or may not be lasting.

Janis Abrahams Spring, PhD, author of *How Can I Forgive You?*, outlines four approaches to forgiveness. With **cheap forgiveness**, the person who cheated does not address the pain they have caused, and the betrayed is so worried about being abandoned that they quickly forgive to keep the relationship together. **Refusing to forgive**, on the other hand, keeps the betrayed partner in control, safe and protected. Betrayed people who refuse to forgive want to punish the offender and retaliate for the pain they have experienced. They are resistant to offering compassion and are not sure they want to repair. **Acceptance** is the healing gift you can give yourself and says nothing about the other. Acceptance means you accept what is. Acceptance can come quickly, or it can be hard won after wrestling with reality, wishing it weren't so. From an approach of acceptance, you are free to continue the relationship or leave it. Acceptance is rare in the early phases but comes more fully as you leave the map of affair repair and work on marriage transformation. **Genuine forgiveness** involves both partners working toward a better relationship. Genuine forgiveness is a mutual effort; it is conditional and must be earned. *As the partner who had the affair works to heal the wound, the betrayed works to let go of resentment and need for constant amends.* If either party fails to do their work, genuine forgiveness cannot be achieved.

Key Concepts

The key feature of the journey through crisis is the activation of the fight-or-flight system in *both* partners as the meaning of discovery begins to sink in. Crisis is the most acute, painful phase.

- Two immediate actions you can take to make things more secure are to end the affair and spend as much time together as possible. If this cannot happen, be authentic and truthful.
- The **betrayed** is experiencing a physiological response to threat. This can include fight, flight, freeze, or fawn.
- The **betrayer** is also experiencing a physiological response that includes fight, flight, freeze, or fawn.
- There are four types of betrayer responses in crisis: regretful, uncertain, doubtful, and forced.
- Preexisting ways, patterns, and problem-solving strategies will affect how crisis is handled.
- A *healing sacrifice* is the pain and difficulty each partner accepts as part of the healing process.
- *Trickle-down truth* is truth that is revealed little by little over time.

- Some couples will experience *hyper-healing*, which is intense emotional and physical closeness.
- Forgiveness in crisis is likely a survival response and should be given time to develop one way or the other.
- **Average Duration:** Crisis can last two weeks to two months or even longer if there are preexisting patterns, trauma or addiction preventing sharing and hearing truth. Crisis cannot go on forever because your body cannot maintain this high level of alert.
- **Goal:** To establish as much truth as can be known. The faster you get the truth out, the shorter the crisis phase, and the better able you will be to deal with the next phase of your healing journey.
- **Do:**
  - Get an STI test
  - Move to another room or home if necessary
  - Spend productive time together
  - Seek a neutral, nonjudgmental, supportive and trustworthy person to share your feelings
  - Get professional help
- **Don't:**
  - Immediately get a divorce
  - Confront the affair partner
  - Tell everyone
  - Seek passionate, sympathetic friends to validate your position
  - Rush to forgiveness
- **If you are the betrayed partner,** accept the truth as an explanation, not an excuse for the betrayal. Your imperfections are not a reason or excuse to lie. Be mindful when you are so upset you cannot take in the information and communicate productively.
- **If you are the betrayer** who was involved in the affair, end the affair or be honest you will not. Be brave. Stay calm and present using suggestions offered in this section if necessary. Tell as much of the truth as possible.

Chapter 9
Affair PTS

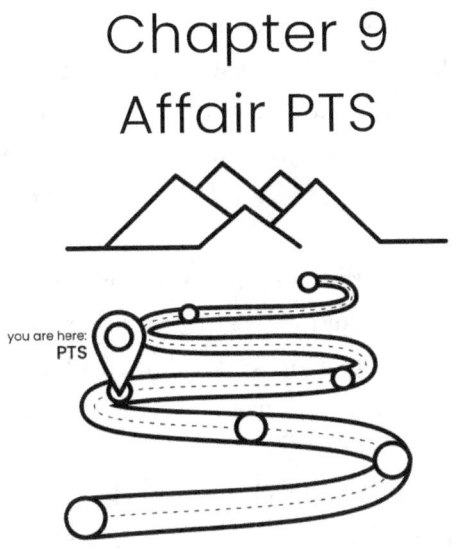

you are here:
PTS

*The challenge of the affair PTS phase
is to understand and recognize when it is happening.*

Your body cannot maintain the intense state of fight, flight, freeze, or fawn that is crisis. Your body will move *from dealing with pain to guarding against it* which marks the beginning of affair post-traumatic stress (PTS). Affair PTS is characterized by **uncontrollable, on again-off again** activation of your body's fight-or-flight system. Some triggering is obvious like accidentally running into the affair partner. Often thoughts alone will activate the system. With affair PTS even a random signal from the body such as the release of adrenaline can cause a sense of alarm. Affair PTS is like battling an enemy ambushing your thoughts, hijacking your mind, and surprise-attacking your system at any moment. Though affair PTS is uncontrollable, it can be addressed, managed, and will ultimately fade away.

Now that you have moved past discovery and crisis, the betrayed partner can be considered the **wounded partner.** If you are the wounded partner dealing with affair PTS, you are no longer in shock but remain in pain. Focus on keeping yourself safe and working toward healing, regardless of whether the relationship survives. In the affair PTS phase, the betraying partner becomes the **responsible partner.** As a responsible partner you are committed to repairing the damage that was caused by the betrayal as best you can. You are not necessarily committed to the marriage but are committed to repair. Trust has not yet been established for either of you. You will decide over the course of the map of affair repair if you would like to journey on to marriage transformation.

Both the wounded and the responsible partner are suffering from affair PTS. The wounded partner is suffering directly. The responsible partner is suffering by association and will do well to understand what is happening. Both partners' experiences will be addressed separately and together.

Affair PTS is not an official psychological diagnosis but based upon what I and other therapists observe in practice, the symptoms are strikingly like those suffering from post-traumatic stress after a life-threatening event such as war, an assault, or a major accident. An affair is a threat to the wounded partner's psychological existence, and the experience of pain travels along some of the same nerves and registers in some of the same areas of the brain as physical pain. Even soldiers have said the bullets they took overseas were not nearly as painful as the betrayal at home. Emotional betrayal is experienced in our bodies as life threatening. A wounded partner is no longer safe in the world.

Wounded partners cannot control affair PTS and neither can their responsible partner. Together you can address the symptoms. When you leave the wounded partner to deal with affair PTS on their own it is like abandoning them again and again. Taking a break from affair PTS is a luxury the wounded partner does not have. They cannot escape. The responsible partner has a critical role in helping the affair PTS go away by being present.

Kimmy broke out in quiet tears at the kitchen table. Johann wanted to run away. It had been two months since he had ended his affair. He felt guilty and frustrated, which only made him angry. She was not trying to make him feel guilty. Only a thought of he and the other woman having dinner together had come into her mind and the tears followed. They sat together in silence. Johann reached for her hand.

Wounded partners experience *ongoing, uncontrollable, and disturbing uncomfortable thoughts* (**triggers**) regarding the betrayal. Shared memories and experiences prior to discovery of the affair are now ruined and can no longer be revisited without pain. For Kimmy, memories of the special dinners she and Johann had shared will trigger images of him and the other woman. The affair rewrites the meaning of every memory because of what happened next. In Kimmy's rewrite, the dinners she and Johann shared were not special enough because he enjoyed them with another woman later. It will take a while before the memories can be healed.

Triggers bring about **aftershocks**, which is a re-experiencing of the pain of betrayal, like a flashback with traditional PTS. The body will physically react to the trigger. Pain will rise, and tears, like Kimmy's, will flow as the aftershock is felt.

Other affair PTS symptoms that are like those of traditional PTS include avoiding the source of the trauma and ongoing negative thoughts. Wounded partners may avoid being open to their responsible partner out of fear and pain. Kimmy could not bring herself to speak to Johann. Exaggerated feelings around guilt, shame, and the cause of the affair cloud everyday thinking. She wondered what was not good enough about the dinners with her that caused Johann to have dinner and more with another. Wounded partners experience emotional numbing to manage the ongoing, uncontrollable triggers. Like traditionally understood PTS, the ability to enjoy life as Kimmy had before the traumatic event was lost.

The hypervigilance of affair PTS can begin to tear down the relationship and prevent the wounded partner from experiencing a sense of safety and calm from which they might be able to securely attach. Mara, in the Forget Forgiveness for Now story, was unable to trust Greg after his repeated infidelity. Affair PTS would not go away for good reason. It kept her safe. However, it also held her back from seeing that he had really changed. Greg understood that his actions were the source of her affair PTS and was patient.

The wounded partner must work to respond productively when dealing with affair PTS. The wounded partner cannot just let their emotions fly and expect healing to occur. If the wounded partner is emotionally out of control or continues to be inconsolable, both will end up destroyed. There is only one logical choice for a responsible partner in an unsolvable situation and that is to pull away. Kim was unable to speak but able to allow Johann to hold her hand. Everyone succeeds when you can self-regulate and work together through affair PTS.

The goal of this phase is to learn to manage the pain and fear of each affair PTS moment until symptoms are gone. Just as massage or analgesics might be used to aid in reducing the pain of a physical wound, the techniques suggested here can help in the healing of an affair. If you are dealing with affair PTS right now, you may not believe this to be possible, but it is.

Affair PTS symptoms last more than four weeks and, though they may fade, they can continue for six months to a year or more. Affair PTS disrupts the wounded partner's ability to work, relate, parent, and generally live life as they did before the affair. Though it is difficult, affair PTS also gives the couple an opportunity to work and heal together.

Hypervigilance

Hypervigilance is an intense checking for safety. This includes looking at phones for communication with the affair partner, checking locations, confirming whereabouts, and questioning. The relationship is now in a state of high alert, and **as long as one person is activated, the relationship cannot move forward**. Greg had to be patient with Mara after his multiple affairs which made her hypervigilant whenever he left her sight. The wounded partner is anticipating another attack, and the responsible partner feels under surveillance. Every minute late, unaccounted whereabouts, or slip-up in a sentence is cause for alarm. Hypervigilance is part of affair PTS. The wounded and responsible partner should both be patient as they work together to manage the symptoms.

Triggers

Triggers for the wounded partner are *repeating, involuntary, and disturbing* thoughts about the affair. Triggers activate the body's nervous system, causing irritability, rumination, and distress as the body struggles to protect itself and find safety. Triggers happen over and over about the same issues, topics, or questions. Triggers are intense and will not simply go away with a logical explanation or personal will.

Some triggers can be foreseen, such as an anniversary, location, or the ping of a text notification. Often, however, triggers pop up randomly. Something as routine as a passing silver minivan (if the affair partner drove a minivan) can trigger affair PTS. Just having a quiet dinner at home triggered Kimmy to tears thinking of Johann and his lover at a similar table in her apartment. A random thought or physical sensation can send a cascade of affair PTS. The mind is not always an ally as it interprets these signals, and when triggered it is predisposed to catastrophe. For every real text, photo, receipt, or shared information, there are a thousand imaginings. The imagination is often worse than reality. Kimmy imagined Johann was passionately in love with his affair partner when it was a passing fling and over time, he did not know how to get out of it. He loved Kimmy and wanted a family with her.

Be patient. Wounded partners will ask the same questions over and over in different ways. **The responsible partner will need near-super-human patience to repeat and repeat true, soothing responses until**

the wounded partner will either accept the answers, get used to the feeling of being unsafe, or leave. Dealing with triggers can be so exhausting that both partners will consider leaving.

Aftershocks

Triggers bring about **aftershocks**, which is a reexperiencing of the pain of betrayal, like Kimmy's silent tears when she thought of her partner with another. Aftershocks can be triggered by a feeling of normalcy. The last time the wounded partner felt like everything was safe and normal, an affair was happening. There is an eerie quiet. If you have ever been in an earthquake, it is not the initial earthquake that is distressing. It is the free-floating anxiety of waiting for the next after-shock that is unnerving. It is not uncommon for people to sell their homes and move away from all they have known after an earthquake. Each aftershock is amplified by the remembrance of the first, with the time in between filled with pins and needles. The wounded partner will need the responsible partner to be grounding, patient, and reas-suring that nothing is happening. Or, if something is still happening, be honest, so the wounded partner knows exactly where it is and can make choices to move to safety.

Rumination

Rumination is *thinking and rethinking* about all angles of the affair. Rumination is like a thought rut. The wounded partner is forever revis-iting the what-ifs. Questions continue in the mind. What could I have done? What should I do now? What is (s)he like? How did this occur? Why did this happen? Where did they meet? Where was I? What was (s)he thinking? Everything and anything affair related is revisited. Few other topics enter the mind of a ruminating wounded partner beyond the affair. Life seems to be on autopilot as the wounded partner goes to work, picks up the kids, or attends social events. Their mind is rumi-nating as they go through the motions.

Ruminating brings back the trauma of discovery again and again establishing neurological pathways in your brain, deepening grooves, and making it harder to break out of that thought pattern. Rumination makes you feel helpless in controlling your mind because you can't get out of the rut. The responsible partner has a responsibility to help because the wounded partner never would have fallen into rumination if the affair hadn't happened. The wounded partner also has the responsibility to work on stopping the rumination. The responsible partner can continually provide facts and encouragement. The wounded partner can strive not to fall into the ruts and accept the help.

For the fourth time in the same conversation Kenji asked Ryan, "Why did you take him to our favorite restaurant?!"

Ryan remained calm, knowing Kenji was dealing with rumination, replied, "Ken, I love you. I will tell you again, but do you remember what I have said?"

"'You couldn't think of another restaurant!'"

"Yes, and I wasn't thinking what that would mean to you. Do you have other questions for me?" Ryan's calm voice helped Kenji trust he was telling the truth and turn his mind to another question that would move them along in healing.

Good Guy/Bad Guy Thinking

When we are feeling threatened, there is a "good guy" and a "bad guy." Guess who is the good guy? This answer is deep in our bodies, not in our heads. The affair may be over, but our bodies are still judging. The responsible partner is instinctively framed as the bad guy. This is particularly strong in wounded partners who have a clear sense of right and wrong.

Rose, a lawyer, said to her husband, Sol, "I wish you hadn't done this because now you can never be right." She felt that because Sol had had an affair, she now had the edge in all disputes from co-parenting to how the home should be run. After the affair, anytime Sol failed to pick up the milk or became grouchy, the small bit of irritation pulled the emotional thread of the deep well of pain and became another example of letdown.

One bad thing reminded Rose of another and another. On the negative emotion highway, all roads led to Rome, the capital of betrayals, which is the affair. Snoring too loudly ended up in a fight about Sol's infidelity. If you are the wounded partner, you must work to curb the cascade of judgment and criticism. If you do not entertain the possibility that your responsible partner is capable of being a good guy, they can never become your repairing partner who is working toward establishing trust, and your relationship cannot heal.

Key Concepts

Affair PTS is characterized by *uncontrollable, on again-off again* activation of the body's fight-or-flight system. Affair PTS responses are impulsive, subconscious, and for the wounded partner's protection.

- The betrayed partner evolves to the **wounded partner** allowing their hurt to be addressed.
- The betrayer evolves to the **responsible partner** willing to address the wound.
- Neither the wounded nor the responsible partner can control affair PTS.
  - **Triggers** for the wounded partner are *repeating, involuntary, and disturbing* thoughts about the affair.
  - Triggers bring about **aftershocks**, which are a reexperiencing of the pain of betrayal.
  - **Hypervigilance** is intense checking for safety that includes constant communication and wondering about the whereabouts of the responsible partner.

- o **Rumination** is *thinking and rethinking* about all aspects of the affair.
- Affair PTS causes good guy/bad guy thinking that will take time to get past.
- **Average Duration:** Affair PTS can last two to six months; can be longer if there is trauma in your past or addiction that can complicate the healing process.
- **Goal:** The goal of the affair PTS phase is to learn to recognize it when it is happening.
- **Do:**
  - o Have patience
  - o Learn all you can about the symptoms
  - o Learn from the upcoming chapters about managing the symptoms
  - o Know affair PTS will abate as you move through the rest of this phase
- **Don't:**
  - o Let yourself act out of control
  - o Abandon your wounded partner to manage the symptoms
  - o Blame your wounded partner, affair PTS is uncontrollable
- **If you are the wounded partner**, work to manage the triggers and aftershocks as well as possible. Communicate when you are reexperiencing the trauma. Avoid the all-out fight-or-flight responses such as attack, fawn, or shutdown if possible.
- **If you are the responsible partner**, understand your partner cannot control affair PTS. Triggers are everywhere and cannot always be foreseen or intercepted. Be present during an aftershock in a patient manner as best you can.

Chapter 10
Healing Affair PTS

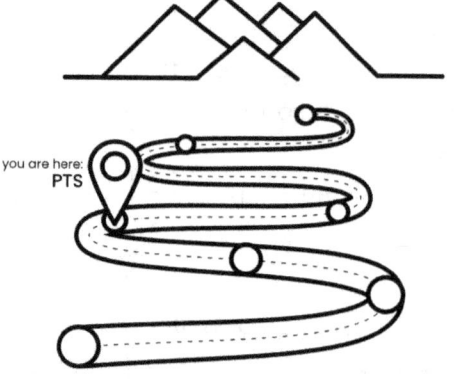

you are here:
PTS

The challenge of healing affair PTS
is to learn to experience and manage the symptoms.

Emotions in the affair PTS phase can be like the weather—beautiful and sunny one moment, with a sudden burst of lightning and thunder the next. Triggers and aftershocks do not go away; they lessen over time. Affair PTS is healed when the wounded partner builds a tolerance to the symptoms they are experiencing. The facts will always be the facts. The affair has happened, and any thought of it will bring some reaction. The goal is to be able to tolerate the facts so that you can decide if acceptance is worth the gift of a better relationship or moving on. That calm clarity comes much later in the marriage transformation phase. First, you both must manage the affair PTS in the body and mind.

"Us" and Trauma

When two "me's" enter a relationship, there is an "us." Like conjoined twins, a couple shares an "us" body. Some conjoined twins can be separated safely; others cannot. One partner may be okay without the other, but a vital organ may have been taken in the separation caused by the affair. Even if both partners can survive without the other, there is a wounding in the separating surgery, and it is painful for both.

The "Us" Body

Emotions are felt in the body. The trauma felt in one person can be felt in another, even if only vaguely via mirror neurons. **Mirror neurons** are neurons in our brain that fire when we see another person do or express something. For example, when Johann saw Kimmy silently crying at the dinner table, he felt her pain. He wanted to run away from the pain and she did, too, but she had no choice. The pain was in her body. Rather than leave the table not wanting to deal with the pain, Johann reached out his hand. Mirror neurons aid in empathy. Neurodivergent people may not be able to interpret these signals. Most people can interpret the signals from their mirror neurons and experience in their own bodies, even in some small way, what others experience. We are connected to others.

In betrayal, the emotional shared body has been wounded. One part may hurt more than the other, but the whole body is hurting. Just as when a leg is broken and the other extremities are intact, the body itself is in no way "fine." Kimmy was hurt more than Johann, but he was sad that she was sad. With an affair, the couple has suffered a wound, and it will take both partners to heal it.

In addition to experiencing the other person in the "us" through mirror neurons, there is neuroception. **Neuroception** is the body's way of determining if things are safe. Neuroception is the response of a system of nerves grounded in the polyvagal nerve which runs from the base of the brain down the spine. Neuroception comes before, and overrides, thinking. Polyvagal theory explains why a baby will coo with its caregiver and cry with a stranger. The baby's safety is not threatened logically or even actually, but the baby's neuroception is telling it something is off. Without her direct control, Kimmy's body is using neuroception to determine if Johann is sincere or if he is now a stranger to her. Over time, the wounded and vulnerable small self within her will learn to better interpret outside cues to determine if the relationship is safe or not, but the first response comes from her body. Johann's calm presence, loving eyes, and warm, open hand were a safety Kimmy could feel.

Bottom-Up Healing

Bottom-up healing begins in the body, not the mind. Bottom-up healing is when the *body* experiences safety. Bottom-up healing for the "us" body can be experienced directly via physical touch or neuroception. Our bodies can sense the sincerity of our partners. Kimmy could feel Johann loved her though her mind was racing. Johann knew she was struggling, but she was not pushing him away. The couple was beginning to experience bottom-up healing in the "us" body.

Couples can deepen their experience of the "us" body through **sustained eye-contact**, **rhythmic breathing**, and **intentional touch**. These experiences can be intimate and intense. Do not be surprised if these exercises are uncomfortable. Many people prefer to be in the "me" body. These exercises must only be done with mutual agreement. Do not force, push, or pressure your partner.

Eye Contact

To practice being in the "us" body through eye contact, pick a time both partners are feeling calm and open. Sit facing each other in a comfortable position and gently look into each other's eyes for two minutes without talking. Become aware of how you are feeling. Are you comfortable? Feeling vulnerable? Avoiding the moment with humor? Squirming? See if you can move past it to experience acceptance. If you or your partner becomes too uncomfortable, take a break and try again later. Be non-judgmental and don't pressure the exercise. Go slowly until each of you feel safe and comfortable in sustained eye contact.

Rhythmic Breathing

Couples can use rhythmic breathing to activate a state of calm in the "us" body. Sit or lie down together. Lie in a comfortable position, holding hands, and synchronize your breath. Inhale deeply together through the nose for a count of four, hold for seven and exhale through your mouth for a count of eight. Repeat this exercise for five to ten minutes. Humming together on the exhale together will further stimulate the vagal nerve.

Intentional Touch

Finally, intentional touch or massage can reduce stress and increase feelings of safety in the "me" and "us" body. Intentional touch is holding hands, hugging, or spooning. You can also put a hand on your partner's back, arm, leg, or shoulder letting them know you care. Massage can also be healing beyond words. Take turns giving each other gentle hand, foot, or shoulder massages. Use slow, soothing strokes. Strive to be fully present in giving and receiving. Proceed slowly and take a break if either of you is not feeling safe or wholly present.

Do not attempt any of these exercises if either of you is feeling unsafe or unable to tolerate the closeness. Wait until there is inner calm and strength or preparedness to enter the exercise.

Top-Down Healing

Top-down healing occurs when the mind concludes it is safe so that the body is not continually triggered by thoughts. Just because you feel a sense of safety does not necessarily mean the affair has ended. Safety means you know the truth so you can make decisions to keep yourself safe. Traumatized minds need a story that makes sense and a clear understanding of what happened so they can make decisions for the future whether you stay together or not. Top-down healing occurs when what the mind predicts is what happens. Astrid could never heal from the top down because though Jay held her, came to therapy, said he loved her, and wanted to repair, she could see via the text messages she was secretly reading that he was still in contact with his affair partner.

If the story makes sense, the wounded partner can make decisions to self-protect or move to safety. Ellie, in the Bubble Bath Miracle story was honest. She cut contact with her affair partner, but she wasn't sure she wanted to repair the marriage. Knowing the truth empowered Aaron to make predictions and protect himself as necessary. Together with honesty, presence, and safety, the couple found their way. Truth is the bedrock of top-down healing.

Window of Tolerance

The **window of tolerance** is the state of being where you can *think and feel* at the same time. Healing cannot happen outside the window of tolerance. Affair PTS is upsetting at least one member of the "us" body, so both partners must learn to bring the mind and body back into the window of tolerance for healing to occur.

When a person is within the window of tolerance, they are **regulated** and can think and feel. If a person is only thinking but not feeling, that is **dissociating**. When your partner dissociates, they will mostly be talking about logic, protecting their feelings. For example, a frustrated and dissociated responsible partner might say with little emotion things like, "I have my location services on. Everything is fine. It's over." Or a dissociated wounded partner might say, "I am okay. I can just look at your location, no problem." These sentences in the affair repair phase are fine if there is care, concern, or vulnerability expressed. But if they are emotionless; they are dissociated.

If a person is only feeling without being able to moderate those feelings, that is **dysregulating**. When your partner is dysregulated there will be no talking sense to help resolve the problem.

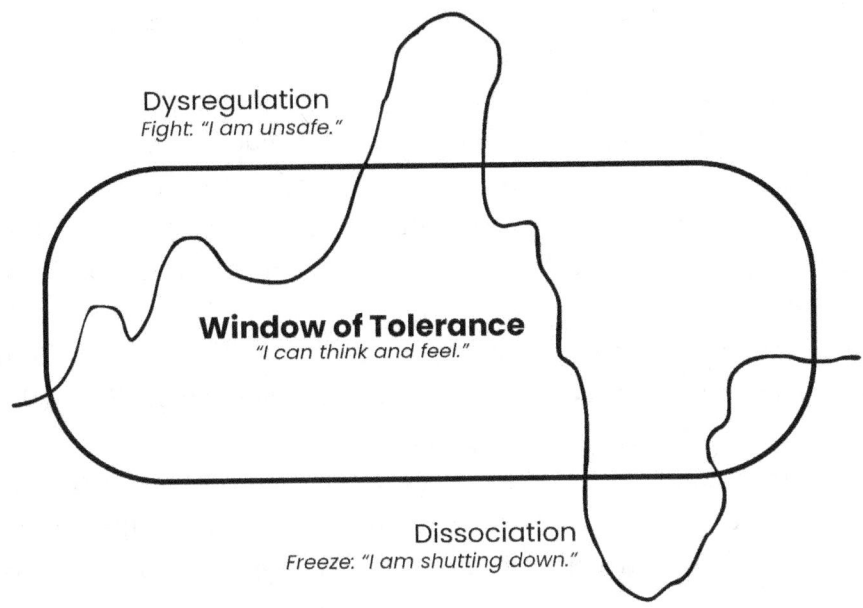

Dysregulation
Fight: "I am unsafe."

Window of Tolerance
"I can think and feel."

Dissociation
Freeze: "I am shutting down."

Greg knew Mara was so hurt by his multiple infidelities that even the sight of a blonde woman in the next line at the grocery store would be a dysregulating trigger. "Do you want to get her number?" she would loudly ask. Rather than engage Mara in the moment, he would remain present until she returned to the window of tolerance to soothe her.

Do not try to judge the size of the trigger by how important it may or may not seem in the grand scheme of things. Judge the size of the trigger by the reaction of your wounded partner. The goal is not to argue the truth of the trigger; the goal is to come back to the window of tolerance so the information can be shared and safely experienced.

The window of tolerance is wide. Sometimes you may need to dissociate a little so that feelings can be tolerated and managed. You may dysregulate a bit so that feelings can be experienced, expressed, and known. Extreme dissociating or dysregulating is outside of the window of tolerance. No communication or healing can begin when we are completely shut down or overcome by emotion.

How to get back into the window of tolerance

If one or both partners are outside the window of tolerance, take a breath. It is better to say, "I am outside my window of tolerance, and nothing I say will be productive," or "I am outside my window of tolerance, and I can't think straight right now," than to continue a fruitless conversation (or fight) that will lead to more miscommunication and bad feelings.

If a breath doesn't work, take a break. During the break, take the opportunity to self-soothe. Go for a walk, write in your journal, or spend some time doing anything that calms your body.

If a break doesn't work, get professional help. When our emotions are upset, our bodies are upset. Do not use substances or other destructive choices to calm yourself. Calm your body and your mind with exercise, meditation, or conversation with a neutral someone who can help bring you back to your window of tolerance. (That neutral someone brings their calm nervous system into your presence so you can calm your own.)

Once your body is calm, sort out what is making you elevated. Brainstorm productive ways to communicate your needs versus replaying what went wrong and how your partner must change. Avoid rumination by imagining successful conversations and thinking about what *you* need to do to get the outcome you want. Together in the window of tolerance you can make positive changes.

"Me" and Trauma

You cannot be half of a whole if you are not whole yourself. If one of the "me's" in an "us" is hurting, the "us" is hurting. Your other half can help, but it is important you do what you can to heal the "me" that is you. You are not responsible for the trauma that happened to you, but you are responsible for your healing. You may decide you need rest, support, time to think, or take leave. There are steps you can take to help heal your affair related trauma.

Individual Bottom-Up Healing

Bottom-up healing focuses on calming the body first. If your body is on alert status, you won't feel better, no matter how much truth, change, or apologies are provided. Sometimes your body's response is not triggered by an affair PTS thought, but by sleeplessness, alcohol or drug use, or a thought may simply appear out of nowhere when the body releases a hormone.

You can reduce trauma symptoms by calming your body, a moving to a safe place, being in the presence of those who love you, or immersing yourself in peaceful nature. Now is a good time to try psychotherapies that supplement talk therapy such as hypnosis, neurofeedback, and eye movement desensitization and reprocessing (EMDR). You can engage in body-calming activities such as aromatherapy, rocking, humming, controlling your breath, meditating, eating or drinking comforting food, and going for a walk or other exercise. You may or may not feel comfortable with massage. If you have found yourself overeating, exercising, sleeping, or doing other calming activities post discovery of the affair, this is your body seeking soothing and healing. Respond to your body's needs in healthy moderation.

Fortunately, as much as the body can influence the mind, the mind can influence the body. You can use your mind to bring awareness to the body's response to stress and make decisions on how to handle things. You can identify what works to calm your body and directly influence your mental health by taking action. Now is the time to incorporate self-care into your daily routine. Be sure you are getting enough exercise, eating well, time to journal, think, meditate, pray, and as much quality sleep as you need. A poor diet, too much alcohol, lack of sleep, and a disconnect from whatever gives you meaning in life can throw you into depression. Without this important self-care, your body will be signaling depression and distress that will be lumped in with the grief and sadness of the current challenge. Take care of yourself so you can sort things out. The more confident, fit, and calm your body feels, the better you will be able to participate in the healing of yourself and your relationship.

The Relaxation Response

Under stress, without your conscious thought, your body increases your heart rate, delivering more blood and oxygen to the brain. You can consciously lead your body to calm by activating the relaxation response, bringing it out of fight-or-flight activation, and back into the window of tolerance with a breathing exercise.

Affair repair is a stressful experience, often activating the fight-or-flight response in both partners. Try relaxing your body anytime you feel anxiety or stress arise—or anytime you want to calm your body—using this quick breathing exercise.

- Inhale deeply through your nose.
- Pause for four seconds.
- Exhale through your mouth for a *longer period of time* than your inhalation.
- Repeat three times or until you feel relaxed.

Meditation Practice

A regular meditation practice helps build the muscle of your mind to release thoughts at will. The ability to release the impact of a sudden thought allows you to put a pause between stimulus and response. In the pause you remain safe and can decide what you want versus react without thought in a fight or flight mode.

A regular meditation practice increases your ability to maintain a calm, self-aware, and self-controlled state of being. Here's how:

- Sit comfortably with your eyes closed.
- Pay attention to your breathing and repeat a word or phrase or prayer silently to yourself as you exhale.
- When you notice your mind wandering, (and it will), just notice it and passively bring your attention back to your breathing.

- Build up your practice to approximately twenty minutes every day (or at least three or four times per week). Don't set an alarm but sit with a clock in view if necessary.

There is a growing body of research on the positive effects of meditation and the brain. Consistent meditation demonstrated a thickening of the myelin sheath of the nerves in the brain, improving nerve signal transmission, reducing anxiety and inducing a state of calm. Meditation has been used as treatment for PTSD for soldiers returning from war. Many books, online videos, and apps are available to introduce you to other ways to meditate.

Medication

Medication is a reasonable thing to consider when dealing with affair PTS. Medication, like meditation, can put a pause between stimulus and response, giving you the ability to stay within the window of tolerance and make wise decisions. Some people have worried they will suffer from "med head," a sense of fog. This does not always occur, and if it does, you should consult your prescriber. Medication won't totally disarm the alarm system, but like a fire alarm that will not shut off, constant arousal no longer serves a true function and wears you out. Medication can help calm your system enough for it to reset. Medication may be considered like a plaster cast to support you through this time as you heal. Medication is not required or even recommended here, but it is offered for consideration. Your medical provider can help you decide if and which medication is right for you.

Alternatives to Medication

There are homeopathic and behavioral options to replace medication. Your local naturopath can recommend herbal remedies for stress that are gaining validity through evidence-based research.

Exercise has been proven to increase mood-lifting dopamine and norepinephrine neurotransmitters in your brain and can be as effective in treating depression as antidepressants. A long bike ride, quick run, or walk can do a lot to reduce stress and improve your overall health. Exercising also gives you time to think and process. Not all exercise is aerobics. There are other forms of exercise that include meditation like benefits such as yoga, fishing, and hiking. Take the opportunity to calm your mind and body as you work through the map of affair repair.

Individual Top-Down Healing

It takes time for a wounded person to move through affair PTS. Neuro-imaging of brains in highly emotional states show that intense fear, sadness, and anger cause the brain to move from using the frontal lobes of logic to the midbrain of emotion. People in this state literally lose their minds. They startle easily, are quick to enrage, or may detach and become frozen. Brains in an activated state will quickly revert to survival mode. A classic example is startling because you thought you saw a snake when it was a coiled hose. Your brain knows it's safer to suspect a snake and then learn it is a hose. That same mechanism is involved in affair PTS.

People can learn to tell the difference between snakes and hoses and react differently. Couples can use their intellect to avoid or prepare for affair PTS triggers such as people, places, things, and dates associated with the affair. The mind can get ahead of trouble, anticipating or iden-tifying pop-up triggers. It can look at the unlocked phone and verify there is no continuing communication. It can also navigate whether this is a random intrusive thought or a new angle that needs further investigation. And when the mind starts to spiral, it can become aware of itself and use counter facts or mental toughness to regain control.

Sanity Check with CBT

Cognitive behavioral therapy (CBT) directly challenges faulty thinking so you can better identify a snake vs hose or lie vs truth. Here are ten common mistakes people make:

1. **Black-and-white thinking.** All people think if an affair happens, the marriage is over—until it happens to them. Allow yourself

to weigh all the angles of staying or leaving. Once a cheat is not always a cheat. Repair and transformation can happen. Getting stuck in black-and-white thinking can prevent healing. If you are the wounded partner using black-and-white thinking, you may be unable to forgive. Or if you are the responsible partner, you may feel it is pointless to try to help heal. Avoid black-and-white thinking.

2. **Making unfair comparisons.** Comparing your marriage to the excitement of the affair is unfair. It is not possible for a familiar relationship worn down by drudgery and bad habits to compete with a fresh one full of excitement and new energy.

3. **Filtering**. Filtering is seeing only the negative. If you are the wounded partner, you may only see the failures and suspicious actions of your responsible partner, ignoring the many actions showing a desire to repair. If you are the responsible partner, you may see only the ongoing anger and old patterns of an unsatisfying relationship versus the deep desire to heal and changes that are being made.

4. **Personalizing.** Blaming yourself for the actions of your partner will prevent your partner from taking responsibility and making changes. An affair is a choice separate from making requests for change; it is not the wounded partner's fault.

5. **Mind-reading.** We often think we know what the other person is thinking and feeling. Mind-reading is particularly dangerous in affair repair as the wounded partner will assume the worst and the responsible partner will lose hope. Assuming the worst and losing hope will make affair repair particularly difficult. Try to avoid mind-reading and focus on authentic communication, telling and accepting the truth.

6. **Catastrophizing.** Catastrophizing is your mind's way of keeping you safe. If you are expecting the worst of the worst to happen, you will be prepared. Catastrophizing can prevent you from seeing where things are getting better and taking steps toward healing.

7. **Overgeneralizing.** Anytime the word *always* is applied to behavior, you are overgeneralizing. Nobody is always angry, always indifferent, or always untrustworthy. Overgeneralizing your partner's behavior will be an obstacle to healing.

8. **Emotional reasoning.** When we take our feelings to be the measure of truth, we can obscure reality. Affair PTS is a good example; a trigger can cause fear, anger, and depression on a perfectly good day when no betrayal is happening. Another example of emotional reasoning is, "She is so angry. This can never be repaired." Overcome emotional reasoning by accepting you are having a valid emotional experience without letting it cloud the reality that things are on the mend.

9. **Labeling.** "Once a cheat, always a cheat" may be a thought you cling to, to keep yourself safe, but it will prevent healing. Further labels that could prevent overcoming the affair are frigid, whore, bastard, or any other demeaning name that prevents you from caring about a whole person capable of change and growth.

10. **Expecting life to be fair.** The wounded partner may think the responsible partner should come crawling back after the awful thing they have just done, but your partner may be uncertain (which is most common). The responsible partner may feel the wounded partner is overreacting and withholding forgiveness after all the apologizing. Clinging to a thought that life is fair will only make things more difficult.

The strength of CBT is that the approach focuses on reality. Addressing faulty thinking empowers you to make decisions based upon what is actually happening, not upon a story you have in your mind or emotional feeling. Review this list and consider which of these faulty thinking patterns you most often fall into. Try to catch yourself in the act and notice how it affects your journey on the map of affair repair. Become aware and plan to address how faulty thinking affects your feelings before acting.

Key Concepts

Managing and healing affair PTS involves bottom-up and top-down approaches for the individual "me" and shared "us" body. What you feel in your bodies must match what you think in your minds. Truthful communication and calm presence will help manage and heal affair PTS.

- The **"us" body** shares the experience of your partner via mirror neurons and neuroception.
  - Mirror neurons are in the brain and mimic the experience.
  - Neuroception is the response of a system of nerves in the *body* analyzing the experience.
  - **Bottom-up healing for the "us"** body happens when safety is experienced in the body together. For example, this happens when you both want to hug.
  - **Top-down healing for the "us"** body happens when what the mind understands is congruent with the experience of the bodies. For example, this can happen when you are honest and admit you are angry or unsure you want to repair.
- The **window of tolerance** is the state of being where you can think and feel at the same time. Responding to and handling your disrupting thoughts and body's response with patience and care will reduce the duration of affair PTS. Return as fast as possible to a calm mind and body where you can think and feel.
  - **Dissociating** is avoiding feeling by focusing on thinking and is outside the window of tolerance.
  - **Dysregulating** is letting feeling flow out of control and is outside the window of tolerance.
  - **Wounded and responsible partners** must be in the window of tolerance for healing to occur
- The **"me" body** must be healed to be part of a healthy "us" body.
  - **Bottom-up healing for the "me"** body includes important self-care practices such as healthy eating, sleeping, moving, and meditating.

- ○ The relaxation response, medication, and alternative medicines can be used to overcome affair PTS.
- ○ **Top-down healing for the "me"** body includes challenging faulty thinking.
- **Average Duration:** You will be managing affair PTS for two to six months or longer if what the body feels does not match what the mind is told.
- **Goal:** Heal the "us" and "me" body by calming the body, telling the truth, and helping the body and mind experience safety.
- **Do:**
  - ○ Remain in the window of tolerance
  - ○ Be authentic
  - ○ Focus on how your body feels and mind thinks to provide a strong foundation to continue on the map of affair repair
- **Don't:**
  - ○ Dysregulate or dissociate
  - ○ Lie
- **If you are the wounded partner**, strive to heal your "me" body. Work to stay in the window of tolerance and take in what your partner is saying and doing. Become aware and challenge any of your faulty thinking. If your body and mind are activated, you will not be able to get an accurate read of who your partner is.
- **If you are the responsible partner**, take care of your "me" body and show up as authentically as you can in the "us" body experiences. Strive to stay in the window of tolerance as you take in the experience with your partner. Your partner is reading your verbal and nonverbal cues. Make them honest and authentic.

Chapter 11
Affair Limerence

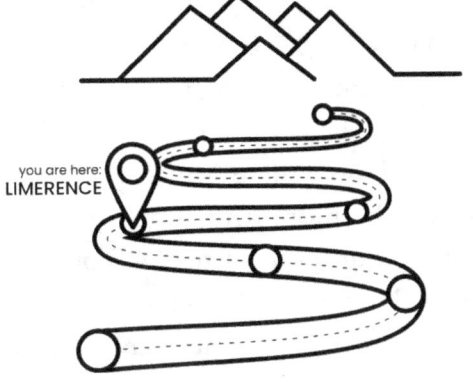

you are here:
LIMERENCE

*The challenge of affair limerence
is for the responsible partner to reflect
upon themselves and the loss of the affair.*

This chapter is for the responsible partner. While your focus should be on helping your wounded partner move through affair PTS, you likely will be dealing with your own painful experience. Missing and wanting your affair partner are socially unacceptable feelings nobody wants to talk about. Your wounded partner will likely experience any attachment, sympathy, or grief for the affair partner as further betrayal. In this leg of the affair repair journey, you travel a side road alone. You're not keeping secrets, but your wounded partner cannot help you.

Affair Limerence

If you cannot stop thinking about your affair partner, you may be dealing with limerence. **Limerence** is a longing for someone that becomes all-consuming. You just can't get them out of your mind. Affair limerence is limerence felt for your affair partner, the **limerent object** (LO). Thoughts of the LO, like affair PTS, are uncontrollable. You may not be thinking of the LO when out of the blue they pop into your mind. If you are trying to break off the affair, this may be surprising, as the feeling of longing is not your intention, but your intention is overridden by affair limerence.

Like affair PTS, affair limerence is not just psychological, it is biological. Affair limerence involves increased levels of neurochemicals—norepinephrine and dopamine—in your brain that cause an experience of pleasure. The more, the better. The desire sparked by these thoughts increases your levels of testosterone resulting in an all-around conquer-the-world feeling. Depression disappears, and superhero energy appears. Limerence is an incredible natural drug.

Withdrawal of this strong biochemical cocktail means loss of all the good feelings and experiences which makes you want it even more. If you decide to continue the relationship openly (an honest situation), every contact with the LO will strengthen affair limerence. Ellie had to work even harder in her repair process as she continued to see Mark struggling between limerence and love. If you continue the affair secretly (continued betrayal) your affair limerence will be doubly magnified with the pleasure and forbidden fuel of secrecy. It only takes a quick internet search to find stories of people who have destroyed their families and careers under the influence of limerence.

Affair limerence is beyond infatuation. Infatuation is usually short lived and based upon innocence that fades away or is shattered by new information. It can be dispelled by an ugly pimple, a disagreement, or an embarrassing moment. Under the influence of affair limerence, people downplay the risk to their careers, families, and reputations.

Affair limerence minimizes faults and exaggerates gifts to keep the good biochemicals flowing. Proverbial red flags are readily overlooked. The spell of infatuation is broken the moment you smell bad breath or learn of the maxed-out credit cards; affair limerence barely notices these obstacles or finds ways to overcome.

The Affair Limerence Story

Sam and Megan worked at the same nonprofit organization. Both were dedicated to the mission and regularly volunteered. Sam's wife, Rachel, never questioned the time spent away, as she knew how important work was to Sam. Rachel and Sam had been together for over twenty-five years. Together they had a shared mission of their own, investing blood, sweat, and tears in their farm and four children.

Now Sam had started an affair with Megan. Megan and he had spent long hours at the office and in the field, bonding over the mission, sharing victories and defeats. Megan was compassionate by nature and understood Sam. Emotional connection was easy.

Rachel was loyal in her support, maintaining the farm and family to free Sam. When Sam turned toward his work, she turned toward her responsibilities. The couple was together but apart.

Work and Megan became Sam's source of inspiration. Hours at home were endured until he could go back to work. He would hole himself up in his study after dinner, secretly texting Megan. If she didn't respond, he would worry and become irritable. He would get up early to get to work, often arriving a full half hour before she did. Sam's mind was consumed with arranging his work and life schedule to find time to be with Megan.

Sam and Megan spent hours, even overnight weekends together, under the guise of work. They clustered their weekends away alongside work events. Sam would go to the beach, a leisure desti-

nation he loathed, just to be with Megan. She refused to go on hiking trips he suggested.

After a full day at the beach, where Megan would shush Sam while reading her book, Megan would dodge meal prep by taking her time in the shower, applying luxurious lotion, and putting on fresh clothing. Meanwhile, Sam would plate their meal and sit down with her in his sandy shorts, energized by their chemistry.

I asked Sam about the incongruencies, but he brushed off my concerns, saying he felt so loved and alive with Megan. He didn't mind the beach, being patient while she read, and preparing the evening meal by himself. He did not have "that feeling" when he was with Rachel.

Affair Limerence ... or Love?

All new relationships sparkle with a bit of limerence. All old relationships become a bit dull. Love often starts with limerence, so it may be very hard to determine if your affair relationship is love, especially under the influence of limerence.

Limerence kept Sam chasing "that feeling" at the expense of his family, his character, and his preferred interests. In short, he sacrificed his true self. He hated the beach, ignored the fact he was doing all the work, and gladly suffered sandy shorts. Limerence made him unable to see these things.

A fundamental difference between love and affair limerence is self-will. There is no self-will in affair limerence. Self sells out, binding and blinding its will and better nature for the thrill of limerence. Love permits choice; limerence leaves no choice. With limerence, you not only can't live without the LO, you also can't think, function, or be. Sam endured being at home, he could not be present.

Sorting through your feelings in the affair PTS phase is skewed by pain and limerence. Soul searching is not a quick process, but it is necessary for everyone involved. Only a small percentage of affairs end in marriage, and the statistics of staying married become grimmer with each successive marriage. Second marriages are more likely to end in divorce than the first, the third more likely than the second, and so on. You want to know, is this limerence or love.

I have seen people find their forever love in an affair, but it is rare. In this case, the responsible partner took time to try to repair with their spouse and come to know their own self. It was not easy for the affair partner, but it was love. The responsible partner did some serious personal self-reflection. They spent time trying to help their wounded partner overcome the betrayal and worked to see if the marriage could be transformed. In their case, it couldn't. I would encourage responsible partners to repair the hurt they have caused and work on marriage transformation to see if the evolved relationship can be what you need. There is nothing to lose but time, which will pay dividends in the secure knowledge of knowing you did everything to make things right.

Overcoming Affair Limerence

It is impossible to simply stop affair limerence. "Just say no!" is the prevailing advice. However, we have learned in treating addictions, a lot more than willpower is needed to interrupt a craving cycle sustained by neurochemicals. You may be able to stop contact with, but not the thoughts of, the LO. Overcoming affair limerence is disenfranchised grief work. There are things you can do to address the intrusive thoughts and sadness.

No Contact

Eliminating contact is the best first step. Out of sight helps keep out of mind. If you relapse and contact the LO, it will be harder to break the pattern. No contact is the number one way to extinguish limerence. Some people can go cold turkey or make a habit change with a flip of a switch. Most cannot. Accept that overcoming affair limerence may be hard, and you may need other strategies to succeed.

Once no contact is established, you will have some relief because you no longer need to maintain the illusion. Supporting two worlds is exhausting. After a while, this no-contact situation may become difficult. The absence of that good feeling, emotional boost, and excitement of the LO will be felt. Cravings can set in. Your mind will come up with a hundred good reasons to do a bad thing. Breaking the commitment to go no-contact and work on the marriage is the wrong thing, no matter how many reasons. If you break contact, tell your partner. Breaking your commitment is a significant harm to your wounded partner and yourself.

Break the Lock

Try to break the lock of affair limerence by focusing on the reality of the LO. Affair limerence prevents you from seeing the warts and only the beauty. What red flags are being overlooked? Is there financial irresponsibility? Inattention to health or fitness? Cultural or religious differences? Are there personality quirks or attitudes you would find intolerable in another person? Affair limerence will minimize or flat-out refute reality.

The initial comparison of your wounded partner and the LO will likely not be favorable to your long-term partner. Reality rarely outshines fantasy. Turn the tables. Break the lock of limerence by asking what might you miss about your wounded partner. What special memory, activity, talent, skill, or characteristic would you miss? It might not be enough to stay but try to identify what is good about your wounded partner. Affair limerence can skew perspective. *Write down* the strengths of your wounded partner and the weaknesses of the LO. Limerence will bias your view. Writing this information down (not just acknowledging it in your mind) can help break the bias. As you journey on the map of affair repair, try to turn your attention to who your wounded partner is becoming. People change.

The Break the Affair Limerence Lock Story

Sam was overriding many of his standard sensibilities. A land-lubber and family man, he was having an affair with Megan, a woman who loved the beach and was generally self-focused. Sam felt connected to Megan. They shared the same work ethic and dedication to the philanthropic mission where they were employed. The sex was good, even though she was less giving than he and was not his usual body type. The time together was precious—because it was limited.

Sam could not see any red flags, so I asked him what he would miss about his wife, Rachel, once he left. Sam thought about the years he and Rachel had labored together for family and farm. He recalled her solidarity and always having lunch packed for him. She never forgot the pickle. Rachel was a good cook. He and Rachel had hiked the entire Appalachian Trail before they married. They had hoped to hike the Pacific Crest once the kids were older. Hiking would be over with Megan. Megan refused to venture into the woods and resented the time Sam spent away from her. Sam thought of Rachel's body, which he always appreciated. Megan's was different and Sam was surprised how limerence stoked desire.

Sam began to realize he had put his feelings for Rachel in a can, shut the lid, and buried it. He realized he had contributed to the distancing and was unable to be open to the new Rachel, who was making changes to improve their relationship.

One Saturday, Megan got angry at Sam for not coming to the beach. Sam had to chaperone his twins' Boy Scout camping trip. Badges were being awarded, and Sam was leading several activities for the troop. Sam realized with Megan, there would always be tension between him and what he loved. Sam ended it with Megan.

Stop Thought Technique

A significant source of power for affair limerence is the creativity of the brain. The stop thought technique can be used to stop the ongoing, rewarding, and reinforcing thoughts of the LO. Here is how this simple, but powerful technique works:

- The instant you have an intrusive thought, imagine a stop sign popping up right in front of your eyes.
- Ask yourself: What color is the sign? What shape is it? What color is the border? What letters are on it? How big is it?

Your mind cannot think of two thoughts at once. You cannot simultaneously be thinking *red*; *octagon*; *white* and imagine the LO at work, ruminate over pain, or daydream of what it would be like to be together.

Ending limerence is hard. The stop thought technique may need to be employed over and over, repeatedly flashing the stop sign in front of your mind's eye. Once your mind has stopped indulging in the reward of limerence, be prepared to redirect your thoughts. You will best succeed if you already know where you want to lead your mind (versus be led by it.) Plan ahead. If your mind becomes overrun with obsessive thoughts, what will be the better thoughts? Create a list of your replacement thoughts. You might redirect your thoughts to the task right in front of you in the moment. Another option is to turn your mind to your next meal, workout, or upcoming meeting. Mantras or prayers can be used to anchor your mind. Consider directing your mental energies to a creative challenge or endeavor. Losing oneself in a book or phoning a friend are also healthy ways to channel your mind. Avoid thinking about what is wrong. Think about what is neutral or good to stop the thoughts.

Rebuild Your Life

Once you have eliminated contact with the affair partner, you may experience a letdown from the absence of all the energy that was fresh, exciting, and different. The return to married life, with its drudgery and current trauma, cannot compare. Now is the time for you to commit to being creative about what you will do to make *this moment* better.

Commit to the map of affair repair. Take advantage of your freedom from the shackles of secrecy. Before you were carefully planning and shamefully hiding. Now in the open, you can pursue new, healthy passions. You are free to create the life you want. You are not going back to the old you and the old relationship. New passions will bring fresh energy but should not be another escape. You might throw yourself into a home or self-improvement project, or best of all, time with your wounded partner in a productive way. Your new life should include work on your relationship.

Starve Out the Passionate Fire

The Latin root of passion is *passio*, which means "suffering" not hot desire as most people think. Passion is the high-octane fuel that was driving you to the LO. Passion ignites a fire. For some of us, the pain is worth it. For others, the blaze leaves a wake of destruction behind.

Starve the affair limerence fire by depriving it of **uncertainty, hope**, and **rumination**. Uncertainty is the oxygen that keeps the fire going. No contact is the fire road that cannot be crossed. Make it clean and wide. Clear commitment to repairing your relationship starves the fire of oxygen. Uncertainty leaves scattered glowing embers that can roar into a flame just by chance. Hope is like tinder, a quick-burning fuel that keeps the fire going. Shut out any hope of rekindling the relationship. Finally, rumination is the deep, slow burn of the log. The heat of the fire emanating from thoughts of the LO will feel warm and draw you near. Rumination will lock your mind into thinking the LO is the only answer and the spouse is not. Don't let those thoughts sit smoldering. Stop the rumination and toss that log out. Just as your wounded partner must resist the pop-up thoughts of the betrayal, you must resist pop-up thoughts of the LO.

Poo Brownie

A poo brownie is the best brownie you could ever imagine. Whether you like your brownies frosted, baked with nuts, or filled with chocolate chips, this brownie tastes amazing! You never felt so high, alive, and vibrant as when you are eating this brownie. There is only one small ingredient you might not like, but don't worry, you can't taste it. You won't realize you are getting sick. Do you still want it? An affair is a poo brownie.

You can be the best parent, lover, provider, caregiver, citizen, leader of the church, and overall amazing person, but the tiniest bit of treachery ruins it all. Affairs involve good people making one bad decision that compromises everything.

The poo brownie was shared. Your affair partner has also enjoyed the brownie knowing the ingredients and taking the risk. Your affair partner was always in the shadow of your marriage, kept in a box of secrecy. Despite feeling special by the heightened desire, there is an edge of not being "the one." This book will not focus on the pain of the affair partner, but there is real hurt, regardless of whether it is just desserts. Sometimes the thought of your affair partner's pain offers a sense of moral balance that helps soothe your wounded partner.

You are likely aware of the suffering of your affair partner and have some empathy toward it. Affair limerence is hard to break for you and your affair partner. The pain of your affair partner may make it hard for you, knowing two people are now hurt, but hopefully this knowledge will help you do the important personal work of becoming clear about what you want and communicating with honesty. The most helpful thing you can do for your affair partner is to eliminate uncertainty and hope, so that you can give yourself some time and they can move on and heal.

Disenfranchised Grief

Disenfranchised grief is the socially unacceptable sadness over losing the affair. Most likely, you, as the responsible partner, were in some way emotionally attached to the affair partner and that attachment was ruptured at discovery. Your attachment may range from general concern to deep love. With the ruptured attachment, you are overcoming psychological wounds that you can feel physiologically. Your grief needs to be understood and addressed.

You may just want to rip the bandage off and not acknowledge your grief, knowing it was your decision that caused such pain. It may be noble to take responsibility and move forward, but it is not healthy to completely disown your feelings. The affair happened for a reason, and those reasons should be examined. If you were seeking an outlet or using another person, you should reflect upon that. If you were connected to another human being, you should allow time to sort out all the complicated feelings. Seek a friend who can listen without judgment and provide support while you sort out your thoughts, or better still, a good therapist.

You will have many voices ringing in your ears as you deal with disenfranchised grief. Ellie, of the Bubble Bath Miracle story in the beginning of this book, spoke with friends, family, and her therapist (me.) Some friends gently pressured her to return to her marriage; others held her in unconditional love. Her mother encouraged her to do what made her happy. I supported her in her discernment processes, helping her identify what she needed. No matter who you speak with, you will do what you really want in the end. Having someone you trust to help you sort things out will help you move forward faster with more clarity and less suffering.

As you sit with your disenfranchised grief, consider what parts of the loss you are feeling were tied to the affair partner themselves and what is now the gaping hole that the affair once filled. Those empty, unfulfilled areas may have been a loss of confidence, loss of job, feeling not enough or ignored, boredom, addiction, overwhelm with family responsibilities, or any other reason.

Avoid focusing on the shortcomings of your wounded partner when sitting with your disenfranchised grief. Those shortcomings will be addressed later. Focus on what you were seeking, needing, and expressing in the affair relationship that you were not in your marriage. Consider what *internal psychological* factors chipped away at your ability to honor your promise to your marriage and excused your decision to cheat. Likely those factors prevented you from confronting or handling problems in the relationship. You will need to know what you want and how to get it without compromise going forward.

Your wounded partner may be able to help process the grief of those gaping holes that were problems for you without touching the grief of ending the affair. For example, you may identify one of the factors that led to the affair was a sense of not feeling good enough or unappreciated. Your wounded partner can be supportive of the pain in feeling inadequate or undervalued, but not of the loss of the affair. The work you do now with your disenfranchised grief will yield insights you can share when your partner is ready to move forward with affair repair and transform your marriage.

Some insights and memories are for you to keep. Memories of passion, friendship, and happiness can be accepted but not acted upon by you. Smile and be grateful for the good you experienced, then put it to rest. You do not need to cling nor shove it away. Memories with the affair partner can fade and be overwritten by the richness of having a transformed relationship that comes with its own long history, gifts, and treasure.

If you are asked about any feelings you may still have for the affair partner, be honest. But remember, the work to resolve your disenfranchised grief should be done with a trusted friend, family member, or better yet, an experienced therapist.

Key Concepts

Affair limerence is an intense longing for the **limerent object (LO)**, aka the affair partner. Dealing with affair limerence is the work of the responsible partner.

- Like affair PTS, thoughts prompted by affair limerence can be repeating, disruptive, and involuntary.

- Thoughts themselves are enough to keep affair limerence going.
- Affair limerence, like affair PTS, is psychological and physiological.
- Affair limerence vs. infatuation and love
  - Affair limerence is not infatuation. Infatuation can be dispelled.
  - Affair limerence is not love but is often involved in the beginning of pair bonding. You likely experienced some limerence with your spouse.
- Affairs are like poo brownies; they are wonderful except for one very small ingredient: the decision to cheat.
- **Disenfranchised grief** is the socially unacceptable grief and loss the responsible partner feels for the affair partner.
  - Dealing with disenfranchised grief is the work of the responsible partner.
  - Understanding the loss includes grieving whatever was missing that the affair covered or fulfilled in the responsible partner.
  - Some memories are for the responsible partner to keep.
- **Responsible partners** can overcome affair limerence by:
  - Eliminating contact
  - Focusing on the reality of the LO
  - Using the stop thought technique
  - Getting a life outside the affair relationship
  - Eliminating uncertainty, hope, and rumination which keep affair limerence going
- **Wounded partners** should not be involved in resolving affair limerence or disenfranchised grief.
- **Average Duration:** Starting from the last contact, the first ninety days will be the initial work of breaking affair limerence. Affair limerence will be a potential challenge for six months to a year. Disenfranchised grief will lessen over time and more quickly as your marriage transforms. It is not uncommon to have occasional reoccurring thoughts of your affair partner now and again.

- **Goal:** Understand disenfranchised grief and recognize affair limerence symptoms.
- **Do:**
  - Recognize the influence of affair limerence
  - Take time to process your grief and loss
- **Don't:**
  - Continue contact with the LO, making it harder to clear space for you, the responsible partner, to think and act clearly
- **If you are the wounded partner**, acknowledge that affair limerence is hard to break but expect your responsible partner to work toward its end. Understand that disenfranchised grief is normal. Avoid internalizing this grief as rejection of you.
- **If you are the responsible partner**, acknowledge that affair limerence is powerful and work to address its effects. Seek help from a trusted friend or, better even, a helpful professional. Understand that disenfranchised grief is normal and something for you to work through individually.

Chapter 12
Affair Repair

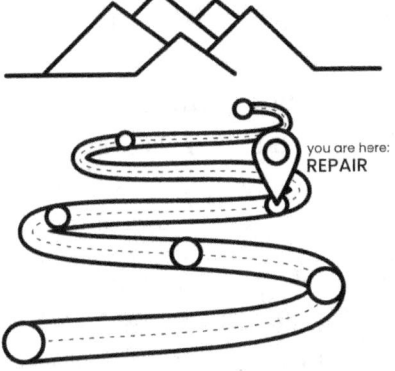

you are here:
REPAIR

*The challenge of the affair repair phase
is to seek understanding
while sharing conflicting experiences.*

The affair repair phase can begin as early as six weeks post-discovery, but more commonly couples start communicating better around three months. Most couples who pick up this book are in the earlier affair PTS phase of their healing journey. If you jumped to this section, please go back and review affair PTS, as *you will struggle to effectively engage in affair repair if you cannot recognize and manage affair PTS.* Affair PTS will pop up now and again until it lessens and ultimately becomes nearly nonexistent. It is important that couples understand when affair PTS is happening.

Couples should **work through the affair repair phase, even if you intend to divorce.** The partner who was hurt deserves to heal, and the partner who was involved in the affair can know they did what they could to repair the hurt they caused. For the moment, set aside whether you intend to stay together or separate. Focus instead on repairing the wound. That way, if you do part ways, you will have been honest, taken responsibility, and done what you could to restore a sense of safety and selfhood.

Affair repair can be the most frustrating phase because you have moved through crisis and affair PTS seems to have died down, but the wounded partner is still unhappy and the responsible partner is wondering why things are not getting better. What more can be said? How many more times do we need to talk about this? When will we be past this? The truth is that affair PTS is almost always just under the surface. Triggers and aftershocks will continue as you two transition to this affair repair phase. Should affair PTS arise, switch the focus of your discussion to addressing the symptoms versus trying to push forward with affair repair.

The purpose of affair repair is to *experience truth together*. You cannot experience the truth if you are not honest with yourself and your partner. Experiencing truth is both physiological and psychological. Over the course of the healing journey, you will come to know each other more deeply and decide whether you want the reality of the relationship as it really is. In this phase, each partner will explore what was happening before the affair and what effects the betrayal has had on you individually and as a couple. Experiencing the truth, painful or not, provides a sense of grounding, mutual understanding, and shared foundation from which you can move forward.

White Lies and Feigned Sincerity

Affair repair discussions without honesty are dangerous. Bald-faced or even white lies are setbacks to further healing. Be as authentic as possible, even if you are scared and can't say everything right now because you are confused. Half-truths or untruths create damage in this phase that will set you back in the next. Healing will be delayed or may not happen at all. Insincere discussions will result in trickle-down truth where portions of truth are revealed a little at a time. As we saw in the crisis phase, trickle-down truth is retraumatizing, causing the wounded partner to wonder what will be discovered next. It's better for either partner to say, "I can't make that promise right now," "I am not sure how I feel after all the hurt we have been through," or "I am not sure if I want to repair the relationship," than to lie.

One Foot in, One Foot Out

Sometimes a responsible partner genuinely wants to repair the relationship for the sake of helping the wounded partner and to see where things go, but they have not fully severed ties with the affair partner. They are one foot in and one foot out. The wounded partner often knows that the affair is continuing. If their sixth sense doesn't tell them, tracking devices, phone checks, and information from others will confirm the reality. The wounded partner will continue to play the game, maintaining their access to reality, while working to save the marriage. This is common and very painful. A one foot in, one foot out partner is not yet repairing nor healing but considering their next steps.

The One Foot In, One Foot Out Story

Regardless of whether he stayed or went, James wanted to make amends for the hurt he had caused Allison. He wanted to answer his own guilty conscience. He thought of himself as a good man. Having an affair was not aligned with his core values.

James continually apologized and expressed regret to Allison as the couple worked on the strategies suggested in an out-of-phase approach. The couple focused on marriage transformation. James needed to know forgiveness was possible and that the marriage was going to be worth coming back to.

He put the affair on hold with occasional relapses. He wanted to be sure happiness was possible with his wife before he officially ended things with the LO. James was going through the motions of affair repair with honest intention, but dishonest action.

No matter how many times James said all the right things, Allison could not fully credit or trust him because she knew he was still cheating. His frustration grew as he was doing everything asked of him as the responsible partner, but because he had not acknowledged the affair was continuing, he was living in an illusion Allison was not. He could not yet become a repairing partner.

James's affair repair efforts didn't succeed because Allison knew the affair was continuing. His risks were hedged at her expense. He was not completely dedicated to repairing. Allison could tell James had sincere feelings for her and could see he was making changes, but she could barely tolerate the process of his personal growth that involved complete safety for him while she risked everything to trust again. She was trying to save her marriage by engaging in affair repair, but there was a limit to how vulnerable she could truly be. Allison could not hope to become a healing partner ready to establish trust because James was one foot in and one foot out. James needed to do his personal work and be more honest with himself and Allison.

The Responsible Partner's Path

As the responsible partner, your work in this phase of the journey is twofold. Looking inward for **self-understanding is extremely important, but your outward efforts should be toward healing the wound** you created. Your wounded partner may be in so much pain at the beginning of the affair repair journey that they may not want or have capacity for empathy for you, the responsible partner.

"I can't believe you cheated," Miguel cried through the tears. "My heart is broken."

"I am in pain, too!" Chase snapped back.

After an affair is discovered, the wounded partner lies destroyed in a metaphorical body cast, moaning from what just happened. When they ask for soothing and their responsible partner answers, "My leg is broken too!" nobody is cared for. Responsible partners cannot fully help heal their partner until they are healed themselves. So, let's heal your leg, but keep the healing priority in order. Like disenfranchised grief, much of your work will be done individually.

If you are the responsible partner, you may want to journal about your hurts, needs, and wants, to help sort things out. It is a good idea to seek professional support from a therapist. Your work in self-understanding will bring clarity and calmness to the healing journey. Do this work now so that when your wounded partner asks you questions like, "Why?" "What was wrong with me?" "What was going on with you?" You will have well thought out answers. Insightful and authentic explanations provide an understanding of who you are as well as who you are becoming because of this experience.

When you can respond with thorough, honest answers, your wounded partner will experience a sense of safety that leads to healing. When you understand yourself better, you will be able to make clear requests, share your needs and wants for the future without leaving the window of tolerance. Your answers will not eliminate the pain of affair PTS or affair repair talks, but your answers will be laying foundational groundwork for establishing trust and marriage transformation. You will be experiencing truth together. Healing can begin.

Become Aware of the Illusion

Affairs happen when one partner convinces themselves it's okay to hide the truth instead of being honest, working toward change, or ending the relationship respectfully. Cheating enables a person to maintain an illusion and avoid responsibility for reality. Often there are good, understandable reasons for maintaining the illusion. If you are the responsible partner, you likely don't want to lose your family or hurt your spouse. To maintain the illusion, you must rationalize your reasons for lying to keep the affair going and sustain a positive view of yourself. Self-loathing is naturally avoided by all humans, which is a good thing. Self-loathing can be unhealthy and lead to negative consequences. Everyone engages in self-deception from time to time, and when you become aware of it, be gentle and honest with yourself. If a person is going in the wrong direction, the fastest course correction is to stop and go the right way. Looking for a loophole or turn-around delays progress. Don't waste time getting stuck in excuses or beating yourself up.

Now that the affair has been discovered, it is time for you, as the repairing partner, to begin to dismantle the web of rationalizations. Common rationalizations to excuse lying include not getting your needs met in your marriage—it was just physical, you deserve to be happy, or you are a good person in other ways. It is important that you unpack all your rationalizations, otherwise you risk maintaining the illusion.

One way to maintain the illusion is to dump all your resentment on your wounded partner, which is a way of saying they are responsible for your actions. Dumping like this can result in either anger or an unfair sense of failure in your wounded partner. As a responsible partner, you need to radically accept responsibility, forgive yourself, and move forward doing the right thing. Your wounded partner may or may not forgive you. That is not something you can control. Your responsibility is to do the right thing, not for the results that follow.

Revisit Limerence

As the responsible partner, you should revisit affair limerence discussed in the previous chapter. Unlike affair PTS, the intrusive thoughts of limerence are pleasant. Limerence intrusive thoughts provide relief from the stress of trying to repair. Limerence is an involuntary attraction. Under the influence of limerence, your brain and physiology are drawing you toward the LO and away from your wounded partner.

Limerence takes hold in the cracks and weakness of your psyche. Despite the pull of limerence, however, underneath the pleasantness, there is the anxiety of trying to sustain two worlds. Addressing cracks and weaknesses is part of your work to heal self, become whole, and move from illusion to reality. Become aware of and reflect upon any lingering limerence. How much limerence is still going on? What part of yourself has been lost to limerence? What was gained through the limerence experience? What did you experience in the affair that you must continue to have in your life? Renewed energy in fitness, health, playfulness, travel, adventure, and sexual intimacy are examples of positive experiences that would be desirable in the future. Make a list. Consider what role you played in the loss of excitement and novelty in your marriage. What did you do or not do, and what do you need to do to inspire that spark in your spouse?

Consider Your Contribution

As the responsible partner, closely examine and challenge your reasons for the affair and the problems in your marriage. What was your contribution? Did you really try to communicate with your partner, or did you participate in an unhealthy pattern? Were you really present in the bedroom, or did you contribute to the lackluster experience by your own indifference? Was all your energy going into the affair, with the leftovers, or worse, brought home? Were you as attentive to your partner's needs as you expected them to be to yours? How has limerence influenced your actions in response to these questions? How does limerence inhibit affair repair efforts?

Consider Your Personal History and Motivations

Alton had come to my office for Divorce Busting™ coaching. He desperately wanted to improve his marriage with his wife. She was unhappy with him and threatened to leave. Alton recalled the devastation he had experienced when his parents divorced.

His father's affair devastated his mom, him, and their extended family. His world was fractured. All that Alton believed to be safe, secure, and true was destroyed in his childhood. Alton would do anything to keep his marriage versus relive the breakup of a family.

Alton threw himself into solution-focused action steps. He stepped up doing the dishes, being sure to leave the baby bottle nipples out to dry and not putting them in the dishwasher. He was sure to separate all the colors of the laundry. He got up in the middle of the night with the baby and went to work early. He planned date nights and tried to please his wife, who never seemed satisfied. Alton felt low self-esteem for failing in his marriage and never having gone to college. He came regularly to therapy to work on himself and to improve his marriage.

One day Alton came and revealed he had been caught having an affair. All this time, he had been struggling to maintain the illusion while he was trying to improve his marriage. The comfort of the affair had been so great, he could not bring himself to share it in therapy. He had been too ashamed to voice the truth, and he needed the limerence of the affair to sustain him, as he had failed in every other area of his life. With the affair partner, he felt wanted, desired, and enough. He could not give up the affair, though he loved his wife, and he was doing exactly what he resented his father for having done. He not only broke his wife's heart, he broke his own.

Now that discovery had occurred, Alton had to deal with the pieces of his own shattered life. Alton had betrayed himself by doing the one thing he thought he would never do, which was to have an affair like his father. Alton now had to do the hard work of examining what the affair meant to him.

What was hurting so deeply that he was able to override his values and make the affair acceptable? If it was not a need, how had he allowed himself to compromise? If it was not a compromise, how was it that he felt so entitled to deceive? Alton had to come to terms with his marriage. Was he doing all he could? Were his wife's expectations too high, or did they need to be more honest in their communication and negotiation?

Alton's illusion and self-delusion was fortified by guilt and shame. Alton was struggling with low self-esteem, a sense of failure, and rejection. Self-centeredness is not limited to the overly confident. People can become so self-focused in a negative state that they cannot access help. Rather than face the risk of vulnerability, they will stay safe behind closed lips.

Upon discovery, the veil hiding your affair has been lifted, and there is a stark reflection in the mirror. Look in the mirror with compassion, curiosity, and accountability. You may want to seek a good, nonjudgmental therapist to help navigate self-reflection. It is very hard to see oneself without an accurate mirror.

Find your voice. What have you been trying to say to your partner that was ignored? Did you say it? How did you say it? Did you hear your partner's response? What rationalizations did you use to maintain the illusion? What did the illusion look like? What purpose did the illusion serve? How does your behavior align with the person you believe yourself to be? What caused the gap? Where did these patterns of behavior come from? How can you close the gap between who you are and who you want to be?

Grandiosity and Worthlessness

Getting caught in an affair can provoke feelings of grandiosity or worthlessness as ways of coping with the pain. Grandiosity shows up as image management. If you are having a grandiose response, you may compare yourself to other people noting that you make more money, are better looking, or are more socially powerful. These things may be true, but you are shoring up yourself to feel as though you are not *that* bad. You may also compare yourself to others who have cheated or are struggling with problems such as addiction or financial challenges, again to reduce the seriousness of your transgression by measuring others against your own better-than, grandiose stature. Without comparing yourself to others to minimize your mistake, try looking deeper. Work past grandiosity to see where you tripped. Taking full ownership of your contribution to your dry or disappointing marriage can be difficult. Grandiosity often masks a deep-seated sense of being unacceptable as you are. The glory of grandiosity is that it outshines any unacceptable parts of yourself with dazzling accomplishments and comparisons.

An opposite reaction to grandiosity is worthlessness. The overwhelming pain of being caught in an affair brings out loud, condemning voices in your head that you cannot escape. You may want to avoid intimacy because of feeling so unworthy, but your wounded partner needs you. Your healing is important. A **betrayal moral injury** occurs when your choice to have an affair goes so deeply against your own values that you experience a lasting psychological injury to your psyche, self-image, and worldview. Not all responsible partners will experience a moral injury, and that is good.

Moral injuries can be very difficult to overcome. Betrayal moral injuries can cause feelings of guilt, shame, anger, sadness, anxiety, disgust, and worthlessness. Betrayal moral injury may cause you to go into isolation, experience anxiety and/or depression. If you are a responsible partner so overwhelmed with worthlessness that you struggle to function socially, at work, or at home, or are considering self-harm, please seek professional help.

The Wounded Partner's Path

Affair repair is a tandem process. Ideally your responsible partner strives to repair the wound, and you, as the wounded partner, strive to feel strong and safe enough to accept the repair. *Your relationship cannot heal if you remain stuck in a space where you are unable or unwilling to accept the sincere efforts of your responsible partner.*

It's Not All about You

Wounded partners comparing themselves to the affair partner is normal but self-harming. It's natural to compare yourself to the affair partner and wonder what they had that you didn't. These thoughts make you feel less-than, cast off, or second choice. Worse, it is painful to think of the two of them talking about you.

No matter what was right or wrong in your relationship or what you did or didn't do, the decision and responsibility for cheating lies with your responsible partner. The affair was more about your responsible partner's failing than about your desirability.

Affairs can cause a **narcissistic wound**. A narcissistic wound is an emotional trauma that injures your pride and self-worth. A narcissistic wound can leave you feeling humiliated, degraded, hollow, and empty. The trauma of the affair can cut your connection with your natural born identity which is lovable, capable, content, creative, and confident. If being lovable is your natural state, you may wonder, how could the affair have happened in the first place?

It is narcissistic to feel you are so lovable that it would mesmerize and solve all your partner's problems, and they would forsake every need or want for the love of you. People fail. It's not that you are not lovable, it's that your partner is human. It is not narcissistic to expect people to keep their promises. Your attributes of being lovable are still intact, just buried under a history full of life experiences, challenges, and a relationship pattern to which your partner contributed.

Do not let the narcissistic wound become a scar. A **narcissistic scar** forms when shame runs so deep that it blocks you from ever feeling truly okay about yourself, even when that shame isn't justified. Betrayal is not about you. Rediscover your self-identity apart from your relationship and responsible partner's efforts. Seek healthy affirming friends, relatives, and situations. Work to remember all that is wonderful about you. It's still there.

Jealousy

Jealousy is a passion that can consume you, the wounded partner. The Latin root of the word passion is *passio*, which means suffering. Passion brings pain. Jealousy of the affair partner is not often discussed but is usually present in the affair repair journey. Some wounded partners are blind with it; others are more focused on safety and dissociate or disconnect so they don't feel it at all. As a wounded partner, become aware of your feelings of jealousy. How do you acknowledge and address them? Admitting jealousy is admitting vulnerability and power over you, which may make you want to fight. How do you feel about being jealous? Sometimes wounded partners unleash their jealousy on the responsible partner. Other times they turn that hurtful burning passion on themselves, tearing themselves down for not being "better" than the affair partner. Jealousy can be a destructive force. Become aware of how jealousy is driving your behavior, and work to be productive, not destructive with the energy.

What Was Your Contribution?

Asking you as a wounded partner what your contribution was to the negative patterns in the relationship comes dangerously close to blaming you for the affair. To be clear, the responsibility for betraying lies squarely with your responsible partner. Your partner could have communicated better, fought harder, or found better ways to pursue happiness. Some or all of those strategies may have been tried and were unsuccessful. They could have left. You are not responsible for their choice to cheat. Nonetheless, you, as the wounded partner, must reflect from a safe space what your contribution was to the negative patterns in the relationship. The purpose of your reflection is not to shift blame but to help set a course for affair repair and marriage transformation. Your insights will guide what kind of communication and relationship patterns you want going forward. Do not settle for less. Now is the time for you to make your own changes as you hold the expectation that your responsible partner will make theirs.

Makiko's Contribution

Makiko was adamant she had done nothing wrong. Her and Steve's life had been perfect, but he had built it on illusion, and then it came crashing down. Steve had provided a jet-setting life-style, private education for their four boys, and limitless funds for their needs. Makiko did not want the funds; she wanted him. He would be gone weeks at a time for work. Now she discovered he had cheated, they were in financial distress, and he had a drinking problem. Makiko claimed he had ruined their perfect life.

Gently I challenged her: had she ever found signs of his drinking that he tried to cover up? She said, "Yes! When I took the recy-cling to the bin, it was full of empties! He had been throwing his bottles away before I ever saw him drink." I reflected that she had known something was wrong but for many understandable reasons ignored it. Challenging her husband's drinking problem would have brought down the whole house of cards. She had colluded by default and left it to her husband to maintain the illusion.

As a wounded partner, take the time to self-compassionately reflect upon what you accepted, let go, or did not fight. Makiko overlooked weeks away from home and a drinking problem that were not accept-able to her. Consider what and why you did not challenge things in the past. Perhaps you did challenge, but the lies continued. Perhaps your challenge was too critical, aggressive, or negative. Identify what needs to change to make your relationship reliable and desirable again.

Clarify What Is Wanted and What Is Not

As you try to heal, emotions send you in every direction like a pinball bouncing from bumper to bumper, triggering lights, bells, and whistles until it tilts. Rage wants your responsible partner destroyed. Love wants them back. Despair wants to crawl in a hole, while fear wants to cling. Justice demands your responsible partner leave—but first make amends. Revenge wants them stuck in the trying, watching them squirm, knowing they will never be forgiven, and vengeance wants them ruined. Hope wants to resurrect the life that went to ashes in the fallout of discovery.

Luke Realizes What He Doesn't Want

I first met Luke and Grace when they were on the brink of divorce. Counseling was successful, as they made changes in themselves that brought out the best in each other. Their twelve-year marriage was better than ever before. Then, two years later, Luke came back in for some individual sessions. Their old habits had returned. Grace was overspending, and he was yelling. Then Luke discovered Grace was having an affair.

Grace was regretful. She worked hard to repair the damage she had done, taking full responsibility for her poor choice, though the marriage had relapsed to its old patterns. She tried to make as many changes as she could to demonstrate to Luke it was worth coming back, but he was angry. He was conflicted and did not ask for a divorce. He wanted his marriage back but was not sure how he could get over the pain and disappointment.

Luke began a text conversation with Grace's sister, Emma. Emma was a comforting ear, knowing Grace's many shortcomings and of her betrayal. Emma had lived with Grace's disorganization and poor housekeeping skills throughout college and a little beyond. Emma had been the maid of honor in their wedding and had known Luke his entire married life. Emma felt compassion for Luke's pain in the betrayal and frustration in the relationship. Soon Emma and Luke were meeting for coffee, having long talks, walks, and ultimately sex.

Luke realized he and Emma couldn't be together, but he didn't want to leave her. He didn't know if he really wanted Grace. He was open and exploring all options but was not ending the relationship with either woman. Even though Luke acknowledged what he was doing was wrong, he felt justified because Grace had broken the vow first. Further, after deeper reflection, he acknowledged that though Grace had done everything to repair the affair, he was not willing to do what it would take for marriage transformation. He did not want to redo all the original work they had done, and had not maintained, to improve their marriage.

As the wounded partner, you should take some time to consider if you really want your responsible partner back. It is hard to know because the pain is blinding and confusing at first. You may want payback but try not to let it compromise your own behavior or waste time. Wounded and responsible partners deserve a repair process, even if you two decide not to stay married. If you can, try to imagine that one day the pain has gone away and you two have established trust. In this image where the relationship is fully repaired, is it wanted? What would have to be regained or different to make affair repair and marriage transformation efforts worth it?

What If I Can't Forgive?

In the affair repair phase, it is too soon to expect yourself as a wounded partner to be able to forgive, though some may be able to. Allow time and space to be self-compassionate and honest about how you feel. Work can be done on your relationship before forgiveness has occurred. Strive to strengthen positive feelings such as hope, partnership, shared responsibility for the home and children, or peaceful stability for now. Identify negative emotions such as revenge, vengeance, and rage. Work to reduce their influence. If justice is important to you, what role does it play? How can you protect yourself, receive justice, and repair your relationship? What role does mercy have? Is mercy love?

The What If I Can't Forgive Story

"It's been six years," said Priya. "And finally Ramesh is willing to get divorced, but now I am not sure what I want."

Priya and Ramesh separated after she discovered his affair. Ramesh had dragged his feet, delaying the process. He did not want to divorce. He spent six years pursuing Priya and had finally come to accept she would not forgive him.

Priya was rattled now that he was moving on. She did not want him back; she could not forgive him. Yet, she did not want him to leave. Part of her still had a sentimental attachment to him, but she was concerned if she indulged in that sentimentality, her friends who had been so supportive of her would feel betrayed.

Ramesh was making one last-ditch effort to get Priya to come to marriage counseling with the new therapist he had been seeing for the past year who had helped him gain insight and personal growth. In counseling with me, Priya disclosed she did not want to go. She worried the new therapist would be looking to see what was wrong with Priya that had caused Ramesh to stray. I assured her that no matter how she had failed, it did not excuse or warrant betrayal. It was okay for her to admit shortcomings and work on them. Such a willingness deserves compassion and support. It is not an opportunity to shift blame.

Priya was zealous in protecting her right to vengeance as an innocent victim of his betrayal. Not forgiving kept Priya safe, though she loved Ramesh.

Some people are fighters, some are fawners or people pleasers. Fighters tend to seek retribution. Fight was part of Priya's makeup. Priya acknowledged vengeance was not a healthy emotion, but it was the one she had. I encouraged radical acceptance. It is not a problem to have the feeling; it is a problem to act unproductively. Priya could work to note when vengeance was coming up for her, ask for what she needed from Ramesh, or leave the situation. Priya could ask for an apology, a deep discussion, a compliment, or words of appreciation to dampen the flames of vengeance. Vengeance masks hurt and vulnerability. Working with the feeling versus trying to deny, judge, or take away Priya's natural fight instinct had a better chance of keeping her safe and repairing the relationship. Perhaps Ramesh would be willing to work with her vengeance in productive ways. He had waited six years, and his sincerity was obvious. Maybe marriage counseling with the new therapist would help.

Letting Others Down

Priya was afraid to betray those who were supportive during the crisis and affair PTS phase. The reality is that true friends want you to be safe, happy, and have everything you want. If you as the wounded partner can repair your relationship and be safe and happy, those who love you will be supportive in the end. Children want their family back and will have their own work to do with the repairing parent. Unless your relationship was violent, do not let the potential judgment of friends prevent healthy repair.

The Shared Path of Affair Repair

Your individual paths are intertwined on the map of affair repair and marriage transformation. Together both of you will be working on forgiveness, maintaining hope, ensuring an end to the pain, and knowing why you continue. Forgiveness is a process you will work on together. You will find glimmers of hope and justifications to call it quits. Identifying your reasons to repair will sustain you as you make decisions along the way.

Forgiveness is a Process

You as a couple may overcome an affair PTS trigger, but the pain pops back up again. Be patient. You two will manage triggers and pain repeatedly. Sometimes the challenge will be over the same issue and sometimes something new. Forgiveness is a process. As much as the responsible partner must continue to work on repair with ongoing demonstration of changed behavior, the wounded partner must continue to offer acknowledgement or forgiveness as much as they can.

The wounded partner's heart may say, "I forgive you," but the head may say, "Don't be a fool." The head may say, "I forgive you because it is the 'right thing to do,'" but the heart says, "How could you leave us to be hurt again?" The wounded partner may go back and forth. The wounded partner may have to forgive not just seven times, but seven times seventy as the affair PTS continues to resurface. The wounded partner may think they were over something but then the pain returns. The responsible partner will need patience, strength, and support to see this process through.

Wounded partners with a black-and-white sense of right and wrong may particularly struggle with the repeated cycle of forgiveness. If you have a strong sense of right and wrong, you may have a hard time seeing your responsible partner's point of view. It is wrong to cheat and nothing past that will be considered. This will increase the challenge for your responsible partner to be seen, understood, and possibly forgiven. In this rut of black and white thinking, repair gets stuck in a loop of pain-apology-repeat. Repetition will be necessary but strive for a breakout.

Responsible partners can be equally black and white. The responsible partner may feel they have apologized enough. They know they did wrong and have taken responsibility, so it's over. Responsible partners may feel guilty but also justified in doing what they did to meet their needs. In black and white thinking, things are settled, so why press the point? Until both partners come to a mutual understanding and acceptance, repair is not complete.

Couples who are black-and-white thinkers struggle to empathize deep enough to balance their understanding. People who are clear on what the "right" answer is, have little patience for or understanding of any other contingency or conclusion. Black-and-white thinkers may be able to articulate what their partner is thinking or feeling, but when it comes to discussion or negotiation, their own logic and experience supersedes all others.

Healthy people can keep a balance in their understanding. Unhealthy people sway to an extreme by either giving up or enforcing their point of view. Wounded partners should focus on what the responsible partner is doing to make things better. Responsible partners should accept responsibility but also work to establish better mutual understanding.

Glimmers

Both partners can focus on **glimmers**. Glimmers are the opposite of triggers and are indications of potential healing. Glimmers help people experience a sense of safety. Glimmers are often subtle, like a smile from your partner, sitting together on the sofa, or hand holding. Cognitively, a person might not *think*, "I feel safe and connected in the world," but their *body* begins to experience connection and safety. This experience is taken in by the senses before it is labeled by the brain. Becoming aware of glimmers, noticing when you *feel* safe, and looking for those experiences can help calm your system overall, reducing the sensation of being on constant alert and strengthening your baseline feeling of safety.

Nurture yourself by noting and affirming any glimmers of things going well. Being aware of glimmers will help you stay within the window of tolerance when a trigger threatens to knock you out. It is a superpower if you can identify a glimmer when emotions are high. If you can catch your partner's soft eyes or notice they called you honey when things were tense, you will grow stronger. Noticing a glimmer does not mean you believe everything is okay; it means you see all is not lost.

Kill Switch

Sometimes you just need a kill switch for the pain. The affair PTS won't stop, and you can no longer endure the free-floating anxiety of whether your relationship will repair. I always empower my clients by reminding them that they can end the marriage at any time. No one is truly trapped. But for many reasons they don't want to end the relationship yet. They know they don't want to leave today or tomorrow, maybe not in a week or a month, but an indefinite horizon in limbo is too much to tolerate. A kill switch can be a date, action, or series of dates/actions that when flipped will prompt you to end things. Either partner can adopt a kill switch.

A **kill switch date** is a date set in your mind for when you will be done. You will accept you have tried everything you can until that date arrives. Identify a kill switch date and mark it in your mental calendar. Know that the date can slide forward (or backward) anytime if anything changes. The kill switch date could be after the holidays, your child's birthday, the big vacation you had been looking forward to, or the commission bonus that will be coming at the end of the quarter. Any reason to move the kill switch date allowing you to continue to work on the map of affair repair is a good reason. Be sure to be productive in trying to repair your relationship versus waiting in misery.

A **kill switch action** is an action you won't tolerate. Make it clear to your partner what you will not tolerate. An obvious kill switch might be ongoing contact with the affair partner after committing to end things. Other kill switches might be exposing the children to the affair partner, giving the affair partner money, or not following through on pursuing addiction recovery. It is always permissible to reset your kill switch. It may be that your relationship has progressed but not completely healed. There is reason to hope, but there is nothing complete.

Establish safety with if/then statements. If you confirm your partner is cheating again (not a reveal of more information about cheating you already knew about, but current cheating post this discovery), then you may take a kill switch action. Settle yourself with that thought so you feel safe. You may decide you will separate. You may move out or choose to divorce if you discover that cheating continues.

You must be serious about your kill switch but not so rigid you end things prematurely. Stephanie, in the Stop! Do Not Divorce story earlier, was clear that if Chuck returned to the affair partner, she would divorce him, and it would not be pretty. He believed her. It took all her personal strength and focus not to divorce him when she caught him again. His relapse made the repair all that harder, and he knew he was lucky she gave him a shot. Stephanie took a risk that paid off; there was no guarantee. You may not choose to take that risk when the moment comes; the key is the resolve. Chuck knew it, and Stephanie knew she could if she wanted to. She kept the power.

A **kill switch chain** is a series of dates and/or actions to move you toward safety in or out of the relationship. You may set a first step date in your kill switch chain. For example, you may have a target date in mind to move to separate rooms, see a lawyer, or start the separation, followed by divorce if things don't get better along the way. Dates can be rescheduled if good things happen or you regain strength or hope.

Anchors

When you are bobbing around in the raging waters of affair repair, being tossed and feeling out of control, you need an anchor. An **anchor** is the reason you stay. When your fight-or-flight system is activated and emotions overrun you, you need an anchor. An anchor is a non-triggering thought in your heart that reminds you why you are doing this hard work. You are not a fool; you are choosing to work through the map of affair repair and marriage transformation for a reason. Your reasons might include you are doing the right thing as you see it, you are working to keep the family intact for the children, it is cheaper to stay married, the grass is not greener, and most of all, you may still actually love your partner.

The reason you continue to work on repair does not have to be pretty; it just needs to be true. I have seen each of these reasons in various combinations get a person through the darkest trials of the healing journey until they came to the other side and found an even better reason to stay. Anchors are one of the many tools you can use to sustain you on your healing journey through affair repair and marriage transformation.

Key Concepts

The affair repair phase is where you two experience truth together by honestly sharing your conflicting yet connected journeys. This sharing of truth builds a history and foundation you can move forward from.

- Wounds can heal and partners can repair.
- Affair PTS symptoms can arise at any time and must be addressed before affair repair can proceed.
- **White lies** and **feigned sincerity** will be setbacks in the long run.
- It is common for either partner to be **one foot in, one foot out**. Strive for honesty.
- **Responsible partner's personal work:**
  - Help heal the wound you created
  - Become aware of the illusion you created
  - Revisit the effects of limerence
  - Consider your contribution to the lack of fulfillment in the relationship
  - Address any feelings of grandiosity or worthlessness
- **Wounded partner's personal work:**
  - Understand that the decision to betray is not about you
  - Confront jealousy
  - Consider your contribution to the lack of fulfillment in the relationship

- Clarify what you really want
- Consider if you can forgive
- Do not worry about letting others down
- **Both partners** must work together, be aware of each other's process, and not move ahead of the other. Together they can:
  - Re-dedicate time and time again until affair PTS fades
  - Look for **glimmers**, which are signs of hope and opposite of triggers
  - Determine **kill switch** dates, chains, or actions to reduce free floating anxiety that things will not get better
  - Stay connected to **anchors**, which are the reasons to stay dedicated to the healing journey
- **Average Duration:** Affair repair work usually begins six weeks to three months post discovery and can go on for six months to a year, depending on the couple.
- **Goal:** Work together to communicate and understand each other as you move toward healing.
- **Do:**
  - Remain in the window of tolerance
  - Be authentic
  - Address your own personal work
- **Don't:**
  - Dysregulate or dissociate
  - Lie
  - Expect your partner to be further along than where they are in getting past the affair or recommitting to the relationship
- **If you are the wounded partner**, do not try to control or push your partner's process. Accept and make decisions for yourself in response to where your responsible partner is at emotionally. Continue to do your own personal work.
- **If you are the responsible partner**, be prepared, not afraid or holding back, to move through any pop-up affair PTS symptoms. Honesty and patience are the best efforts toward healing the wound. Continue to do your own personal work.

Chapter 13
Affair Repair Talks

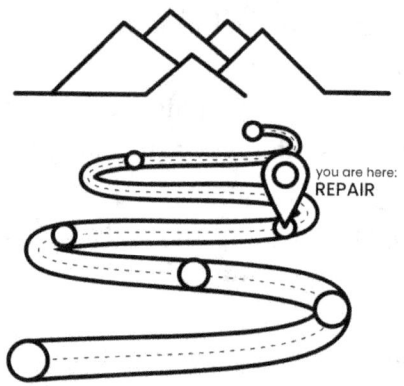

you are here:
REPAIR

*The challenge of affair repair talks
is to ensure your talks are safe and productive.*

The foundation of affair repair is cemented in the talks you and your partner have. Affair repair talks help resolve the trauma by giving the experience of a beginning, middle, and end. When people get stuck in trauma, they cannot move past discovery. There is no end. Both of you will need a clear understanding of strong communication skills to establish a shared understanding and meaning of what has happened.

Unlike the crisis or affair PTS phase, the affair repair phase is characterized by an *extended* ability to tolerate uncomfortable information. When you can hear and/or say the truth without becoming dysregulated, you two can experience a new relationship.

In the window of tolerance, you can feel intense hurt, anger, or fear and still communicate. You can hear what your partner is saying, and you can articulate what you are feeling. From this safe foundation of co-experienced truth, you can proceed together in a new, shared reality. The co-experienced, regulated honesty provides insight into yourself and your partner.

Affair repair talks can be intense and draining because emotions are powerful and take energy to manage. Feelings cannot be ignored, or they will surface in other areas of your life or physical health. Wounded partners need the relief of an affair repair talk, so they look forward to them. Responsible partners need the hope that the difficult discussion will be worth the pain.

Affair repair talks are time spent talking about the affair within the window of tolerance. Neither partner is too emotional or shut down to share and engage with one another's feelings. Affair repair talks can last a few minutes to a few hours but should not exceed either party's window of tolerance. Some may say that an affair repair talk should not exceed ninety minutes, yet if you are having a good talk where there is safety, sharing, and healing, there is no need to limit. If you are having a talk where there is escalating anger, conflict, and hurtfulness, it is better to take a break and calm your emotions so you can reengage productively. Remember, dysregulation can include shutdown. Just because someone is not yelling or crying does not mean they are in their window of tolerance.

Healthy Affair Repair Talks

A healthy repair talk can be painful but ultimately brings a sense of peace, clarity, or acceptance of difficult truth. At any time, affair PTS can upset either partner. If either of you becomes dysregulated, return to the soothing techniques of the affair PTS phase. Healthy repair talks are authentic and honest without meanness. Dishonest communication creates distrust.

Dishonest communication involves lies. In their book, *Tell Me No Lies*, Ellyn Bader, Judith D. Schwartz, and Peter Pearson, write that everybody lies. A **lie invitee**, they point out, is someone who invites lying. Lie invitees encourage lying by becoming emotionally dysregulated, seeking promises, withdrawing, shutting down, pretending to listen, or resorting to addictive behavior. Some responsible partners like Tara, who was caught cheating with her brother-in-law, would break down crying out of guilt every time a discussion became difficult. In response to her invitation, her wounded partner, Alby, stopped asking the questions to which he really needed answers and told her it was okay. Most lies, according to the authors, are said to maintain the relationship. In affair repair talks, lies may be an attempt to prevent further hurt, avoid conflict, or find a back doorway out of the relationship. Lying is a mistake and will only set back your affair repair process.

Some lies are small, to avoid hurt, such as "Your penis is bigger," or "I never think of the affair partner." These are called **loving lies**. Lies are told to maintain the illusion of fantasy or perfection and are often a characteristic found in new relationships. After a while, as the relationship becomes more familiar, lies are told to maintain the status quo, rather than deal with problems.

Partners may tell **passive-aggressive lies** to avoid taking responsibility and dealing with differences. An example of a passive-aggressive lie in an affair repair talk is promising to share your location or not to snoop when neither of you has any intention of following through. Partners telling passive-aggressive lies do not want to tell the truth so they can protect the illusion that the relationship is functioning.

People will lie directly or by omission to avoid conflict. People can even lie to themselves to maintain the relationship and avoid doing the work to repair it. A **conflict-avoidant lie** might sound like, "I'm not thinking about your affair anymore," "I don't really need to have affair repair talks if it stresses you out," or "I am okay with the sex we were having." A conflict-avoidant lie by omission is not telling the wounded partner you saw the affair partner at the grocery store or you deleted a text from them without answering. A healthy repair talk does not involve lying or inviting a lie.

The Healthy Affair Repair Talk Story

Cris and Scott had been moving forward in therapy. Scott was no longer seeking fulfillment outside the marriage. Cris trusted he was coming home to her and the kids. Still, they were stuck in their roles, living parallel, conflict-avoidant lives. They were not connected. Repair and transformation had not yet come to fruition. I asked about physical intimacy. There was none.

Scott acknowledged he had wounded Cris and, though he did want physical connection, he did not want to pressure her. He had also done some introspection and found he no longer needed the attention of a woman as he had in the past and that what he really wanted was family. He was willing to wait. Scott's sharing of insights during their affair repair talk brought up a wellspring of feelings for Cris.

When she and Scott first met, he had said he wanted a family, but when Cris was pregnant with their first child, he was in the arms of another woman. Other distractions followed, such as work and time with friends. Though she desperately wanted to, how could she believe he really wanted a family? Cris, a normally well-composed woman, began to cry. She was struggling with affair PTS. Her strong inner walls that used to block him out were beginning to crack as she considered the conflicting realities of him wanting their family and what had happened the last time she believed him.

Scott was able to be present with Cris as she spoke of her pain. She was not dysregulated, but very hurt. The moment was intense and emotional. Scott resisted his usual defensive reaction. In previous sessions, he would explain his actions or point out that he had not done anything untrustworthy in more than a year. Finally, in this affair repair talk, Cris felt heard because Scott was able to listen without the defense that brought her protective walls back up. The couple moved forward on their healing journey.

Unhealthy Affair Repair Talks

Unhealthy repair talks involve lying, emotional dysregulation, and/or purposeless pain. Unhealthy talks do not repair, they activate, shred, and leave both parties exhausted and upset. Avoid trashing your partner and reducing them to less than human. The expression of anger or hurt no longer brings soothing to the wounded partner or resolve of guilt for the responsible partner. No matter how many times the responsible partner apologizes, cries, nurtures, or breaks down, there is no resolve.

An unhealthy cycle begins with each partner returning every offense with their own hurt. "I need you to understand how devastated I was," is answered with, "I know you were, and do you know how long I suffered with your mother living with us?"

When the pain of affair repair talks is unproductive, the wounded partner is left in emotional turmoil and the responsible partner in the darkness of shame and hopelessness. There is only one way out of an unhealthy repair talk cycle—detachment. Both partners want to quit. Purposeless talks lead to resentment and separation, not repair and trust.

If you are in an unhealthy talk, don't escalate or detach, **take a break**. Consider if you are activated by affair PTS or are simply dysregulated. If you are dysregulated, review some of the suggestions in affair PTS for self-regulation and co-regulation. Work to bring yourself back into the window of tolerance. Keep reading to learn how to avoid unhealthy repair talks.

Avoid the Drama Triangle

The concept of a drama triangle pattern was originated by psychiatrist Stephan B. Karpman. The **drama triangle** describes the dance a couple does when they are driven by and respond out of emotion. There are three roles in the drama triangle: rescuer, persecutor, and victim.

A couple, in an escalated, dramatic, and unproductive argument, will chase each other around the corners of the triangle, championing their positions as they say things like:

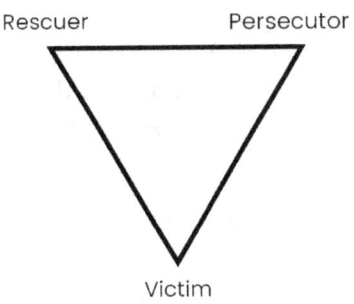

"How could you do this to me?" (Victim making the other a persecutor)

"If we had had sex more than once a year, I wouldn't have sought someone else." (Role reversal, persecutor becomes victim)

"You will never see your children again!" (Persecutor creating victim)

"I realize I never paid attention to you, which left you feeling lonely." (Rescuer creating victim)

In the drama triangle, there is no meeting in the middle, no balance of power, and no ability to see each other as having a valid perspective. Of course, it is normal for couples to fall into the drama triangle pattern, saying things like the statements above when emotions are high. This is particularly common in the early phases of the map of affair repair. However, over time, a healthy repair talk keeps the drama within the window of tolerance and becomes a sincere expression of pain or remorse, not victimhood or rescuing. In a more stabilized, productive affair repair talk, emotions are no longer weapons or entrenched positions, they are honest expressions.

In healthy relating, there is adult-to-adult communication in the window of tolerance.

In adult-to-adult communication, each of you can self-regulate. You are responsible for your own actions. You can help but you cannot control your partner. Healthy adults are aware of what they want, but they do not force one another. They can take acceptable risks. Adults have an emotional range and can use emotion as information, not be overwhelmed by it.

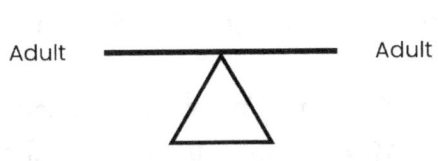

A rewrite of the above scenario might look like:

"I never imagined this would have happened. I am devastated." (Adult expressing fact and emotional experience)

"I felt abandoned without physical touch and sex in our relationship. I went behind your back." (Adult taking responsibility and expressing emotional experience—not excusing)

"I am so angry and want to protect our children from getting hurt more." (Adult expressing emotion without using the children as weapons to punish)

"I realize I never paid attention to you, which left you feeling lonely. I can change that going forward, but I am going to need some help getting over this." (Adult taking responsibility, but not excusing and requesting amends)

Guidelines for Affair Repair Talks

Guidelines can help your affair repair talks be more productive. Avoiding difficult discussions is as bad as having emotionally charged arguments that go off the rails. Use the following guidelines to keep yourselves moving forward on the map of affair repair.

Is This a Good Time?

It is perfectly acceptable to have an impromptu affair repair talk. It is not okay to ambush your partner. Unlike affair PTS, the prompt to have an affair repair talk is manageable. An idea or thought may come to your mind, but the hallmark of the affair repair phase is that you remain in the window of tolerance for long periods of time. You may be upset, but you are not overwhelmed. You may be curious, worried, wondering, or simply fact-checking, but you are not ruminating, overly anxious, or angry. There is no reason, if the timing seems right, not to initiate a talk.

Right timing means there is privacy and time. The two of you should be alone. It is a good idea to remove any distractions by turning off cell phones, computers, and TV. There must be enough time to process the topic you would like to discuss. So be mindful not to start this conversation right before leaving the house, having visitors, or heading out to a social gathering. Initiate an affair repair talk by asking, "Is this a good time to talk, and if not, when would be?" If now is not a good time, set a time when you will not be distracted. If you think a discussion may go beyond the time you have, consider scheduling a time.

Set a Schedule

Affair repair talks can happen anywhere or anytime there is privacy and opportunity, but a schedule can be helpful, particularly in the beginning of this affair repair phase. The beginning of this phase will overlap with the ending of the affair PTS phase. Affair PTS cannot be scheduled; it can be managed. If affair PTS arises, revert to the strategies of the earlier phase as necessary. If you are processing an affair of the past that seems long gone, be prepared for affair PTS symptoms to surface.

Set a schedule for affair repair talks at least five to six times per week at the beginning of this phase. Consider scheduling talks for breakfast, commute time, or lunch, when there is a hard stop and a potential transition to another activity. Avoid scheduling your talks too close to bedtime. It is hard to end the talk when you know you can just push back bedtime. Even if you can end the talk, who can sleep after all that emotion has been stirred up? Try to schedule your affair repair talk to start right after dinner and end an hour before you go to bed so you have time to release some of the tension from your body.

Setting a schedule alleviates the free-floating anxiety of the wounded partner who fears you two will never talk about the affair again. Not talking about the affair gives an appearance that everything is okay. This appearance and lack of talking leaves the wounded partner alone to deal with the pain. Setting a schedule removes the free-floating anxiety of the responsible partner because they do not need to worry when the next difficult conversation might occur. Setting a schedule for affair repair talks also sets a schedule for all the time you are *not* going to be talking about the affair.

Avoid letting affair repair talks drag on into the night or pop up at unscheduled times. This will help establish some normalcy in your relationship without pretending that everything is okay. Allowing normalcy such as just watching TV, cooking together, or being with the kids gives everyone a break. Pockets of normalcy also offer some hope that things can be all right even while you are working on repairing the relationship.

Save one day for taking a break from the topic of the affair if you can. Five to six scheduled talks per week may seem like a lot, but if you stack them up front early in this process, you will more quickly move through this phase and onto the next, establishing trust with a firm foundation. Over time, you may reduce the number of talks you schedule. Do not rush. You may find that after several weeks, not months, you both will not want to talk about the affair so often.

Set a Time Limit

Set a time limit for your affair repair talks. A time limit will prevent burnout for either person, especially the responsible partner. Honoring time limits will reduce the dread of the talks because the intense work will have an end. The time limit depends on the topic. Some talks may be limited to five minutes because that is all the discussion will require. Or five minutes may be all that can be endured before one person leaves the window of tolerance. Generally, talks should be around ninety minutes. After ninety minutes, people can become physically, mentally, and emotionally tired. The adrenaline of the topic may sustain you for longer, but be mindful of exceeding this time. Agree to a limit and stick to it. The time for discussion should include your ritual in and ritual out.

Set a Ritual In and a Ritual Out

Set a ritual in to mark the beginning of your affair repair talk. The ritual demonstrates your intention to be purposeful and present. Rituals train your mind and body for the moment. Consistent rituals make things automatic and help you more quickly leave other distractions behind. Your ritual in may be that you always go to the living room and sit on the sofa facing each other. Or you might always sit and have coffee or go for a walk. Your ritual in should include a warmup statement such as "Thank you for having these difficult conversations." Or "I know this is hard for you. I am ready to listen and answer your questions." You may exchange opening statements such as "I love you and I want to overcome this together." Or "This opening ritual feels odd to me, but I am willing to try whatever works for us."

Your ritual out may be a simple hug. If you are not ready for a hug, you may try a closing statement such as "Thank you for this time in talking. It means a lot." A good ritual out would include acknowledging each other for the work you are doing to repair the relationship.

Don't Burn Your Partner Out

Don't burn your wounded partner by avoiding every little thing. Your wounded partner may not want to ask questions because they don't trust you as the responsible partner to stay within the window of tolerance or answer truthfully. The problem with not addressing what seems like a small thing is that it festers. This small question, feeling, or emotion burns deeper in the heart like a painful ember. *Not having affair repair talks is a way to burn out the wounded partner.*

More commonly, wounded partners burn out responsible partners by revisiting details repeatedly until their responsible partner is near exhaustion and shuts down. This is most common in crisis and affair PTS phases but can continue here in affair repair talks. Repeatedly asking the same question is the wounded partner's way of putting their world back together. Information needs to be confirmed and recon-firmed, however, there comes a tipping point, where you as a wounded partner are causing more hurt than healing by continually seeking the nonexistent, one bit of information that will make sense of everything and remove the pain.

If you are wearing each other out—even if both of you are within the window of tolerance—it is a bit of lingering affair PTS. When you two find yourself banging your head against the same wall and your partner withdrawing, consider taking a break from discussions. Engage in a distracting activity and work on acceptance. There is no answer that is going to make what happened okay.

Asking Questions

Information is necessary to establish an accurate understanding of what was real and what was an illusion in the past and in this moment. The healing factor in this transformative event is the personal and shared growth you *experience together*. Together you make sense of what was, is, and can be as you move forward. The questioning and answering process is the affair repair talk. Affair repair talks are often where the responsible partner's insight and personal work can be continued with their partner versus individually. The responsible partner can spend more time sharing their process, which provides safety for both of you and can be very healing, even if the honesty is difficult.

Post-discovery, there are innumerable questions of many types. Some questions will seek detail such as, "How many times did you have sex?" Some questions will involve meaning, such as "What were you getting out of the affair that you were not getting with me?" Who, what, when, where, and why will be asked over and over again from different angles. Each question serves a purpose, and each can exceed a tipping point. Repeatedly asking a question can be affirming and helpful, but it also can be ruminating and exhausting.

Some questions may not be necessary. Consider the value of asking questions to which you may not need or really want to know the answer. "Did he have a bigger penis than me?" Or "Was she in better shape than me?" may lead to painful answers that won't necessarily help you repair the relationship. What is the value of knowing a short-coming when your responsible partner is choosing you?

The Twenty-Four-Hour Rule

Some questions may bring answers you, as the wounded partner, would rather not know in the long run. Once the information is known, it cannot be unknown. Such questions tend to be in the comparison category such as "Was she prettier?" or "Was he a better lover?"

Since each question should be answered honestly and you do not want to invite lies, it is important that you are prepared for the answer. If there is any concern, the person answering the question may invoke the twenty-four-hour rule which simply puts a twenty-four-hour pause between the question and its honest answer. The person answering the question may say, "Are you sure you want to know that?" If the answer is, yes, then the answerer may say, "I will give you the honest answer, but I would like to wait twenty-four hours for you to consider what that answer may mean to you." If the question remains, the answer should be given.

Questions You Might Ask

Factual Questions

How did you meet? How often did you meet? Where did you go? Do you still communicate? Do you still have their contact information (phone, email, etc.)? When was the last time you communicated? How long have you been having the affair? How long had it been going on before I found out?

Did you give them money? Did you expose the children to them? Did you make plans with them to spend your lives together? Who was the backup plan, me or them?

Had you thought of having an affair before? How often? Have you cheated on anyone else before? Are there other affairs I do not know about? How long did you think you could get away with it? How did you think this was going to end?

Reasons for the Affair

Were you looking for an affair? Why him/her/them? Was this a midlife crisis? Were you bored? Were you feeling isolated? Were you feeling less of a man/woman/person? Were you needing attention? Did you do this to hurt me? What needs were met by the affair partner that were not being met in our relationship? Was I not good enough to be respected? When were we done in your mind? What went wrong in our relationship?

About the Affair

What did you experience with the other that you don't have with me? Did you have fun with him/her/them? What did they offer you that made it worth having the affair?

Vulnerability

Does this person know about us? How much does this person know about me and our family? Did you think about me and the children? What was it like to come home to me after having been with this person? How do I know I can trust you now? When did you think of them when you were with me? Were you ever communicating with them in my presence?

Fear of Divorce or Abandonment

Were you trying to leave me? Did you hope I would leave so you wouldn't feel responsible for breaking up the family? Why didn't you just dump me if you were going to cheat? Did you keep me just as a second option? Would you have ended it if I hadn't found out? Did you think I would leave if I found out? Did you hope I would find out? Would you respect me less if I were to forgive you?

Sexual Questions

Did you have sex? Did you use protection? What kind of sex were you looking for? Was the affair strictly physical?

Emotional Questions

Did you fall in love? How did you feel when you were with this person? What feelings did you have for them, then and now? Do you have any regrets about the affair?

Commitment Questions

What steps are you willing to take to regain my trust? What do you need from me? How can we work together to rebuild our relationship? What are your long-term commitments to prevent future affairs?

Insight Questions

What did you like about yourself during the affair? What did you not like about yourself during that time? What do you like about yourself now? What did the affair mean about you? Us? Me? What is the reason you couldn't talk to me about your feelings? What was the moment you decided to have an affair? What kept you from keeping your commitment you made to me? How do you suggest working on our relationship? Why did you continue when you knew it was wrong? How do you feel about the affair now? How could you lie to me every day? Did you ever feel guilty? Do you feel guilty when I question you? How could you have meant it when you said *I love you* to me when you were with your affair partner?

The Question Asking Story

> Kelsey was still. She paused to take in what Emma had just said. She sat quietly for a while. Her eyes were moving left and right, back and forth as she thought. (This was a sign her brain was processing the trauma.) We sat for a little while. Allowing space and silence for her to take it all in.
>
> She came out with a question, a pointed question that would further settle the trauma. "Where did you go after dinner that Saturday night?"

"She went home, and I went to my brother's to drink," Emma replied, providing the fact that helped Kelsey piece together the reality of what had happened. Kelsey relaxed and thanked Emma for the truth. Kelsey reaffirmed she still wanted a divorce and felt pressure to stay. Emma acknowledged her feelings but remained honest in her anger about the situation she was unable to repair completely. She was not blaming Kelsey for her feelings while acknowledging her own anger.

This couple's emotional intelligence was high. Their affair repair talks were effective in helping to heal the wound and create a new shared foundation from which they could clearly decide whether to move forward. Kelsey and Emma were each doing their own work. Emma's was to find a way to heal and Kelsey's to take ownership of who she was and what to do now.

Key Concepts

Affair repair talks are the bulk of the work of affair repair. Affair repair talks give the trauma a beginning, middle, and end, helping to settle the truth and build a foundation for the future together or apart.

- Lying sets back affair repair.
  - Avoid being a **lie invitee** with communication behaviors and tactics that invite your partner to lie
  - Avoid telling **loving lies** which maintain an illusion
  - Avoid telling **passive-aggressive lies** which evade taking responsibility
  - Avoid **conflict-avoidant lies** which delay affair repair
- Avoid the roles of the **drama triangle:**
  - **Victim** who needs rescuing
  - **Persecutor** who is irredeemable and awful
  - **Rescuer** who has no needs of their own
- Adopt **adult-to-adult** relational stance, communicating within the window of tolerance. Adults can have needs and are known to do bad things, but adults communicate in a mature manner.

- Guidelines for healthy affair repair talks:
  - Ask if this is a good time and if not, when would be
  - Set a schedule for talks, to prevent avoidance or limitless discussion
  - Set a time limit to reduce exhaustion and increase willingness to engage
  - Set a ritual in and ritual out of the talk to help engage your brain and body for repair
  - Don't burn out the **responsible partner** by processing too much information or the **wounded partner** by processing too little
  - Keep the children out of it
- Asking questions is necessary and informative, but not transformative. The *experience* of affair repair is transformative.
  - **Wounded partners** should consider the value of the questions they ask. Repeatedly asking a question may be affirming and confirming, but there is a tipping point where it becomes ruminating and exhausting.
  - Consider the **twenty-four-hour rule**, which may be invoked by the **responsible partner** to delay response and give the **wounded partner** some time to think if they really want the answer.
  - All questions should be answered honestly.
  - Questions may be factual or emotional and can fall into different categories such as insight, sexual, vulnerable, or fearful. This section contains a list of possible questions you might ask.
- **Average Duration:** You will use the skills of affair repair talks for the rest of your life. Do not worry, the need for affair repair talks will lessen over time and once you master them they will be more efficient, powerful, and effective.
- **Goal:** Communicate honestly and in healthy ways with your partner to work through the trauma of the affair.

- **Do:**
    - Have as many affair repair talks as it takes
    - Remain in the window of tolerance
    - Tell the truth
    - Adhere to schedules and time limits
    - Maintain adult-to-adult roles in communicating
- **Don't:**
    - Lie
    - Avoid affair repair talks
    - Fall into the drama triangle rolls of victim, persecutor, or rescuer
- **Actions for the wounded partner:** Be open to the truth. Do not invite lies. Do not burn your responsible partner out by exceeding schedules and limits. Do not let your partner avoid affair repair talks. Ask as many questions as you need. Become aware if you find yourself in a regular role of the drama triangle and work toward adult-to-adult communication.
- **Actions for the responsible partner:** Tell the truth. Do not lie. Better to say in honesty, "I am undecided," or "I worry the answer will hurt you unnecessarily," and invoke the twenty-four-hour rule than lie. Participate in as many affair repair talks as it takes. (It will exceed your patience and capacity at times.) Adhere to schedules and time limits to avoid unnecessary burnout. Become aware if you find yourself in a regular role of the drama triangle and work toward adult-to-adult communication.

Chapter 14
Affair Repair Communication Skills

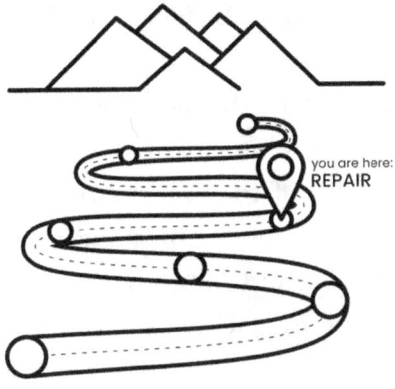

*The challenge of affair repair communication skills
is to practice better ways of sharing experiences.*

Even if you are a good communicator, consider this section as offering small ways to improve your skillset. Communication, like exercise, raising kids, or managing money, is something we think we intuitively know how to do. However, in all these areas, it is a good idea to learn and apply expert knowledge to take it to the next level. Even pro athletes have coaches.

I Statements

I statements are also known as I messages. I statements help you express your feelings, thoughts, and needs clearly while minimizing defensiveness and blame. An affair is a volatile topic where things can quickly relapse into an argument.

When you use I statements effectively, you focus on expressing your emotions, beliefs, or desires without accusing or criticizing. Good I statements usually begin with "I feel" or "I need," followed by a specific statement or request. "I feel/felt _____ when _____." For example, you could say: "I felt crazy every time you went to work. I worried you were meeting him again. I felt angry and hated you." An unhelpful statement might be: "I know you were fucking him while we were on vacation—with the kids! How could you do this to me, you whore!"

I statements, when said in the window of tolerance, provide the opportunity for the responsible partner to step in and offer healing. I statements in the window of tolerance allow the wounded partner to hear hurtful information without internalizing it as personal to them. "I felt needful of attention, so I sought it elsewhere," is an example of an I statement that owns your feelings without blaming the wounded partner.

I statements promote open dialogue and self-awareness. Sticking to I statements in affair repair talks helps to keep the environment constructive. By taking ownership of your feelings and needs in the window of tolerance, I statements build trust and safety in your relationship.

Four Horsemen of the Apocalypse of Communication

"If you knew you would have to go through all of this, you would never have had the affair."
John Gottman, PhD

Dr. John and Dr. Julie Gottman of The Gottman Institute are well known for their scientific research in couples' communication. They have been observing couples' interactions for more than thirty years. Over the course of their work, they identified four negative communication styles and what to do to correct them. The Gottmans' four horsemen of the apocalypse of communication are: **criticism**, **defensiveness**, **stonewalling,** and **contempt**. Focusing on the body's physiological response and avoiding the four horsemen of the apocalypse of communication will help keep you communicating within the window of tolerance.

Criticism

Criticism often begins a sentence with "You." Criticism labels and feels like a direct attack. It negatively frames someone into a caricature they can never escape. Criticized people are rendered unidimensional and incapable of change. Examples of criticism a wounded partner might say are, "You have ruined everything," or "You are the worst father." Criticizing looks like trash talking. "How many times did you spread your legs for him, you skank?" "You're such a loser, sex addict." A critical responsible partner might say things like, "You are always unsatisfied," or "You never listen to what I am saying." Criticism can also look like gaslighting, which is denying the reality of the other person's experience, by saying things like, "You are crazy," or "You're overreacting."

Antidote: Avoid criticism by focusing on I statements that reflect what you are feeling and begin communication with a gentle start up. Whenever possible, follow your I statement *with a request*. Examples of I statements followed by gentle start up and request might be, "I don't know how I will get over this and I know this discussion is hard for you too. Can you tell me again what made you do this?" "I am so disappointed. I know you are sorry. Can you give me some encouragement that this won't happen again?" "I can't make sense of what is happening. I want to help. How can I comfort you?" or "I am unsure how to help you. I know you are frustrated. Can you please tell me what I can do?" Remember, it is not only the words, but also the tone and physical expression of delivery that help in healing. Better to say you are having a hard time feeling open, nurturing, or present than to force a mixed message.

Some will say criticism, though painful, is true. That may be a fact, but criticism is not helpful in encouraging change, repairing hurt, or rebuilding a relationship. Criticism is like lobbing verbal hand grenades over the wall to get someone to change. When we are walled off, we are not open to relationship with our partner. Making a request is vulnerable. Making a request is allowing the other person to come close and meet your needs. Criticism breaks communication, amps up emotions, and threatens to throw both of you out of the window of tolerance.

The Criticism Cycle Story

Allison had grown up in a highly critical environment where nobody yelled but it was understood you must be perfect. At any moment Father might be disappointed, which would send the family scrambling to make things right. Allison was excellent at anticipating James's needs and was the perfect wife. He was the perfect husband. Both were nearly perfect in their behavior, work ethic, parenting, and physical appearance.

Problems arose when there were slight disagreements or chinks in the armor. Both were highly critical. Over time, this drove the couple apart as they tried to stay in their perfect roles, unable to process disagreements and feel acceptable to the other.

James could not understand why she took his feedback so harshly. (He was not taking Allison's experience of growing up in a perfectionist family in his understanding of her.) He began avoiding conflict and his wife altogether. He lost himself in work and found himself with another woman. In affair repair, Allison could not understand why James did not do everything to make amends. She criticized James's behavior, look, and emotions. She was trying to repair the relationship. When things were wrong, she had a hair-trigger response to make amends. Why didn't he?

Over the years, James had developed a hair-trigger response to all criticism. As soon as she made even the slightest comment, he snapped back and often yelled. The couple got stuck. When Allison was critical and released her pain over the affair, the obstacle for James, though genuine, was that he was triggered by the criticism and became highly defensive. Progress stalled as the criticism/defensiveness cycle continued.

Wounded partners must learn to receive apologies without adding further criticism. When possible, offering forgiveness, support, or praise for the apology or truth telling will help responsible partners be open and vulnerable. Critical partners often don't feel support is warranted for doing the right thing, but if they want more repair, they will need to do what works, not what they think they should. Responsible partners must learn to repair so that the wounded partner can respond to it. If the wounded partner becomes critical, it may be helpful to say something like, "I know you are hurting. I want to soothe you," to help them become more vulnerable and open.

Defensiveness

Defensiveness is often a good offense, justification, or explanation to avoid taking responsibility head on. A good offense sometimes looks like an emotional outburst. In this case, a person will flood the moment by breaking out in tears or anger, turning the focus to their regret, pain, or outrage rather than taking responsibility for the issue at hand. If this happens, slow everything down. Go back to the successful emotion regulating actions from the affair PTS phase. An emotionally reactive person needs to learn to moderate feelings and physiology to stay within the window of tolerance and move toward healing. Emotions cannot be used to avoid discussion. Take your time.

Defensiveness by justifying behaviors can be as bold as "If you hadn't been working all the time, I wouldn't have been so lonely and had this affair." Or, in a more subtle form, defensiveness may look like an explanation. "I was so lonely, that was why I had the affair." Both sentences avoid responsibility. One is blaming, the other excuses. Defensiveness breaks communication, amps intensity, and threatens to throw the couple out of the window of tolerance.

Antidote: The antidote to defensiveness is to first take full responsibility for one's action. "I did break your trust and had the affair." Or "I was lonely, so I chose to have an affair." Taking full responsibility when things are heated often helps the wounded partner maintain calm. Taking full responsibility is not an opportunity for the wounded partner to become emotionally abusive in response to the truth. When things are calm, the couple can explore the explanation. An explanation is not justification or an excuse. An explanation is the truth, and the truth is healing on the map of affair repair.

Stonewalling

Stonewalling occurs when one person is outside their window of tolerance. Stonewalling is the opposite of loud, out of control emotions; it is detachment and shutdown. A person who is stonewalling is shutting down because their nervous system is so physiologically aroused, they need to disengage. This disengagement may look like offering one-word answers, silent treatment, hanging up mid-conversation, or walking out.

Antidote: When you feel you are about to fall into stonewalling, take a time-out. The person who feels the need for a time-out says they need a break and *sets a time to return*. Setting a time to return is critical, otherwise the person who would like to continue the conversation feels cut off, disrespected, frustrated, and abandoned. The time to return may be in fifteen minutes, after dinner, after you take a walk or a drive, or the next day. Anytime within twenty-four hours is acceptable. The other person *must respect the time-out*.

One partner should not pursue as the other withdraws to the time-out. Pursuing is a doomed attempt to co-regulate emotions with the partner who has already made it known they are flooded beyond their window of tolerance. Pursuing will not go well. The pursuing person, must learn to self-soothe until the conversation can productively begin again. Stonewalling and pursuing will break communication, escalate frustration, and will threaten to throw you as a couple out of the window of tolerance. Take a time-limited break and return to a healthy affair repair talk.

Contempt

Contempt, according to Gottman research, is the number one predictor of divorce. Contempt is eye-rolling, name-calling, mocking, and belittling. Contempt dehumanizes and characterizes other people. A common subtle form of contempt when couples are working through an affair is taking moral high ground. "I have heels higher than your standards. You are pathetic. I never would have done this to you. Even when you lost your job, and I had all the opportunity with your brother, I didn't cheat. You're pathetic." This is belittling. Sometimes humor can be used to defuse a moment, but often it is cloaked contempt. "I know, I know. Your father always called you Little Miss Polly Perfect. If you're offended by my opinion, you should hear the ones I keep to myself."

Antidote: The root of contempt is dislike and disrespect. Rather than focus on how much you dislike your partner, focus on your own feelings and needs. Form an I statement that reflects the feeling you are struggling with. "I am so hurt this has happened to me. I feel unjustly wronged, and I don't know how to make it better. I don't even know what to ask you to do. I am so disappointed." Or "I am just so tired of apologizing and going over this. I am sorry I mocked you. I don't know if I can do this anymore." I suggest you make contempt a rule like "we don't drop babies." No matter how angry we are, even at the baby, we don't drop them. Don't excuse and indulge in contemptuous communication. Dig deeper into your motivations and communicate better. Contempt is a hurtful action.

Truce Signals

When things become a little tense, which could happen at any moment in an affair repair talk, look for a truce signal. A truce signal is a small comment, gesture, or word that indicates a softening of attitude toward you. When dogs fight, one dog may whimper or gesture by exposing part of their neck, or roll over onto their back to signal submission. The other dog, unless rabid or raised to fight, will stop the aggression while maintaining a readiness. These dogs are elevated, defending their boundaries, but they are not "going for the kill." *They back off.*

Acknowledging a truce signal does not mean the discussion is over or has come to a satisfactory conclusion. Acknowledging a truce signal means you see your partner is working to stay within the window of tolerance and connected to you. A truce signal is simply a subtle cue to keep the aggression at bay and focus on the productive communication tools of I statements and avoiding criticism, defensiveness, stonewalling, and contempt. Truce signals are small signs to keep the discussion open, vulnerable, and safe.

People offer truce signals naturally. They just don't consciously say, "I am sending you a truce signal." An example might be, "I know, honey, you have told me a thousand times how hurt you are." This may feel like a dismissive response because it is not the soothing comment that was hoped for. It was not soothing. However, unless it was said with a contemptuous tone, this is a truce signal. The pet name, honey, signals care, connection, and nurturing, while the rest of the sentence acknowledges fact and expresses exhaustion. When this occurs, rather than go for the jugular at the failure to soothe, note the truce signal. Respond non-attackingly. You might respond in a calmer tone, "I know you are tired of this, but I am still hurting," and if you are able to respond to what your partner said, "Maybe we should take a break." Make a request, use an I statement, or take a break in response to a truce signal. Don't escalate.

Humor is sometimes a truce signal. Humor breaks a bit of the tension without disengaging completely from the discussion. However, humor can also be used to deflect deeper thinking. Don't allow humor to completely throw the discussion; instead, welcome a bit of lightening up to keep both of you in the window of tolerance. Smile, take a pause, and then ask your comic relief partner if they are ready to continue with a more serious discussion.

If your argument begins to heat up, listen for words such as "I'm sorry," or "I understand." These words are non-attacking and bridge across to you in the discussion. You may also hear words of vulnerability such as "I was weak," or "I am ashamed." Don't go for the kill; accept the signaling of peace. Truce signals in gestures may be touching, defenseless body posture such as drooped shoulders and head down, or vulnerable facial expressions. Offering a cup of tea or breaking the silence with a comment about the weather in a bid for connection is a truce signal. Attacking when someone offers such truce signals will not move toward repair. It will cause damage and retraction. Do not ignore truce signals.

How to Know Your Affair Repair Is Working

You will know your affair repair efforts are working when the talks are filled less with anger and guilt, and more with mutual sadness. Initially, your talks will swing from extreme sadness to deep love, from absolute readiness to leave to a resolution to persevere and many other opposite emotions. Over time and with purpose, your swings will be less extreme until you jointly settle into grief over what has happened. Rest there until clarity comes and you can move forward.

In the beginning of the affair repair phase, you may have had a list of questions you would like to explore. Over time, you may have no specific questions. Keep your affair repair talk appointment at the scheduled time and allow for free flow of conversation. You may have good things to talk about, such as new memories, successes, or appreciations for the progress made. Allow the discussion to wander, but avoid logistics or problems not related to the affair. This is a time specifically to talk about overcoming how the affair has affected your relationship.

If you literally have nothing to talk about, take it as a good sign. This means the affair PTS is being managed. No one is in crisis and the affair repair process is beginning to work. You are getting better like a broken leg that no longer aches but is not quite ready to have the cast taken off and head out for the one-mile run. If you do not have anything to talk about or do not feel up to a draining conversation, take the time to play a game, go for a walk, hold each other, or some other activity that provides a safe opportunity to be together and connect.

Key Concepts

Everyone knows how to communicate, but just as professional athletes hire coaches, consider affair repair communication skills as valuable tips and tricks to take your communication skills to the next level for success.

- **I statements** help to express feelings and requests while minimizing criticism and defensiveness.
- Avoid **the four horsemen of the apocalypse of communication:**
  - **Criticism** can be avoided by using a gentle start-up, I statements, and making requests.
  - **Defensiveness** can be avoided by taking responsibility and not offering excuses.
  - **Stonewalling** can be avoided by taking a time-out *and setting a specific time to return to the discussion.*
  - **Contempt** can be avoided by describing your own feelings and needs. Don't describe your partner.
- Look for and honor **truce signals** in heated discussions or arguments. Truce signals can be a verbal agreement, change in tone, smile, pet name, or any gesture seeking to soften the argument or discussion.
- **You know your affair repair efforts are working when** your affair repair talks move from angry and intense, through sadness

and guilt, to purpose and acceptance. You know you are moving forward when you quickly manage affair PTS symptoms, maintain the window of tolerance, and communicate effectively.

- **Average Duration:** You will use affair repair communication skills for the rest of, and in all areas of, your life. These communication skills are transferable to all relationships, from personal to the community at large.
- **Goal:** Continually hone your affair repair communication skills to improve effectiveness and shorten the time needed to process difficult discussions.
- **Do:**
  - Learn and apply the skills
  - Remain in the window of tolerance
  - Hold yourself accountable in your communication
- **Don't:**
  - Allow any of the four horsemen of the apocalypse of communication to creep in
  - Ignore truce signals
- **Actions for the wounded partner:** Be mindful to use I statements and avoid criticism. Look for truce signals to deescalate conversations. Respect time-outs and do not pursue.
- **Actions for the responsible partner:** Be mindful not to be defensive—even if you have a good reason. Take ownership quickly to move the discussion along. Take time-outs but be sure to set a time you will be back to the discussion.

Chapter 15
Establishing Trust

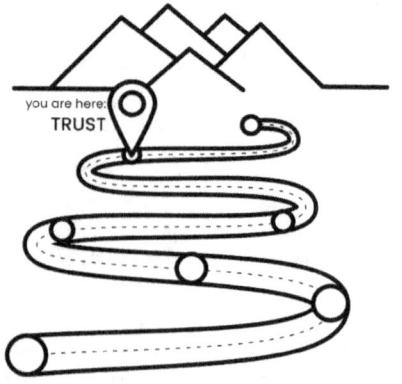

*The challenge of the establishing trust phase
is to provide safety through honest and calm presence.*

There is such a thing as sustainable hurt. Upon entering the establishing trust phase, the wounded partner commits to becoming the **healing partner,** and the responsible partner has developed the skill set to become the **repairing partner.** You as the wounded partner may have experienced betrayal trauma, but you do not need to be defined by it. A person can heal from trauma. Healing does not involve forgetting, it involves overcoming. You didn't have a choice in what happened, but you do have a choice in how you respond. A person who betrayed may never betray again and can make amends. Trust is built by repeated experiences of safety so that the traumatized nervous systems can rewire to the new state of being.

As a repairing partner, you can demonstrate authenticity no matter how difficult reality is. In previous phases of the map of affair repair you examined your conscience, discerned what you want, and have learned how to have hard, truth-telling conversations. You no longer need to live an illusion but can move forward with integrity toward what you really want.

You two will continue to have affair repair talks as often as needed, gradually reducing frequency and duration, ultimately to an as-needed basis. Over time, you may find that the topic of your talks will shift.

Establishing trust is an emotional and mental healing process that occurs in the heart and the head. Trust can be felt in the body, but since discovery, intuition has felt like shaky ground. Intuition is not failsafe, nor is logic. Many facts were left out or lies were told to mask the affair. Affair repair that is based solely on intuition, feeling, and perceiving with the right side (emotional center) of the brain is subject to imagination and manipulation. Affair repair that is based solely on observing, thinking, and judging with the left side (logic center) of the brain is subject to coldness and information control. **Establishing trust requires a feeling of bodily safety and mental verification of facts.**

Establishing trust is ongoing. The verification process is intense at first but lessens over time. The foundation of trust evolves through a long series of repeated exposure to the truth and discovering **false positives**. False positives are times when the healing partner is sure the repairing partner is lying, but upon investigation, finds their fears are proven false. Counter evidence proving nothing is wrong is very helpful in healing.

Healing partners may be convinced repairing partners are texting the affair partner, but when they look at their partner's phone and see nothing but a text to a sister and another that they are on their way home, the healing partner must accept that their preconceived notions were wrong. Like scientists examining all the facts, healing partners will test every possible angle to prove something else is involved until there is nothing left to accept but the truth. The fastest way to shorten the journey in establishing trust is to expose the truth.

Establishing Trust and Preexisting Trauma

Before transitioning to a healing partner status, betrayed people feel chronically out of sync with their partner. People who have been traumatized in other ways often feel out of sync with everyone. Preexisting trauma for either partner can make it harder in the establishing trust phase. For human beings to feel close to another, they must widen their window of tolerance, not shut down or dysregulate, so they can experience intimacy, even when their defense system is slightly activated. Traumatized individuals remain in an ongoing subtle state of alert that prevents them from truly being vulnerable and getting close. They are unable to have intimacy without edges of fear. Preexisting trauma may be related to a prior betrayal history or some other trauma such as assault, childhood sexual abuse, war, an accident, bullying, or a natural disaster.

Understanding how you or your partner coped with the previous trauma can provide insight as to how they may behave now. For example, Cecilia had a volatile first marriage that ended with her partner's cheating. She shut down her emotions and used the cheating as a way out of the marriage. Her coping strategy was useful, until she became aware she had avoidant tendencies that were limiting sexual intimacy in her current marriage.

Unresolved trauma can cause people to instinctively resort to old coping strategies under stress. Conversations involving establishing trust are highly stressful so those old response strategies will appear. It is a real challenge for someone who has experienced trauma not to react with a coping strategy they developed to successfully survive the original trauma. As you work through the map of affair repair, be aware of any activated old coping strategies you or your partner may be using.

Antoni and Clair Together in Trauma

> *Antoni and Clair were eating at a restaurant with some friends when the other couple began to playfully hint at tying each other*

up. On the way home in the car, nothing was said. Antoni, the healing partner, gathered himself and ventured, "Shall we address the elephant in the room and send it on its way?" Clair shut down.

"All I could think about is, 'There goes the next six months,'" she later said in session. Clair was triggered, worried that now the couple would relapse into the previous painful phases of the map of affair repair. She worried that affair PTS would cause Antoni to express anger. Though Antoni's reaction is normal and warranted, male anger evokes trauma memories with associated scary emotions and defensive behaviors in Clair. She so feared reverting to dealing with the intensity of affair PTS and affair repair she was evading.

Clair, a survivor of more than one assault and repeated childhood sexual abuse, went into a self-protective survival mode. She began to panic internally, seeking a way to lie, dissociate, or in any way escape what her body felt was Antoni's uncontrollable power and anger. Clair could not go back to discussing all the facts and experiences of her kinky, risky affair with a random man she met at a gas station, now known only as "Sir."

Clair began to shut down, which left Antoni alone to self-soothe through the emotions that were coming up in him. Antoni took the opportunity to ground her in the reality of the moment, not in the past. "I am not elevated right now, Clair." His voice was leveled and controlled as he acknowledged what was going on for him and her.

Antoni had done some significant personal work in learning about trauma. He learned that her sexual acting out, though hurtful to him, was not about him. He read everything he could about childhood sexual abuse and learned to listen to Clair, when she was able to, talk about it. He learned about the support she did not *have growing up. He learned that his loud anger, though justified, evoked trauma responses, not repairing responses in Clair. He learned that if the relationship was going to repair, he was going to have to help her heal through her trauma response as well.*

Clair could see Antoni was not elevated. She could experience it in her body, though her internal alarm system was going off and mentally she could not understand it. It will take repeated experiences like this and effort on Clair's part to step forward into trust.

Despite Antoni's great patience and the hurt in his eyes, she could not engage in comforting him. After twenty minutes, midway through the session, she said, "I cannot believe you still love me."

Clair is still working through her past trauma, which is repeatedly triggered when dealing with the affair. Her inability to process and resolve all the emotions, memories, and conflicting thoughts about the experience hinders her ability to be there for Antoni. Clair may never be able to be a full repairing partner for him. Antoni has great strength, intellect, and deep love for Clair. He will have to decide if Clair's efforts are enough for him.

Establishing Trust and Preexisting Addiction

Maintaining healthy attachment while working through or recovering from addictions can be complicated. People who currently or have previously struggled with addictions may have a unique challenge in being present with and managing uncomfortable emotions. The nature of addiction is to feel good and avoid feeling any unwanted emotion. Conversations involving establishing trust involve unwanted emotion, the desire to escape may be increased.

Struggling with addiction is not an excuse for betrayal but understanding how addiction influences thoughts and behavior will help couples understand the motivation and decision-making process before discovery and now as you work to establish trust. Substances or processes (i.e. exercising, gambling, and other activities) offer connection, affirmation, or simply fun, to distract you from the current unhappiness. This is true for healing or repairing partners working with addiction. Longstanding addiction can make it even more difficult for a person to connect and deal with their true emotions. When a person decides to stop the addiction, they begin to deal with all the emotions and situations they had avoided in the past. The experience can be flooding and overwhelming and affair repair only increases the intensity. Be aware of all the challenges you are facing on this healing journey.

Mickey Battles to Recover and Repair

Mickey had had several known emotional affairs and potentially unknown physical affairs while his wife was pregnant. Mickey was a man of great emotion, sometimes overwhelming emotion. When the emotions were high, he was charismatic, and people were drawn to him. When he was low, he felt empty and alone. Mickey sought pleasure, soothing, and escape with other women, as well as alcohol. Many betrayals occurred while Mickey was actively drinking.

Discovery brought the threat of the loss of his marriage. Mickey got serious about getting sober. He had to do some difficult personal insight work to understand the overwhelm of emotion and how he was allowing himself to use his emotional gifts to get the soothing he wanted. The selfish side of him excused the drinking, along with the bad behavior because the emotional pain or desire was so great.

Unfortunately, this was not the first time Mickey had tried to get sober. Ava had already supported Mickey through his other attempts, attending meetings, processing feelings, and avoiding alcohol in the home for his sake. Though he had been trying, he had also been cheating. He would feign that he was "working the program" while secretly drinking.

As the healing partner, Ava was trying to recover from two forms of betrayal. Mickey had broken promises of sobriety and fidelity. As the repairing partner, Mickey was confronting the responsibility of what he had done while trying to manage the intensity of his emotions he used to handle with alcohol and the affection of other women. Mickey was well-spoken, open, and painfully honest. It was difficult for Mickey to stay in the present. It was difficult for Ava to trust he was telling the truth.

Ava had experienced his wordsmithing before. She watched and listened as Mickey shared his moving in and out of not wanting to feel, to placate, to being angry at himself and Ava, and feeling guilty. He struggled to be emotionally grounded so he could be that rock for her. She struggled to believe and lean on him.

The depth and authenticity of their conversations was exceptional and intense. It was the only way for the two of them to establish any clarity. The authenticity of not knowing if trust could ever be achieved, if consistent behavior could be established, or if romantic feelings could come back was the clearest truth the two could find. It was real, and it was as healing as it could be. The hallmark of recovery from addiction and establishing trust in affair repair is an ability to sit with the truth, even if you don't like it.

If your relationship has a history of trauma or addiction (they often go hand in hand), seek professional support. Recovering from trauma and/or addiction is possible. A trained individual can speed up the process and validate your experience that may not be understandable to others. Seek additional information and guidance for yourself individually as well as your relationship. Healing and repair can happen.

Closer or closure

Some people are very clear the relationship is over. Most people are conflicted. If you are conflicted or if you are willing to try to work things out for any reason, continue to do your personal work and communicate authentically. Working the strategies in this book can heal and bring you closer. Establishing trust is the last phase of the affair repair journey before marriage transformation.

If you are beyond a shadow of a doubt that you are no longer interested in continuing the relationship, continue with the healing process of affair repair with honesty. Establish trust upon a foundation of truth and genuine desire to repair the damage that might have been avoided with a difficult breakup conversation earlier.

Following through with honest, open, caring, and clear communication will provide closure. There is no way around the pain of ending the relationship. Whichever partner ends the relationship will have the difficult experience of causing a great deal of pain. (Ongoing betrayal would be even more painful and damaging.) If you are ending the relationship, strive to stay connected with your partner in the window of tolerance as you provide safety with an authentic presence, establish trust by being truthful, and work toward closure. Take breaks, be respectful, and be honest.

Key Concepts

Establishing trust is an emotional and mental process that occurs in the heart and the head. Establishing trust requires an ongoing experience of bodily safety and mental verification of facts where the heart and the head match in understanding. The experience is intense at first but lessens as trust is established.

- The wounded partner becomes the **healing partner**, ready to move toward healing.
- The responsible partner becomes the **repairing partner**, ready and welcomed as someone who is trying to repair.
- **False positives** occur when the healing partner suspects something is wrong but discovers everything is ok. Repeated exposure to false positives builds trust.

- **Preexisting trauma** or **addiction** can complicate the process of establishing trust and must be considered in your process.
- Establishing trust can bring you **closer or closure**. Establishing trust involves establishing the truth and coming to a congruent understanding of your partner and yourself.
- **Average Duration:** Establishing trust can take a year or more post discovery. Establishing trust overlaps the affair repair phase and often begins as affair PTS begins to wane.
- **Goal:** Experience trust in your heart and head.
- **Do:**
  - Remain in the window of tolerance
  - Tell the truth
- **Don't:**
  - Focus on the negative to be self-protective
  - Minimize the effects of preexisting trauma or addiction
  - Lie or be incongruent in your signals
- **Actions for the healing partner:** Acknowledge false positives every time. Understand and address any preexisting trauma or addiction that is influencing the ability to establish trust. Proceed slowly and safely.
- **Actions for the repairing partner:** Continue to be as authentic and honest as possible. Understand and address any preexisting trauma or addiction that is influencing the ability to establish trust. Be patient with the process of experiencing truth together.

Chapter 16
Establishing Trust in the Heart

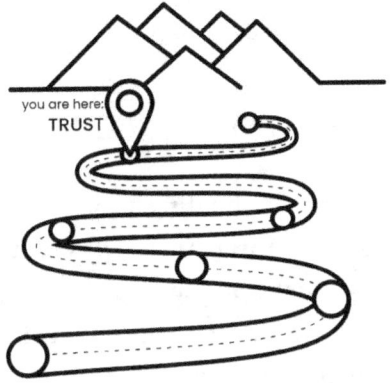

*The challenge of establishing trust in the heart
is to provide safety you can feel in your body.*

Trust in the heart bypasses the logic of our minds and buries itself in our bodies. That trust monitors its surroundings and keeps us safe. Our bodies serve as a fine-tuned receiver and broadcaster of messages, continually tracking energy flows in its environment and within itself. This inborn ability we all have is known as **interoception**. Interoception is the awareness of internal sensations such as heart rate, breath, appetite, pain, heat or cold and emotions. Interoception is so finely tuned, it includes even subtle shifts in pressure, temperature, and internal rhythms.

Your body doesn't merely absorb external stimuli; it also emits signals using its organs and processes to communicate with the world.

Sweating or a flushed face, change in voice intonation, or breath rate can signal anger. Your interpretation of the exchange of information between your and your partner's bodies determines your level of trust and sense of safety. Your body is constantly evaluating the other's signal strength, clarity, and coherence (what is being communicated, matches what is being felt). You would not feel safe if someone said "I love you," and you also felt something insincere in their voice. Your bodily dialogue guides your responses to mismatched signals and helps in understanding your relationship dynamics. For many people, particularly those on the journey of affair repair, honing the body's ability to accurately read the signals is essential for survival and well-being.

Co-Feeling

The most potent medicine for healing from an affair is **co-feeling or** *compathy*. **Co-feeling or compathy occurs when you as a couple share the same emotion in response to a stimulus.** In co-feeling, your bodies' signals are on the same wavelength. Specifically, for affair repair, co-feeling occurs when the repairing partner co-experiences the pain of the betrayal in the healing partner. When the affair is mentioned, you both feel sick. Compathy is not like empathy that is felt *for* the other partner. Compathy is felt *with* them.

Compathy is the *physical* equivalent of empathy. An easy example of compathy is watching your favorite athlete in an intense competition score the winning point. You feel it in your body, your pulse rises, your arms go up, and you experience the rush. The release and excitement is felt with them, not for them. Compathy is particularly deep if you happen to play that sport or have personal knowledge of the athlete's story. You are responding in sync to the same stimuli with their body and emotion.

Another example of compathy is wincing when someone falls. When you are really caught up in a movie, you may be co-feeling with the character. Most of the time movie goers are simply watching the show or feeling an emotion in response to the plot, but when we are feeling what the movie character is feeling, that is compathy. Your palms may sweat, you may jump out of your seat or you may begin to cry. Empathy brings out emotion but does not always prompt physical reaction. Compathy is deeper than empathy.

When establishing trust via co-feeling with your partner you are feeling the same. This experience is so jointly connected, it causes pain in both partners, like emotionally conjoined twins.

When compathy or co-feeling occurs something fundamentally happens within the healing partner. It is as if the pain, in its sharing, is alleviated in some way. The pain seems to transfer from the healing partner to the repairing partner in the shared experience. Repairing partners are skeptical, but healing partners nod vigorously when I suggest co-feeling experiences.

The explosive pain of the betrayal disperses with compathy because now both partners experience fear and pain in the same foxhole together. Both partners are disarmed, hurting, and turning toward each other in the pain. In co-feeling, the repairing partner is joining the healing partner in the scary space, and both know the other never wants to feel like that again. Trust is seeded and attachment begins to grow again. Neither the healing nor the repairing partner should be seeking to rescue the other from the hurt feelings. Just sit and experience compathy in the pain.

Co-feeling sounds simple but is difficult to do, and more than one experience is required. Repeated co-feeling experiences must occur until they are no longer needed for healing. Compathy is difficult for the repairing partner to engage in because it is extremely painful. Co-feeling the pain of the healing partner means sitting not only in the hurt of their healing partner, but also in the guilt of having caused it.

When the healing partner "sees" the empathetic pain and guilt, the healing partner begins to trust at a level deep within their body, past their frontal lobe logic, past their animalia emotion, down deep within their gut and into their heart. *The healing partner experiences compathy with their repairing partner.* The healing partner knows in their body that their repairing partner "gets it." "Seeing" occurs via mirror neurons in the frontal lobes of one person as they look at and experience another. "Seeing" includes actual seeing, the empathetic face, the sad tears, and the look in the eye. The body is interpreting all these signals.

In the past, when betrayal was happening, eyes were often averted, bodies distant, and tones sharp. Allow each other to see what the other is feeling with all the senses. Allow each other to feel a mix of anger, shame, confusion, reticence, regret, and desire for healing. This co-feeling experience establishes a foundation of truth. It puts the healing partner on solid ground and thereby able to trust the two of you are truly connected to each other.

Cultivating Receptivity

Next time you are talking with your partner, and you feel like there's something they're not saying, pay attention to how your body reacts. Notice if you feel any vibrations, thoughts, emotions, or physical sensations. Observe subtle cues that counter their spoken words. Pause and tune in to your body's responses.

If you are within your window of tolerance, gently ask about the disconnect you are experiencing between what your partner is saying and the cues you are picking up. Staying calm will foster a safer space to experience deeper understanding and connection. Allow your partner to be honest in saying they are not ready to talk about something, are confused themselves, or feel conflicted. Remain attentive to both verbal and nonverbal responses, allowing your discernment to inform your interactions.

Reflect on these experiences to deepen your awareness of your intuitive self and refine your ability to navigate interpersonal dynamics in the future. Learn to trust your gut, your body's guiding antenna.

How to Work Toward Co-Feeling

Co-feeling occurs anytime a feeling is shared, particularly around the pain of the betrayal. When co-feeling, it is important that the repairing partner access their most authentic empathetic feelings of regret, shame, guilt, love, openness, or other honest emotion. Do not try to manufacture these feelings or become so lost in your own experience of sadness that the healing partner feels they must rescue you. It takes a great amount of strength to be present and authentic. As the repairing partner, strive to help your healing partner, not to seek affirmation, forgiveness, or soothing for yourself (though this may happen in a compathy experience).

As the healing partner, try to stay in the window of tolerance and receive the experience of your repairing partner. Relationships are an informational and energetic data flow between two people. Maintaining connection will be a challenge, as the nervous system of the healing partner is traumatized and on high alert. Yes, even now in this establishing trust phase, your healing partner is not yet healed. You are almost there. In the meantime, when the healing partner cannot access the authentic feeling of the repairing partner or receives mixed signals while co-feeling, they may feel triggered to shut down and defend. The triggering will leave them agitated and aroused, not open and receiving.

Our nervous system will pick up on forced or faked feelings. What is being said must match what is being felt. Better to be honest and admit feeling conflicted over trying to repair than to try soothing or telling white lies. Better to admit fear of risking reinvesting in the relationship or wondering if there is even a chance of forgiveness.

Working Toward Co-Feeling

Irene was a particularly self-controlled person. She kept her exterior and interior worlds neat. She maintained a clean home, spoke in even tones, and always presented herself as gathered. She and Darren had come to counseling after she had discovered questionable charges on the credit card. Darren had begun seeing call girls on his business trips to Las Vegas.

Darren knew he had crossed the line—his, hers, and theirs. There was nothing he tried to excuse about his behavior. The gift this couple had was that they were able to tell each other what they were feeling; the challenge was that the exchange was very logical, not emotional. They didn't know what to do to heal.

The pain of the discovery made all the self-control walls tumble. Their relationship had been good but distant. Darren had taken advantage of Irene's ability to keep things together. He had let Irene manage the household, his mother's three-month terminal journey with ovarian cancer, the kids, and her own emotions. Irene accepted the role and seemed to be able to handle it all. He did not have to show up emotionally, simply physically. Now, Irene could no longer handle it all.

Irene desperately needed to know where Darren stood. Neither partner was practiced in identifying, sharing, or receiving each other's emotions. Fortunately, Darren was honest and willing to work on insight. He was able to be authentic about his personal limitations, failings, and questionings of the relationship—as well as his own behavior. Irene was able to keep things together as well as request repairs and future changes.

As they let themselves touch their own emotions, they were able to do so in front of each other. They were good witnesses, but more importantly, they responded emotionally to the other's emotion and ultimately were able to experience emotions together. Irene and Darren were guarded at first, then once past the affair PTS and many good affair repair talks, they began to share the pain, which led to trust and, for them, love. Their intellectual discussions were companioned with emotional expression. They learned to co-feel.

Co-feeling can be so draining that the repairing partner may not want to do it often. The discussions are intense, and one dose of compathy does not heal. It takes many applications. If you are unsure if co-feeling works, ask the healing partner how they feel after a co-feeling discussion. They may feel much better and more hopeful about the relationship, while you, the repairing partner feel drained. Take note, progress on the map of affair repair has happened. A little bit of trust has been regained.

Important Limits on Co-Feeling

There is a tipping point to too many co-feeling experiences. If the healing partner does not actually feel better after such a painful discussion, stop! Compathy is costly in emotion and energy. There is no need to immerse yourself in hard feelings with no productive purpose. Unnecessary emotional drama and damage can occur. If the repairing partner is shredded from the experience, stop! There is no value in exhausting, trashing, or breaking down a partner who is working to help heal the relationship.

The fastest way to identify the tipping point is to ask your partner how they are feeling about co-feeling. Is it purposeful? Is it sustainable? Is it helping? Co-feeling is important, but it is intense and should be dosed with intention and reasonable limits.

The Limits to Co-Feeling Story

Luke deeply wanted to repair with his wife Gin after his affair with the nanny. He was willing to work toward co-feeling with Gin as often as she might need, but Gin struggled to trust his sincerity. Luke was a solution-focused, small business owner and his desire to "fix things" got in the way. Luke was so looking forward to transforming their relationship that he struggled to pause enough to feel the pain that is part of co-feeling.

It crushed Luke to see Gin break down during their affair repair talks. He could barely stand it and wanted to solve it immediately. He understood the idea of compathy and was only willing to withstand co-feeling her brokenness if it helped heal Gin. She said it did, so he did.

Luke sat with Gin in the pain, but admitted, "The only way I am going to truly hurt as bad as Gin is if she kicks me to the curb now." Luke had identified an important limit to co-feeling. There was no way for Luke to ever really know Gin's pain. Co-feeling the current pain could get him as close as possible.

The pain of another is unknowable but can be co-felt and soothed to the best of the couple's ability. Co-feeling is worth the effort, despite the limitation.

Key Concepts

Establishing trust is an emotional and mental process that occurs in the heart and the head. Trust is established when what the body feels in the heart matches what the head observes. *The heart can override the head.* Be patient as you establish trust in your heart.

- **Establishing trust in the heart** is an intuitive process involving **interoception**, which is awareness of your bodily sensations like heart rate, breath, appetite, pain, heat or cold. Your body tells you if you are hungry, afraid, angry, lustful, or not safe.
- **Co-feeling or compathy** occurs when you as a couple share the same feeling in response to a stimulus. Compathy is not like empathy, which is felt *for* your partner. Compathy is felt *with* your partner. Something deeply healing is experienced when the healing and repairing partner co-feel the pain of the betrayal.
  - You can cultivate your receptivity by heightening your awareness of your and your partner's signals.
  - Co-feeling or compathy can be intense and tiring. Set a limit to avoid purposeless pain and burnout.
- **Average Duration:** Establishing trust can take a year or more post discovery. Some people trust their hearts more than their heads. Take the time to focus on establishing trust in the heart as needed. Establishing trust overlaps the affair repair phase and often begins as affair PTS begins to fade.

- **Goal:** Experience trust you can feel in your body.
- **Do:**
  - Be in tune with the signals your body sends and receives
  - Strive for co-feeling of the pain of the betrayal
  - Be authentic and congruent in your signaling
  - Remain in the window of tolerance
  - Tell the truth
  - Express honest emotions to establish trust
  - Provide the **healing partner** reasons to trust things will be different
  - Provide the **repairing partner** reasons to hope things will be different
- **Don't:**
  - Focus on the negative to be self-protective
  - Minimize the effects of preexisting trauma or addiction
  - Lie or be incongruent in your signals
  - Wear each other out with co-feeling for extended periods
- **Actions for the healing partner:** Be open to the signals your repairing partner is emitting. Continue to recalibrate your heart and head as you gain new information. Proceed slowly and safely. There is no rush.
- **Actions for the repairing partner:** Be open to co-feeling. Understand that sharing the pain is the surest way your healing partner can know you really "get it" and are not likely to repeat what caused the wound. It is okay to be authentic when it is too much. Better to be honest and say compathy is too much than to lie or make false promises.

Chapter 17
Establishing Trust in the Head

The challenge of establishing trust in the head
is to provide safety through logic and verifiable facts.

In addition to the heart, establishing trust involves knowing with the head. Healing partners must relearn to trust their own thinking. The repairing partner plays a critical role in resetting what the mind perceives as reality. In addition to the information experienced internally with co-feeling, external facts must be bold, obvious, and congruent. *The heart and the head must match.* Establishing trust cycles through trust and verify, trust and verify, until it ultimately becomes trust without question and enjoy in marriage transformation.

Concrete Actions

In the beginning of the establishing trust phase, there are many, sometimes drastic, concrete steps a couple may choose to ensure safety and build trust. Ideally these steps become less necessary as the healing partner begins to feel secure, but there may be a time when the repairing partner feels controlled and become tired of trying—particularly if the concrete step has no lasting effect in establishing trust. Work together to be sure the steps you are taking are helping versus draining.

Here are some concrete actions that can be taken to establish trust:

- You can grant each other access to phone and email.
- You can produce phone records.
- You can turn on GPS location on your phone and car.
- You can send pictures and videos to verify where you are.
- You can delete social media accounts, block contact, and eliminate any potential contact from the affair partner.
- You can be sure not to delete web browsing history or empty trash folders from online accounts.
- You can avoid locations where the affair partner is known to frequent.
- You can ensure you share any contact—even inadvertent sightings—of the affair partner.
- You can allow impromptu visits to work.
- You can avoid places where the repairing partner and the affair partner went.
- You can come home immediately from work or text if there is any delay.
- You can share an accurate itinerary of the day or any travel.
- You can limit travel for a period.
- You can consider an extreme action such as quitting your job or moving to another city to avoid the affair partner.
- You can increase contact by calling or texting your spouse to say hello or share the day.
- You can increase affection in nonsexual ways.
- You can spend more time together sharing hobbies.

- You can continue to have affair repair talks and manage affair PTS when it occurs.
- You can go to couples' therapy.
- You can work the process in this book.
- You can reduce alcohol consumption or pornography use.
- You can replace the bedroom furniture if the affair took place in the home.
- You can brainstorm your own concrete actions or ask your partner for ideas.

What concrete steps are taken and for how long something lasts, you can decide together. No combination of concrete steps will prevent cheating. Concrete steps are not a sure-fire way to affair-proof the marriage, but concrete steps are a demonstration of commitment to be open and to work toward ensuring safety. As you do the work of establishing trust, you will graft together on the journey of affair repair.

Letters of Love

A **letter of love** written by you, the repairing partner, is an emotional unpacking of and taking responsibility for what has happened. It details the rationalizations you told yourself and how those rational-izations helped to maintain the affair. A letter of love relieves your healing partner of responsibility for the affair and is filled with I state-ments. Your letter can express pain, guilt, love, and a pledge to work on the marriage, if those are your honest feelings. A letter of love may may say, "I am working to find my way back to a loving place in our marriage and regret all that has been done." Or a letter of love may be very honest and say, "I would like an open marriage but pledge never to hide from you where I am or who I am with. I will be open with you versus lying. I love you."

Your letter shares insight into your heart. Letters of love are a gift and are not meant to be an opportunity to explain your behavior or beg for forgiveness. Also, letters of love are not an opportunity for your healing partner to attack with challenges like, "This can't be true. If you loved me, you wouldn't have done this."

Letters of love are a concrete expression your healing partner can read and reread to soothe affair PTS, interrupt rumination, and challenge false beliefs. If a letter of love becomes a trigger for affair PTS or a prompt for rumination, it is better not to have a letter of love. If you are willing, ask your healing partner if they would like a letter of love. Written documents are optional. Each couple must decide if that is something that will work for them.

Written Account

A **written account** of every detail of the affair, including dates, locations, money spent, and activities shared can be helpful in establishing trust. A written document like this should be as exhaustive as possible. Your healing partner can return to it for a sense of "this is all there is." There are no more trapdoors hiding information to discover that will re-traumatize. This written account contains the worst of it, and now all the facts are known.

Written documents are helpful when used as a tool, not a weapon. A tool is productive. A weapon is destructive. For example, sometimes information is forgotten and not included in the written document but comes out later. The document is not a weapon to wield. "See, you are a liar! You didn't include that." Rather, it should be used as a tool. Be curious as to why it wasn't included. Do not invite lies with aggressive tones. Take the opportunity to experience the truth. Sometimes information is not included because it was genuinely forgotten, or it was an omission to avoid pain (a passive-aggressive lie). It's preferable to continue to get better at exposing and processing passive-aggressive lies than inviting them to go further underground.

Written documents are optional.

Lie Detector Tests

Many couples have their partners take lie detector tests, technically known as a polygraph. The American Psychological Association publicly states it believes lie detector tests are generally unreliable. Lie detector tests are inadmissible in a court of law in the United States. Even so, lie detector tests have brought some peace to healing and repairing partners.

You can find a person to administer a lie detector test with a quick Google search. There is a strict protocol to administering a polygraph so you want someone who knows what they are doing. Polygraph examiners are professionally trained, earn a certification, and are licensed by your state.

Before taking a polygraph test, the test-taker will be asked to write a disclosure statement. The polygraph test will be limited to what is presented on the disclosure statement. You two can discuss what must be included in the statement and what cannot be included. It is important that what will be tested is clear. Sometimes the details of what is being asked are not recalled or remain a topic of discussion the repairing partner does not want to discuss. Lie detector tests can help establish trust but do not end the pain nor eliminate intrusive thoughts or worries.

Protecting Finances

Your history together has proven it unsafe to bank on love. Some risks on love will have to be taken when we enter a relationship, but partners can avoid taking unnecessary financial risk which is a risk to personal safety. Most couples do not take this step in establishing trust, but both partners should consider reducing their exposure to loss.

Be aware of your finances. Understand your liabilities and monitor if anything shifts. I have witnessed healing and repairing partners quit jobs or require their partner to get jobs to rebalance the amount of alimony that would be paid should the couple split. Liability is reduced not only by quitting jobs, but by taking lesser positions or reducing commissioned earnings by postponing payout or just not trying. Houses have been sold, money transferred or spent, and items purchased to transfer wealth while one partner or the other hedged their bets.

Regardless of whether there is an underhanded long-term setup or not, it is in everyone's interest that both parties be financially stable in the event of a split. A betrayal has happened. Trust has been broken and cannot be reestablished until both partners feel safe. Each party should be mindful of their financial future.

The Financial Future Protection Story

Bradley encouraged Stuart to go back to work. Stuart loved art and creative endeavors; Bradley pointed out that Stuart's talent was wasted at home. Stuart knew Bradley secretly wanted him to return to work, so that in the event of a divorce there would be less alimony to pay.

When they had first gotten together, Bradley encouraged Stuart to leave his job so he would be available to welcome Bradley home and to travel freely. Over the next fifteen years the couple enjoyed friendship, adventure, and intimacy when they could be together. Bradley was a company founder who traveled often for business and leisure. Stuart was often alone while Bradley focused on work. Stuart fell for the attention of another man.

Stuart was aware of Bradley's deep hurt—and sharp negotiation skills he had honed in the business world, but Stuart would do anything to make amends, and he himself felt he deserved to be kicked out for his betrayal. Stuart knew he was reducing his potential future financial support by returning to work, though nothing was said out loud.

It was painful to watch Bradley self-protecting when Stuart was sincere in his desire to repair. It was clear Bradley loved Stuart. Despite Stuart's ongoing authenticity in working on establishing trust, Bradley was yet undecided if he could overcome the betrayal. Stuart knowingly accepted the risk. He wasn't in it for the money.

Postnuptial Agreement

"I have his balls in a vise," Ashley said to me.

I did not think this was the best way to ensure her safety in the relationship, but he had been willing to put them there, so I listened some more. To my great surprise, Jonathan had signed a document that she would receive their entire current retirement savings and half of his earnings upon retirement in five years if he was caught cheating again.

Ashley had struggled greatly with herself to stay with Jonathan. She was vengeful and angry. Her twin sister was imploring her to leave. Staying with him was going against herself and her family. She loved him, but she could not forgive him, nor could she trust him. She needed to be safe and in a position of power before she could begin to love and face her family.

Postnuptial agreements may or may not be enforceable in court. Postnuptials may be seen as a bully club of enforcement carried by the healing partner or a pledge of sincerity from the repairing. Ashley and Jonathan's agreement was strict and severe. Other couples might consider something more balanced.

Fortunately, Jonathan was all-in on repairing and transforming the relationship. He began self-examining how he had let himself pursue a three-year affair when his identity was law enforcement. He knew right from wrong.

He sat with a therapist as he examined the hypocrisy of his family of origin. Growing up, his family had focused on image and used shame and secrecy to hide any less than perfect behavior.

Jonathan shared the painful process of coming to terms with himself with Ashley. Though some old behaviors remained, such as shutting down or making dismissive remarks when distracted, she could feel he was really trying. In fact, he had never tried therapy before. Going to therapy built some trust in the head, sharing fruits from therapy built some trust in the heart.

Little by little, with the postnuptial agreement and tireless efforts to share personally and experience compathy, Ashley and Jonathan were able to complete their journey on the map of affair repair and marriage transformation. In fact, two years later, I received a handwritten note from Ashley, who when I first met her had been ready to destroy Jonathan, thanking me for supporting her in giving Jonathan a chance that ended in a happiness she never thought she could have. I still have that note.

Blackmail

Blackmail is illegal and not a recommended strategy, yet it happens. Stephanie had damning evidence of Chuck's affair that would have ended his political career, shattered his reputation, and devastated the family. Stephanie kept that evidence in a safe and let him know it. Blackmail like this is an attempt to reduce the risk of further heartbreak and ensure safety in the relationship.

The problem with blackmail is that once the cat is out of the bag and the dust has settled, you still don't have your relationship. In fact, you have likely destroyed any chance of repair, and now you have nothing to enforce. Relationships that are shored up with this type of power and control are not on firm footing.

Chuck and Stephanie made it, not because Stephanie had the silver bullet, but because he chose her. He chose his life and history with her over his midlife crisis affair. The blackmail kept Stephanie safe but was also an obstacle to establishing trust. She had to wonder if it was blackmail or true love of her that kept him in the marriage. Blackmail is a safeguard against being hurt, but it is also a block to being chosen. Feeling chosen, versus the second, safe, or fallback choice is a key need of the healing partner. Blackmail is not recommended.

"Surveillance is not trust. If you need a videocam to watch the babysitter, get a new babysitter."
Esther Perel

Key Concepts

Establishing trust is an emotional and mental process that occurs in the heart and the head. Trust is established when what the body feels in the heart matches what the head observes. *The head can trump the heart.* Be patient as you establish trust in your head.

- **Establishing trust in the head** is about logic and verifying concrete facts.
  - There are many concrete actions that can be taken to establish trust, including things such as providing access to phone and email accounts, turning on GPS locators, deleting social media accounts, and the like. Other actions include increasing affection, going to couples' therapy, reducing alcohol consumption, and buying new bedroom furniture.
  - **Letters of love** are honest written declarations of love and commitment to the healing partner. Letters of love include facts, realizations, and reasons for your love.
  - **Written accounts** are detailed statements of every activity of the affair, including dates, locations, money spent, meetings, and other aspects. The purpose of the written statement is to limit trickle-down truth and prevent any surprise new discovery.
  - **Lie detector tests** are not admissible in court and are generally deemed unreliable by the American Psychological Association but have brought comfort to some partners. There is a defined protocol for test administration.
  - **Protecting finances** in the event of a divorce is a good idea for both partners.
  - **Postnuptial agreements** may provide some sense of safety in the event of relapse with the affair partner or divorce.

- **Blackmail** is illegal and controlling. It may provide a sense of safety that the healing partner can trust but is not true healing, is not always effective, and can backfire.
- **Average Duration:** Establishing trust can take a year or more post discovery. Some people trust their heads more than their hearts. Take the time to focus on establishing trust in the head as needed. Establishing trust overlaps the affair repair phase and often begins as affair PTS begins to wane.
- **Goal:** Experience trust you can know in your head.
- **Do:**
  - Be in tune with the signals your body sends and receives
  - Be authentic and congruent in your signaling
  - Remain in the window of tolerance
  - Tell the truth
  - Offer as many concrete actions and expressions of honest emotions to establish trust
  - Provide reasons to trust for the **healing partner**
  - Provide reasons to hope for the **repairing partner**
- **Don't:**
  - Focus on the negative to be self-protective
  - Minimize the effects of preexisting trauma or addiction
  - Panic if your partner is out of sync
  - Lie or be incongruent in your signals
- **Actions for the healing partner:** Continue to recalibrate your heart and head as you gain new information. Proceed slowly and safely. There is no rush. Carefully choose which concrete actions you need to make you feel safe. Avoid unnecessary control.
- **Actions for the repairing partner:** Continue to strive to establish trust as tirelessly as you can in concrete actions. Communicate honestly if any request for concrete action is one that you do not feel comfortable in taking. Try to identify other actions that would establish trust with your healing partner.

Chapter 18
Establishing Trust in the Bedroom

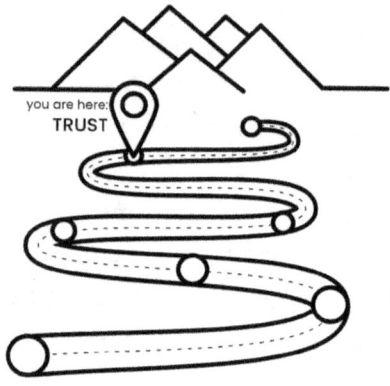

you are here:
TRUST

*The challenge of establishing trust in the bedroom
is to regain sexual confidence and intimacy.*

Erotic injury occurs when a partner's confidence in their sexuality is shaken by the affair. An erotic injury is healed by establishing trust in the bedroom through physical and emotional experience. Before someone can adventure sexually in a healthy way, they need a safe base from which to explore. Secure attachment is a safe base. Secure attachment is built upon trust, honesty, and acceptance. Sexual experience without attachment can be an adventure, but it is not intimate.

The trauma of the affair, if combined with a history of being emotionally detached from your body, may require additional personal work. You may be very good at doing things for your partner or loving them with words, but being physically present in your body may have always been a challenge and now it is even more so. Some people have never been fully present in their body during sex. Being fully present in your body is the first step to recovery from erotic injury. Taking the second step of being present in your body with your partner may take time and should not be rushed.

An erotic injury is healed by experiencing a sense of security and desirability. Feeling insecure and undesirable is overcome by confidence, which starts from within. Healing and repairing partners should consider if they are making love because they are afraid to lose the relationship—or are they making love out of desire for the other? Healing partners may need to push past some fear but should not force themselves to do anything they are not ready to attempt. Repairing partners should not compare experiences but be present in the one they are having. Sex and intimacy may not be as exciting as it was with the affair partner, but it can be good and satisfying.

Create an Erotic Trust Zone

An erotic trust zone can be a location such as your bedroom, where there is no arguing, checkbook balancing, or parenting discussions. Make your bedroom a place of emotional safety and comfort. In the erotic trust zone, you can take your conversations deeper. Establish a **trust position**, which is a way to hold each other that does not feel like a demand for sex in which you can feel closely and warmly connected. Lie in this position anytime you need or want to feel close, especially after a sexual disappointment.

You may start with small steps such as hugging, cuddling, or lying next to each other. Sex is not the only path to erotic recovery. Approach sex less from a goal-oriented process and more from a togetherness experience. Too often in Western society, sex becomes focused on the orgasm. Off come the pants and the all-out race to orgasm begins. Slow the process. Spend time touching, caressing, gazing, and taking in the experience of your partner.

Allow the connection to take hold in a sense of safety. Explore the experience of feeling attracted and attractive. This is intense intimacy if you allow yourself to be present and focused on what is happening. Do you feel attracted to your partner? Can you feel your partner's attraction to you? Is it comfortable, or do you shy away? What happens to you when you pull back? What does it look like? How does your partner respond? Are they aware of you? Are you aware of them, or are you in your own experience? When triggers come up, what do you need from your partner? It is okay to stop. Go slow, stay connected. Try not to completely shut down.

Erotic Date Night

If you are ready, set a weekly date and time for an erotic date. An erotic date is not a regular date where you escape and have fun. An erotic date can be like a regular date but also includes the element of eroticism, getting in touch with not only your emotional romantic self, but your sexual self as well.

Erotic date night does not necessarily mean sex. It means a dedicated time to be together intimately and creatively. After an affair, you might try sensate focus exercises to help repair the erotic injury and bring each other closer together in a trusting experience. Sensate focus exercises use physical touch to help build trust and intimacy. There is no pressure to become aroused. Simply be present during the exercise and allow whatever may come.

If you decide to try a form of sensate exercises, avoid intercourse on the first three erotic date nights. The goal is to establish the routine of the date night and be solely focused on being together. Abstinence provides a safe place to explore and build desire without pressure. Your erotic date night activities should encourage eye contact, presence, sensual awareness, and giving and receiving pleasure. Over the course of each exercise, become aware if you are more comfortable giving or receiving. Strive to grow past and through your discomfort to be fully present, whether you are the giver or the receiver.

A range of feelings may surface during sensate exercises, including performance anxiety, vulnerability, anger, sadness, or dissociation. Become aware and be present with these feelings. Allow and address them within yourself and your partner. It's okay if you need to stop, cry or reach out in passion. All these reactions are normal. Unless someone is hurt, explore the experience together.

During the sensate exercise, the sender focuses on taking in and appreciating their partner and sending pleasure. The receiver focuses on being taken in and receiving pleasure and appreciation. It is a mindful experience. Focus on your breath, and as you inhale, draw in power and awareness; as you exhale, radiate that power and attention through your touch. As you give and receive, you may try to breathe with your partner. Do not force it but notice if you fall into sync. Be aware of what your partner is experiencing and see if you fall into a rhythm. You may find yourself attuning to what your partner is experiencing and adjusting to meet them, enjoying a giving and receiving presence. You may need to slow the touch or pause. You may increase the exploration and smile.

When the exercise is over, share with each other what the experience was like. Was it comfortable? Were you able to trust? Did you feel love? Was the love flowing from you, into you, between you, or both? Were there parts of you that were numb? Did you resent or welcome the touching? The eye contact? Welcome all feelings without judgment.

Five Nights of Sensate

Night one

Sit in your erotic trust zone or a quiet space dedicated to this exercise with your clothes on. There is no talking. Take turns touching each other for ten minutes minimum each. Touch each other for pleasure. Take turns giving and receiving. There is no touching of erogenous zones, including breasts and genitals, and no orgasms, just giving and receiving pleasure.

Night two

Wait about a week and then repeat the exercise. This time, do it in the nude in a relaxed environment, but again avoid touching breasts, nipples, and genitals.

Night three

Wait another week, and then repeat the nude touching exercise, this time while including nipples, breasts, and genitals. Again, do not speak, but give nonverbal feedback. If your partner touches you in a pleasurable way, let them know by moaning softly in pleasure or squeezing their hand.

Night four

After another week with no physical contact, move on to mutual nude touching. In other words, the turn-taking is over, and you can now do anything you want **except oral sex and vaginal or anal intercourse.**

Night five

You should now be about four to five weeks into this process. At this point, you can engage in "non-demand intercourse," which means intercourse without the expectation of achieving orgasm. In fact, if one of you is about to climax, slow down the action and enjoy these moments with your partner.

After completing five nights of sensate exercises, evaluate where you are on your physical connection and trust bond. What improved? What remained untouched? What would you do more of? What would you change?

Considering Nonmonogamy (NM)

It is best if the relationship with the affair partner is ended while working on affair repair. If you are unable or unwilling to end the relationship with the affair partner, at the very least, be truthful with your spouse and consider consensual nonmonogamy (NM). NM is a relationship where all parties are informed. Most repairing partners do not want to mention NM because they doubt their healing partner will accept it. Surprisingly, some do—even if under protest. Many couples, like Ellie and Aaron, have a NM period in their marriage as they work toward repair. Avoiding honest discussion is maintaining the illusion at your healing partner's expense. Try to work up the courage to speak what you really feel.

NM provides information and freedom to choose to be in or out of the relationship. Clear communication enables repairing. With full disclosure, the healing partner has a repairing partner. Deceit sustains betraying. Though NM is a better answer than continuing to cheat, it is not easy. More work will be required to speak honestly and define clear boundaries. Both partners must not only have good self-regulation and an ability to tolerate differences between each other's wants, they must also manage the energy of third parties. Affair partners themselves may or may not be willing to be part of explicit NM once discovery has been made.

In a healthy NM relationship, partners will be talking even more about emotions and boundaries than in traditional monogamy. Dishonesty will set everything back. Partners can sense internal conflict, and this will impede the repair and transformation process. If you would like to know more about NM, consider reading *Polyamory: A Clinical Toolkit for Therapists (And Their Clients)* by Martha Kauppi, Licensed Marriage and Family Therapist, Certified Sex Therapist, and founder of the Institute for Relational Intimacy. Another great resource is by Tammy Nelson, PhD, author, and director of the Integrative Sex Therapy Institute. Nelson's book *The New Monogamy: Redefining Your Relationship After Infidelity* contains guidance and thoughtful questions to better define boundaries around many relationship areas, including emotional connection, sex, and acceptable behaviors.

The (Not) Consensual Nonmonogamy Story

Tyrone wonders how he can work on mending the hurt Laura felt during the marriage when she continues to hurt him by maintaining a relationship with her affair partner. Laura thinks he doesn't know, but Tyrone not only can feel the exciting new relationship energy radiating from Laura, but he is also secretly receiving a copy of her texts and has a tracker on her car. Even with the knowledge of the ongoing affair, Tyrone is fighting for his marriage.

Tyrone loves Laura and is working toward affair repair and marriage transformation. Tyrone feels cast in the shadow of the new relationship. Clinging to her resentments, Laura traps Tyrone in the light of the past and keeps herself distracted from dealing with the guilt and working on the relationship. Tyrone holds back in his affair repair and marriage transformation attempts out of hurt and fear. He cannot let himself go all-in, demonstrating change and offering the loving attention that she says was lacking in their marriage when he knows she is still with another man.

I wonder if Tyrone should consider openly acknowledging what is happening and move forward from there. Other couples, like Ellie and Aaron, chose this route. Aaron was never okay with the other man, but Aaron made it clear he was not giving up on the relationship. Ellie did not commit to ending things right away but did commit to exploring herself and seeing what could change for the sake of history. She made no promises she could not keep and was truthful about what she wanted.

I highly recommend repairing partners end the relationship with the affair partner while they work through the map of affair repair. If it is meant to be, the affair partner will wait. If you are unwilling to end your relationship with the affair partner, make it ethical. Be open and let both of your partners make an informed decision.

Key Concepts

Establishing trust in the bedroom occurs through safe physical and emotional experience.

- **Erotic injury** occurs when a partner's confidence in their sexuality is wounded by the affair. Erotic injury is healed by feeling secure and desired.
- An **erotic trust zone** is a location, such as your bedroom, where there is no arguing, criticizing, or discussing problems like finances or parenting.
- Establish a **trust position** such as spooning or hugging that you can do when either partner is feeling insecure or wants to feel close.
- Take things slow as you begin to reestablish physical connection. (If you have or are experiencing hyper-healing, that is okay too.) Do not force connection.
- **Erotic date night** does not have to include sex but does involve an erotic element. This could include sexy clothing, massage, or conversations.
- Consider **sensate exercises** which build erotic awareness, anticipation, and connection.
- Consider consensual **nonmonogamy (NM)** in which both parties agree and define what a relationship would look like with another party. NM gives both partners freedom of choice and helps in establishing trust, but requires honesty, mutual agreement, and clear communication. Having the discussion does not mean you will ultimately agree upon NM, but it may help build trust as you commit to open and honest communication.
- **Average Duration:** Establishing trust in the bedroom is unique to each couple and can always be taken to greater depths as you move onto marriage transformation. The work done now can set the foundation for growth later.

- **Goal:** Experience erotic trust physically and emotionally.
- **Do:**
    - Establish safe protocols to move forward sexually
    - Make efforts to establish trust in the bedroom; it will not magically happen just because trust is being built in your heart and/or head
    - Try some of the exercises offered in this book or recommended by a professional
- **Don't:**
    - Move forward faster than you are ready
    - Never have sex when you do not want to
    - Don't push your partner beyond their boundaries; be patient, go slow
- **Actions for the healing partner:** Do not go faster than you feel comfortable but continue to seek opportunities to establish trust in the bedroom. Be present in the experience. Be honest if you are or are not interested in NM.
- **Actions for the repairing partner:** Do not go faster than you feel comfortable. Do not push your partner. Be present in the experience. Be honest if you are or are not interested in NM.

Part Two
Marriage Transformation

*"I believe that unarmed truth and unconditional love
will have the final word."*
Martin Luther King Jr.

Chapter 19
Transformation of Reasoning

The challenge of transformation of reasoning is to move beyond fight-or-flight thinking to a deeper understanding.

Marriage transformation requires an understanding of who we were, who we are, and who we are becoming. The affair is over; you now know how to manage affair PTS and can have healthy affair repair talks. You have had healing experiences of co-feeling and can trust with your head and your heart. You are ready to move on to marriage transformation.

According to L. A. Paul, professor of philosophy and cognitive science at Yale University, a **transformative experience** radically and fundamentally changes your understanding of self and the world in unforeseen ways. Affairs can be a transformative experience. The person you were before discovery no longer exists. You may have thought you would never cheat. You may have thought you would never stay. Yet here you are and for reasons you had understood before.

After the affair, you two are new people. Each of you has gained strengths in this healing journey that you will not give up. Neither of you is married to the person to whom you said, "I do." Your marriage will not be as it once was. Fortunately, the good you had in yourselves, and your relationship is not gone but can resurface in vibrant new ways. Like a forest that has sustained a fire, regrowth begins with the same species of plants coming up stronger and in some fresh configurations. Your entire ecosystem—which is the relationship you have with each other, your children, family, friends, and work associates—has changed. It is regenerating. You are different and you can guide the future.

In marriage transformation, you both deal with the circumstances to encourage change in the system. Partners who choose to transform their marriage salvage the good that was in their partnership. Memories and history built together are protected and nurtured, not ended or discarded. Your partner will always be the father of your children. She will always be the one who first believed in you. That partner, for better or worse, is the history keeper of several years of your life. In marriage transformation, you do not need to amputate or section off this part of you. The bend in the trunk or scarring in the rings bear witness to the wound, but the tree continues to grow.

Many transformative experiences do not happen by choice, and even if they are initiated by choice, the effects are unknowable in advance. The person involved in the affair had a choice, the other did not; neither of you could have anticipated the transformation you experienced. Any power you have in a transformative experience is in our response. You can limp along or grow in new ways. Time will indifferently pull you forward from the moment of discovery through crisis and beyond. What you do as time marches on is up to you. A person's freedom, according to Viktor Frankl, a psychiatrist once held in a Nazi prison camp, lies in their response to their condition. You may be justified in your resistance to the experience. That will not change it. Your power in protecting and caring for yourself lies within your response.

Marriage transformation is not about putting your relationship back together the way it was. Marriage transformation is about digging a deeper foundation, really coming to know yourself and your partner. Too often, marriage transformation for the healing partner is limited to feeling a sense of security and desirability again. When in fact for the relationship to truly succeed, it must be regrafted in deeper, truer ways.

The reason people cheat is often complicated and unique to that individual. Affair repair would be easy if life were black and white. It is true that promises should be kept, not broken and hidden by keeping secrets. Now is the time to transform our reasoning—without changing the definition of what is true and right.

Lawrence Kohlberg an American psychologist, laid a foundation of understanding moral development with his famous Heinz Dilemma story. In the story a man, Heinz, could not afford to buy drugs to heal his wife's cancer. Despite speaking with the chemist and trying to raise money, Heinz was unable to obtain the medicine legally, so he broke into the laboratory and stole the drug.

Kohlberg asked many questions of individuals of varying ages, including: Should Heinz have stolen the drug? Would it change anything if Heinz did not love his wife? What if the person dying was a stranger, would it make any difference? Should the police arrest the chemist for murder if the woman dies? Kohlberg found a pattern in the development of thinking across the ages of participants.

The youngest, reasoning at the **preconventional** level, were guided by avoiding punishment and self-interest. Their moral reasoning was based upon direct consequences. Preconventional reasoning mandates that Heinz should not steal, but if he can get away with it, that is an option. At discovery and crisis, people find themselves reverting to the earliest stages of moral reasoning: avoiding punishment and guarding self-interest. This is normal human behavior in a fight-or-flight stage. The person involved in the affair has been avoiding punishment and guarding self-interest. The person wounded by the affair is ready to bring the punishment in their self-interest to protect themselves. Under threat, we focus on survival. Both partners will consider finances, children, and social standing. Loss of money and belonging are direct threats to well-being which will influence your desire to stay or leave the relationship. If you remain at this preconventional level of moral reasoning, there will always be a good guy and a bad guy. One person will forever remain the perpetrator and the other the victim. With this perspective, healing can get stuck and limit transformation. Most people do not stay stuck at this level of moral reasoning.

The next level, **conventional** reasoning, takes a good person or law and order perspective. At this level, if Heinz is a good person, he will live up to social expectations and steal the drug because husbands should save their wives. On the other hand, also at this level, law and order is more important than individuals and must be upheld for society's sake. As the body's alarm system begins to settle while moving through the affair PTS and affair repair phases, couples move more toward the good person or law and order perspectives of the conventional level. The person involved in the affair may reflect upon how unhappy they were and what the affair brought to them. Like necessary medicine, love and happiness are good for people. Yet, betrayal is wrong. During the middle phases of affair repair, there is often a lot of wrestling with "should." You may have considered breaking up or staying together because that's what the rules of culture say and what good people do. "Should" is important, but not enough to sustain you through marriage transformation.

In **postconventional** moral reasoning, social contracts *and* universal principles are applied. As part of the social contract, rules are seen as agreements that can be changed when necessary. Once you have established trust, you are freer to think at the postconventional level. Over the course of your affair repair journey, you began to consider other factors such as a one-night stand or a decade-long sexless marriage. These mitigating circumstances do not justify or excuse an affair but understanding them helps raise your reasoning and decision making to the next level without changing what is right or wrong.

Social contracts and its rules strive to achieve universal principles which are the highest form of moral reasoning. From this perspective, Heinz should steal the drug because human life is more valuable than property rights. Heinz should consider nonviolent civil disobedience or further direct negotiation with the chemist. He should deal with the consequences of his actions to encourage change in the system. In committed relationships, love and happiness are the universal principles, but the pursuit should involve truth, authenticity, and honorable action.

How have you grown through your affair repair journey? The "right" thing has never been in question. Heinz's wife needed medication. Stealing is wrong. Something in your relationship was not well. The affair was betrayal. Understanding how decisions were made and how you grew is important to transformation. Compare and contrast what you first thought and understood to how you perceive and judge things now.

Each partner must evolve in *self* and *other* understanding. Affairs are hard to process because understanding the other person's perspective feels like negating self. Acknowledging and validating your partner's perspective at such a difficult time may feel like gaslighting yourself, but it is not. Acknowledging means recognizing. Validating means understanding how the other could come to that perspective; it does not change yours. Understanding the other person's perspective allows you to integrate it in your thinking. Validating does not mean agreeing, sanctioning, or negating your own experience. It means seeing versus ignoring, overriding, or gaslighting. The journey on the map of affair repair helps the couple integrate two perspectives into one unified truth whether it is ugly or not.

In the establishing trust phase, you built a solid foundation upon authenticity sustained in the window of tolerance. Now you can incorporate concepts such as the social contract (what is good for the family or partner) and self (what is good for the individual). Like Heinz, at the highest level of processing, you nonviolently, openly negotiate your physical and emotional needs. There is no manipulating or controlling.

No lying or guilting, just honest engagement. Heinz's wife needed medicine, you both need a *reliable and desirable* relationship. You are not going to settle for less, and you are going to negotiate it openly. The experience along the map of affair repair can bring you to this place of authentic relationship. Now is the time to have discussions you may not have had before the affair.

The Challenge of Transformation of Reasoning

Joshua was a successful home builder who had proven himself capable of passing inspection tests with high standards but had failed to be faithful. Joshua agreed to therapy because he wanted to do the right thing and his affair was a moral injury to himself. He thought of himself as a good man, husband, and father. His actions were the opposite of who he wanted to be.

When Joshua and his wife, Isabel, came to therapy, she was expecting him to be a regretful betrayer, taking full responsibility and ready to make amends. This was the right way to repair, in her view. Unfortunately, Joshua, like many people caught in an affair, was doubtful. He did not believe Isabel would ever forgive him and was not sure the marriage could be improved so that both would be happy.

Isabel struggled within herself. She couldn't understand why anyone would stay after an affair. Leaving was the right thing to do if Joshua was unwilling to repair in the right way. However, now in the face of reality, the definitions of right and wrong kept her stuck in pain. She loved him and she wanted her marriage back. She raged at Joshua outwardly while inwardly she beat herself up for tolerating his betrayal and disrespect.

In the beginning, their perfect match had been maintained by Isabel's self-correcting behavior and Joshua's hyperdrive toward proving himself. Over time the exhaustion of providing, maintaining the household, and generally trying to meet expectations began to wear them down. The experience within the marriage was a constant sense of failure, frustration, and not feeling appreciated by both partners.

In the end, they had no energy left to nurture each other and resentment had grown between them. Joshua's affair destroyed the punishing standard they each were trying to live up to. For Isabel, it was the ultimate failure. For Joshua it was the release for everyone from a no-win situation.

Isabel was better at suffering than Joshua, who saw a limit to it. The pattern of doing the right thing to be acceptable and loved began in normalcy. When they first met, Joshua and Isabel excelled at meeting expectations in their careers, themselves, and each other. Their partnership had been built upon each doing the right thing, which fed their admiration of each other.

In the first decade of their marriage, their drive contributed to outward success, but over time they became inwardly exhausted and irritated by every shortcoming. A dish in the sink, a bounced check, and an affair were all failures and wrong. Each of them thought:

"Why didn't you put the dish in the dishwasher? It takes two seconds."

"Shoot! I forgot to transfer money; I can't believe I did that! Wait, I have been running around all day getting things done. I could use a little more help."

"An affair can't and shouldn't be fixed without complete show of regret and that is not happening!"

In normalcy, right and wrong had become more important than empathy and mutual support. They would let things go but count *the score. Neither was able to integrate an understanding of the other so that when it was time for affair repair, the marriage could not transform.*

Isabel could not understand Joshua's pain and ultimate act of betrayal. Joshua could not empathize with Isabel's pain because if he did, his justification for betrayal (happiness) would be negated. The relationship could not transform to integrate both perspectives. Each time Isabel acknowledged Joshua's pain in the marriage she felt blamed and, worse, that she had betrayed herself by not holding the right standard for self-protection. Joshua hesitated to empathize with Isabel because he feared he would lose his right to happiness. Love was present which kept them fighting to do the right thing, but the right thing wasn't working.

Do I Want to Repair My Marriage?

Both of you may be wondering if you would like to continue the relationship even after working through affair repair and establishing trust. Affairs involve lying to another and sometimes to self. Now is the time to be honest and live truthfully with grace and strength.

If you are the healing partner, be honest with yourself as to whether you can live with yourself for having stayed in the relationship. Isabel struggled daily to achieve this clarity. If you are unable to accept the past and move forward, the internal conflict will leave you forever unsettled, and your relationship will never be reliable. Self-betrayal is not an option.

If you are the repairing partner and know the relationship can never evolve into what you need, be clear that this is the reason you are ending the relationship. It is important to make it clear to your healing partner that you did not have the affair because there is something wrong with them. Your failure was in betrayal, versus ending the relationship honestly. Now is the time to be truthful. You no longer need to maintain illusions.

Both partners will do well to be honest, kind, and brave. You can repair the hurt and not re-pair in the relationship. It is honest and non-attacking to say, "I know I can never be okay with this relationship." It may be that even though you have done all the growth you can do, it is just not a match. Guilt is a good reason to repair, but not to re-pair.

If you decide to end your relationship after repair, acknowledge the hard, sincere, and good effort you both have made in this healing journey. You may find friendship, empathy, or sentimental connection with your partner, but not want to continue the marriage. The affair may have been the wrecking ball that brought down the illusion holding everything together. Truthfulness is a gift you give yourself and your partner. You are both free now.

The I Don't Think I Want to Repair My Marriage Story

Priya did not want Ramesh to leave her, nor did she want him to change because that would mean the end of their relationship as she had known it.

Priya was stuck clinging to the past, wanting her old marriage back and her wound erased. Priya was aware she was making this choice. She had transformed her understanding of self and acknowledged Ramesh's transformation but could not move forward.

Priya liked the person she had become through this trial. She had gained strength learning to be on her own. Priya had signed separation papers, built a new life in her own place, and surrounded herself with friends. She even began dating a bit. Priya felt she had a sentimental emotion toward Ramesh, but not a true desire to repair and remain. Ramesh hesitated. He did not want the marriage to end. He had grown and hoped to build on their foundation versus losing their entire history and promise to each other.

At last, Ramesh was ready to sign the papers. The reality was like a bucket of cold water for Priya, though she knew she could never completely forgive Ramesh. She thought of the pain of discovery and affair PTS. She recalled feeling out of control and crazy when she found herself driven to snooping, checking emails, and other fact-verifying missions while trying to establish trust.

Priya knew they had successfully moved through those phases and that Ramesh was all-in on the marriage, but she never wanted to experience any of those phases again. Staying with Ramesh would bring back some of those thoughts and feelings even if only now and again and with less intensity. Priya acknowledged that even though they knew how to manage triggers and could communicate better, she did not want to be in the relationship anymore.

The couple was successful in the map of affair repair and marriage transformation. They repaired without re-pairing and transformed their relationship. Their communication was deeper, connection more authentic, and honesty pure. Ramesh was moving forward, treating Priya with respect. They had found a way to be cordial in social gatherings and even went for coffee on occasion.

The healing journey can help you transform your relationship, whether you stay together or decide to part. By working to repair the damage, changing your relationship dynamics with improved skills, and becoming stronger in communicating your needs, you can take your relationship to the next level or leave yourselves better people for the next one.

Key Concepts

Transformation of reasoning is moving beyond the fight-or-flight state of black-and-white thinking to a more integrated, mature reasoning from a place of safety.

- A **transformative event** changes the person you are. The event provides new perspectives (wanted or not) that change the way you understand and interact with the world. An affair is a transformative event.

- The Heinz Dilemma provides a way to understand the transformation of reasoning.
  - **Preconventional** reasoning is black and white and based upon direct consequences. People using preconventional reasoning think affairs should be avoided because they hurt or they think affairs are okay if nobody finds out.
  - **Conventional** reasoning is either good person or law and order based. People using conventional reasoning think cheaters should be punished because they broke the rules. Or that affairs are okay because the person who cheated was so unhappy.
  - **Postconventional** reasoning can integrate multiple factors without changing the definition of right or wrong. People using postconventional reasoning know that:
    - having an affair is wrong,
    - there are many factors that contribute to the decision to have an affair that need to be addressed, and
    - there are better ways to make a necessary change in the relationship.
  - It is normal to progress through all the stages of reasoning in overcoming an affair.
- After completing the healing journey of affair repair, and arriving at marriage transformation, you are in a better place to evaluate if this is a relationship you would like to continue to transform.
- **Average Duration:** Transformation of reasoning has been happening all along the way and your understanding will continue to evolve.
- **Goal:** Understand how your reasoning has changed and value what you have learned.
- **Do:**
  - Respect preconventional reasoning as useful in the early stages of your healing journey

- Allow a transformation in reasoning to strengthen your ability to transform your marriage
- **Don't:**
  - Get stuck in a lower level of reasoning
  - Compromise what is true
  - Compromise what is right or wrong
- **Actions for the healing partner:** Be aware that black-and-white thinking keeps you safe but also keeps you stuck, unable to repair. Allow a transformation of reasoning, grounded in the work you did together on the map of affair repair, to inform your decision making.
- **Actions for the repairing partner:** Allow reasoning skills to evolve in you and your partner. Understand where preconventional reasoning influenced your decision to lie to avoid consequences. Embrace higher levels of reasoning to empower you to tell the truth and expect positive marriage transformation.

Chapter 20
Transformation of Reliability

*The challenge of transformation of reliability
is for you to be able to self-regulate, communicate,
and tolerate differences.*

So far on the map of affair repair and marriage transformation, you have gained experience and tools to make your relationship more reliable, for now and in the future. A reliable relationship is one you can trust to handle any situation. Not only have you established trust that betrayal is no longer happening, but you can trust that truth telling will continue even when things are difficult. As you experience a transformation of reliability, you are better able to self-regulate, communicate, and tolerate your partner's emotions. Reliability is grounded in authenticity and honesty.

In the establishing trust phase, you learned about co-feeling, and without being aware of it, you developed an **integrated brain**. An integrated brain, per Dr. Dan Siegel, clinical professor of psychiatry at the UCLA School of Medicine and executive director of the Mindsight Institute, is *one that integrates all inputs from the various parts of the brain* that register physiological, emotional, and cognitive stimuli. Over the entire course of the affair repair journey you were taking in more and more of what your body felt, what your emotions were telling you, and what was being said.

With your integrated brain, you can become aware when you are getting tense, acting out of fear, and causing your partner to get quiet with your tone of voice. Moreover, you can act on that knowledge, calm yourself, and lead the conversation toward a more productive exchange. If both of you have transformed in this way, the relationship becomes more reliable because your partner can also integrate the moment to help nurture the relationship.

Individuals dealing with a history of abuse, addictions, infection, or other brain-affecting disorders may have unique challenges in fully integrating an experience. Neurodivergent individuals also face unique challenges in processing information and experiences that must be accounted for. Regulation, or your ability to manage attention, mood, thought, memory, relationships, and morality require integration of multiple inputs. Regulation is dependent on how well you can take in and make sense of those inputs. Some people are not noticing key information, others are taking in too much information and still others are focusing on the wrong information.

Your affair repair journey has helped you become better at integrating. By now you have been practicing and hopefully mastering the ability to stay in the window of tolerance, which is a sign of integration. You know how to self-regulate because you can monitor what's going on in your body as well as your mind and emotions.

When you can integrate not only the stimulus from within, but that which comes from without, you are *relationally integrating*. You are integrating information from yourself, your partner, and what's happening in between. In the crisis phase, there was little ability to self-regulate, let alone integrate input from your partner. Energy was volatile and unchanneled. All signals were on transmit, little of you was able to receive. Siegel studies electrochemical energy flowing through and changing the brain. Per Siegel, the brain is energy and "in-formation" flow patterns.

As you progressed through the map of affair repair and onto marriage transformation, the intensity of your energy has died down but is still supercharged. Little by little, you have become able to integrate your own experience to a level where you can begin to integrate the experience of your partner. Your interpretation of stimuli coming from your partner has become more reliable. Your own signaling has become more coherent, and you yourself more reliable. This is the dynamic system of a relationship. Two become new in one reliable, co-regulated, and integrated shared mind.

Integration for Transformation of Reliability

"I am never going to repeat the actions that nearly caused me to drown," said Leonard, a repairing partner. His affair had been a moral injury to himself and he knew MaryAnne was the woman for him. He wanted her back and would do anything to repair and transform their relationship.

Years ago, the couple had tried couples' counseling after the discovery of his affair but to no success. Leonard was able to communicate his experience of regret, unmet needs, and pain of wanting MaryAnne to understand them. He could acknowledge but not fully incorporate MaryAnne's experience in his understanding. He was driven by his own psychological and physiological needs. He was unable to integrate all stimuli as part of the shared reality.

Some of the information was missing. MaryAnne was so wounded by the affair and hindered by a past pattern of not voicing her own needs that she could not trust nor signal louder to break through to Leonard. Counseling failed to help bridge the gaps.

MaryAnne kicked him out and the couple divorced. The settlement was fair and both had financial security. After several years of living apart, Leonard tried again to repair the relationship.

MaryAnne was hesitant and needed time to think. She was cautious, clear that what had happened was wrong, and unwilling to get hurt again. Yet, she loved him and meant it when she had said, "I do." She sought support in sorting out her thoughts and feelings.

Leonard took that little inch she gave him and jumped at the chance to come to therapy. He had no interest in therapy but would do anything to get MaryAnne back. He shared his experience, and after listening, I pointed out that what he was doing to get MaryAnne back made sense but wasn't working. Apologizing, convincing, and pledging true love was not moving MaryAnne. To his credit, he was willing to try something new.

Leonard tackled self-reflection head-on, taking the time to understand what motivated him, drove him, and what he really needed. He integrated all the information he learned about himself. He came to see more clearly how he had been driven to success not only by his early childhood experience but by his own nature. He was obsessively goal focused and action oriented, which blinded him to seeing how others were experiencing him and how his actions affected MaryAnne and their children. He began integrating stimuli from others.

Leonard was anxious to integrate MaryAnne's experience. He wanted to be connected to her. He did his best to hold back his own go-getter energy to provide space for MaryAnne to share her experience. MaryAnne was private, self-sacrificing, and stoic by nature.

Getting her to voice her needs had always been a challenge. This was a pattern problem MaryAnne needed to work on. Leonard *needed to help her unlearn and overcome her reservedness. He had compounded the pattern with years of her not being acknowledged and integrated as part of a co-feeling experience. MaryAnne needed to break the habit of holding back even if it supported Leonard and the family achieve their goals. Leonard had to be aware of the dynamic and support every step she took in the right direction of expressing herself.*

Leonard demonstrated he was ready and able to respond to her concerns with deep listening, reflection, and authentic sharing. Leonard respected her boundaries and wanted to learn more about MaryAnne. He truly loved her. There was no worry that Leonard was not going to share his experience. Together they made their relationship more integrated and have acquired the skills to achieve transformation of reliability.

The Transformation of Reliability but Not Desirability Story

Most commonly, couples' therapy focuses on restoring reliability, presuming that once safety is achieved and cheating will never happen again, desirability will follow. Sometimes that is true, but not always. To transform your marriage, the relationship must be not only reliable, but *desirable* for both partners.

Stuart did not feel sexy or desired and felt that sex since his affair was always a test. Stuart felt Bradley no longer desired him, despite his significant changes along the map of affair repair. Bradley admitted Stuart had made changes and trusted that Stuart was no longer cheating, but Stuart showed no passion.

Stuart explained that it was hard to have passion for someone who does not desire you. Upon deeper reflection, Bradley admitted he was still hurt by the explicit images he'd seen on Stuart's phone. Seeing Stuart desire someone in a way he never had with Bradley, remained an image burned in his mind's eye. The pain of the image caused anger, hatred, and lack of confidence, which inhibited Bradley's desire to reach out to Stuart. "You never took me the way you took him!" Bradley said.

Stuart engaged in the conversation within the window of tolerance to address Bradley's affair PTS.

"I hate going back to this dark place. I want to be past this, but I know this is a hard image to have in your mind, and I did that to you. I regret that. I hate to see you hurt like this." Stuart articulated his own feelings while validating and soothing Bradley's. "I am not blaming it on the drinking, but I was drinking then and making bad decisions. I was under the influence of loneliness, tequila, and sex."

The state of limerence and liquor can be understood intellectually but not by the wounded heart. Bradley could hear the information in his head, but it did not make him desire his partner. Stuart was caught giving focused attention to the affair partner, a man who was not expecting it, but was taking it. Stuart's affair partner mimicked the rejecting love he had experienced growing up. The hook up was a good feeling but unhealthy fit. The affair partner did not really care about Stuart but touched something deep within him in a familiar way. Stuart came to address and take responsibility for this mistake in his personal work, but Bradley still struggled.

The couple's transformed communication brought them closer, but they found themselves in a double bind, each waiting for the other to initiate the spark, the passion. Stuart wanted Bradley, but Bradley, with the images in his mind, could not believe Stuart wanted him like that. Bradley's flat and negative response was not something Stuart could overcome. The relationship was reliably integrated. Cheating was no longer a threat. The relationship was reliable, but not desirable.

Key Concepts

Transformation of reliability means you can trust your partner to be authentic and honest. You can handle problems together versus breaking apart. You are better able to self-regulate, communicate, and tolerate your partner's emotions.

- An **integrated brain** can integrate or make sense of information from all stimuli (inputs) from within yourself and from others.
- You two are safe because you are better at interpreting the stimuli coming from your partner. Further, your own signaling has become clearer, calmer, and more authentic contributing to the reliability of the relationship.
- Two become new in one reliable, co-regulated, and integrated shared mind.
- **Average Duration:** Transformation of reliability is ongoing as you gain experience and become more expert at integrating information.
- **Goal:** Capitalize on all the communication and relationship skills you have acquired in affair repair to ensure reliability.
- **Do:**
  - Integrate all information from yourself, your partner, and in combination to nurture the relationship
  - Use all the communication and relationship skills you have acquired in your journey through affair repair
- **Don't:**
  - Relapse to old patterns of relating
  - Assume reliability is the same as desirability
- **Actions for the healing partner:** Continue to trust yourself and your ability to integrate the signals from your partner. You are transforming. Reliability is necessary in a relationship, but desirability is as well.
- **Actions for the repairing partner:** Continue to communicate authentically and congruently. Integrate your and your partner's

experience to maintain connection. You are transforming together. Reliability is needed in a relationship, but so is desirability.

Chapter 21
Transformation of Desirability

*The challenge of transformation of desirability
is to experience a mutually satisfying
level of desire for each other.*

Healthy relationships are a mix of reliability and desirability. Desire is wanting in the most complete, all-of-you, bodily sense. Unlike zest, which is a positive, energetic, and enthusiastic attitude toward life, desire is a spark for sexual connection. Zest can inspire desire and be more attractive than any level of wealth, beauty, or fitness. Healthy relationships nurture desire to mutually satisfying levels.

While you were dating, there might have been potential partners who offered loyalty and undying love, but there was something average and unexciting about them. These potential reliable partners likely became your friends. Similarly, there may have been someone you desired, but knew there was no way you could build a life with them. These exciting desirable potential partners may have rejected you or been a destructive force in your life. A comedian once said, "You never marry your best lover; that guy is in jail." There can be a stuck feeling about pure reliability and wild destructiveness about unbridled desirability.

Erotic love is different than loyal love. Erotic comes from the word *eros*, which is the energy that sets a couple aflame sparked by a drive for sexual satisfaction. Eroticism is our own thoughts or emotions in response to a stimulus that leads to a sexual desire. Eroticism is not the arousal itself, but the spark. Some people find body parts provoke erotic thoughts. Others need only the thought. Music, dance, dress, and poetry can evoke erotic responses that may lead to desire. Desire can range from longing to craving. What turns one person on may completely turn another off. Much of our eroticism is closeted and learned over time through experience, culture, or imagination.

Desire draws partners closer together, absorbing one in the other. As the flame burns, each is consumed with the thought of wanting. Desire of one engulfs the other, so that in ultimate intimacy, you have loved the other as yourself. Two become one. It is exhilarating to be wanted by the one we want. When two people desire each other, the spark ignites a passionate flame of aliveness. The height of this intensity cannot continue forever. Seriously, at some point, we must put our clothes back on, let the dog out, and get back to work.

Desire Gap

According to Michelle Weiner Davis, in her book *The Sex-Starved Marriage*, one in three marriages has a desire gap, where one partner desires more sex than the other. A **sex-starved marriage**, per Weiner-Davis, is one in which there is sex, but *one partner desires more and the other doesn't much care to change it.* A **sexless marriage** may be considered one in which *sex has not occurred for one year or more.* A **low-sex marriage** is characterized as one that is engaging in *sex less than ten times per year.* Neither experience, sexless or low sex, is a problem unless one or both partners consider it problematic. When it is a problem, more fights will occur, and the marriage becomes vulnerable to affairs and divorce. The remedy is to take small steps together. Transformed marriages address the desire gap in healthy, productive ways.

Per Weiner-Davis, the person desiring more sex, the **high-desire** partner, needs to bring out the F word, which she names as feelings. If you are the high-desire partner, work to communicate how the lack of physical connection makes you feel. Focus on your emotional experience, not sexual frustration. You may need to spend some time reflecting on what sex *means* to you. After communicating the depth of emotions you felt personally, listen to the experience of your partner.

The **low-desire** partner is the person desiring less sex. People of varying sexes and sexual orientations have told me, "I don't care if I never have sex again." Sometimes a desire not to have sex is healthy, such as when you are in an abusive relationship, feeling negative toward your partner, fearing pregnancy, responding to prior trauma, or overcoming an erotic injury related to an affair. Sometimes a lack of desire (hypodesire) is not healthy. Hypodesire can be on a spectrum from tiredness or stress to an underlying medical condition. If you are the low-desire partner, evaluate and communicate the source of your low desire.

The Desire Gap Story

Leonard loved MaryAnne. The sex he had during his affair and the time they were separated was its own experience, but it wasn't MaryAnne. He desired MaryAnne. Leonard also had a unique insight. He shared that he had "done the math." He tallied up all the hours and minutes he hoped to have sex over the course of his life. He determined that even if he had all the sex he wanted—up to one hour every day, that was still less than five percent of the total time of his life on earth. Leonard began to wonder how he let five percent of anything become the most important factor in the relationship. Yes, he wanted sex, but he would not let it become the one thing that could ruin his relationship.

Meanwhile, MaryAnne had discovered a new side to herself with another lover during the separation from Leonard, but an erotic injury and some lingering lack of trust remained that held her back from releasing herself with Leonard. Leonard wanted sex with MaryAnne, good sex. But he did not know how to unleash her desire.

Leonard knew MaryAnne's overall sex drive did not match his. He was willing to accept that his sex drive might be at an eight out of ten level of desire, hers a four, and that they could enjoy somewhere in the middle. He was not interested in her doing something she did not want to do but was hoping MaryAnne was interested in finding a way to a five or six. She was, but there was some work to do.

If you are the high-desire partner who wants to raise the desire in your partner, shift your approach from the position of "my partner needs to please me" to a deeper relationship perspective of "we need to please each other." Listen to your low-desire spouse and do what works. Usually, what works is what your partner is telling you, not what you think will work. If you are a low-desire partner who wants to meet your high-desire partner at or somewhere in between their level, try to nurture your sexual-self back to life and understand your partner's need to express their erotic nature.

Not addressing a desire gap while demanding monogamy is forced celibacy. Forced celibacy is something often accepted by loving, respectful, and suffering partners. Other partners turn toward affairs versus investing in the work it takes to address the desire gap. Carlos did not flirt, tease or sext his wife, Victoria, which could have stoked her passion. It wasn't his habit. Instead, he found an affair partner who did those very things for him. Transformed marriages work to address the desire gap with honesty, care, creativity, and respect.

Arousal Is Not Desire

Arousal, that stirring in your genitals, may lead to wanting sex, but arousal is simply a biological response. Arousal is not desire. Young boys and men wake up aroused. A female or male body may respond during forced sex, but this in no way indicates desire.

It is normal to randomly think about and want sex just for itself. Approximately one percent of the population who is asexual does not think about or want sex. Normally, healthy sex drive is defined across a range of levels with no universal norm or standard. In general, men think about sex (and food) almost twice as much as women. How often someone thinks about sex can be related to age and hormones. Some will think about sex regularly well into their eighties or beyond. Libido is only a problem if it is a concern for you or negatively affects others in your life. Some will seek sex daily, others twice per month, some even less. How often and what you think about sex is unique to you. What you think about sex is influenced by experience, family values, culture, and religion.

Arousal can spark desire for your spouse. Desire is arousal with heart; it is a whole person experience. Wanting sex without relationship is **instrumental**. Instrumental relationships are about gratification, not desire. Gratification is self-based and self-focused. Unlike desire, which is self-based and other-focused. Wanting sexual pleasure to relieve sexual tension, boredom, stress, or anxiety is not desire; that is an instrumental urge for relief, just like using drugs. The hormones released during sex make the unwanted feelings go away.

Instrumental relationships are concerned about another's needs only insomuch as satisfying them meets their own. Jeff wanted to please Candance because her beauty and flirtations made him feel more like a man. Sex was frequent and technically satisfying in their marriage. Outside of sex, his attention to her tears and happiness were only to sustain her attention on him. He had no real interest in how her friends were not true friends or in her small art business. Candace felt loved because he provided so well and made her feel valued (when she met his needs). There was no giving, only trading in an instrumental relationship. Quid pro quo is a status quo.

Limerence and Addiction Are Not Desire

Limerence and addiction are not desire. Limerence and addiction include uncontrolled, obsessive thoughts that affect the quality of your life. Limerence is not sexual fantasy, which is an imagining that can be turned on or off at will. Limerence and addiction are driven by craving and cause impulsive reward-seeking behaviors. Exploring sexual fantasy with your partner as you transform the desirability of marriage should feel exciting but not obsessive, insatiable, or out of control.

The I Want You to Want Me Story

Ashton not only wanted his wife, Kaitlin, to want him, he needed her to need him. Ashton could not get enough of his wife—and not just sexually. He needed to connect with her emotionally, and regularly. He constantly reached out to her via text and became upset when she did not respond. The more he pursued her, the more she felt drained and pulled away.

Ashton tried to back off. He heard Kaitlin when she said being a work-from/stay-at-home mom was too much and she had little left at the end of the day for herself, let alone him. He doubled down on helping with dinner, bathing the twins, and participating in the morning and nighttime routines. He also began dropping their three-year-old toddlers at daycare on his way to work and supported his wife's need for quiet as she accomplished her contract work as a graphic artist on the occasional weekend. He did all of this to gain more attention. The power of his craving gave him the energy to do all this.

Kaitlin's desire did improve, but not to the level Ashton continually requested. He felt unloved, underappreciated, and insecure, despite his hard efforts. The romantic evenings, lunchtime quickies, putting the kids to bed early for time alone, and sexting during the day was never enough.

Asthon remained in pain as he recalled the amazing sex they used to have when they first met. He knew a tigress's desire was part of her. She just didn't seem to want it (and him) like she used to. He was adamant that a healthy sex life was natural and normal for a man. His needs were nothing new. Kaitlin had changed, and he wondered why she didn't want to fix it.

Wanting sex is normal, so is a waxing and waning of desire as we grow older and life changes. However, when the pain of not having sex is so emotionally hurtful, something more is going on. Ashton resisted a request to explore deeper. He and Kaitlin had had a great sex life. All his buddies at work and the gym shared their stories of sexual adventures. Exploring himself deeper was not where he thought the problem lay. He wanted to know why Kaitlin didn't want their great sex life back. He felt her lack of desire for sex was a lack of desire for him as person.

Kaitlin continued to work to meet his sexual and emotional needs because she loved him and was not opposed to seeing if she could enjoy sex more. One month they counted the number of sexual encounters and discovered they were having intercourse at least three times per week. Still the desire for intimacy could not be quenched. Ultimately, both were shredded and in excruciating emotional pain. He was aching for her to desire him, and she was depleted from trying to deliver.

Kaitlin could and would not give any more. Ashton did not want to leave his wife, and if he pushed any further, it was likely she would leave him, so he had no other choice but to examine what his problem was. Ashton's primary problem at home was a lack of desire from Kaitlin. His primary problem at work was stress, but that was offset by how much he loved his job and how successful he was. He was fit and good looking; confidence was not the issue.

Slowly, Ashton came to look at the pain of the betrayal from his first wife. His first wife had begun to pull away from him just before she cheated. She traveled more and paid less attention until he ultimately discovered the texts between her and her boss. That pulling away left a mark in his heart that he never forgot.

Kaitlin's drop in desire rang an alarm of panic that he could not turn off unless he saw the mad passion in her eyes. He still desired the steamy sex the two had in the early part of their marriage, but it no longer sounded an alarm of impending pain. Ashton was disappointed they didn't have the sex they used to, but no longer experienced it as a painful rejection of him when she could not meet his passion.

When the desire to be desired is so extreme, it is painful for both partners. Three nights per week was not enough sex for Ashton. Different positions, toys, and locations were always needed. Daily sexting and affirmation scratched the itch but never satisfied. It wasn't until Asthon looked below the surface that he could address the source of what really needed to be soothed. For Ashton it was prior betrayal, for some it is lack of confidence or change in identity.

Ashton could acknowledge but not integrate that their partner's lower libido was normal and not a rejection of them. If your relationship is suffering with the inability to satisfy one or the other partner's desire, focus on transformation of desirability. Reflect upon, share, and integrate your partner's experience of desire. If you are unable to make things better, consider a sex therapist who specializes in this type of challenge.

Repression

Repression of sexual urges is an attempt to suppress sexual desire. Cultural norms, personal beliefs, or past experiences can cause sexual repression. Sexual repression can lead to anxiety, depression, relationship issues, and other emotional distress. Repression can also cause difficulty in having orgasms, premature ejaculation, pain, or discomfort during sex. Sexual urges should not be repressed but understood and expressed in healthy ways. Accepting your sexuality is important, but not all sexual urges should be acted upon. Fantasizing about or role playing a forced sex act is different than an actual encounter. Discussing fantasy or acting it out with a trusted partner could be very satisfying in a healthy way. Healthy desire includes the ability to express your sexuality in a consensual (mutually agreed upon), respectful, and informed manner, free from coercion and violence.

The Transformation of Desirability Story

Leonard and MaryAnne were responsible and self-sacrificing people who fulfilled their traditional roles well. MaryAnne sacrificed herself for her primary goal of being a good partner and mother. Both she and Leonard had taken oaths and were dedicated to fulfilling them.

MaryAnne cut back on her career, managed the household, and raised their four boys. She was a devoted mother who supported Leonard in his skyrocketing career. MaryAnne worshipped Leonard and, frankly, he was worship-worthy. He was an inspiring individual.

Leonard was committed to MaryAnne but had been driven by unexamined personal demons. He sought success and physical affirmation not only out of nature, but out of an over-the-top need to achieve and be respected due to early experiences in life.

Now as the couple was transforming their marriage post-affair, they knew they could not go back to their near passionless marriage dominated by Leonard's personality and uninformed of MaryAnne's inner experience. MaryAnne had since discovered her passionate self and was not returning to a muzzled role in the relationship.

MaryAnne wanted to be seen and desired completely. Repeatedly Leonard explained to her she was the only one he had ever truly desired, and his affair had been a mistake. She had always been the one for him, but if she said it was over, he would move on.

MaryAnne was hurt that Leonard would accept her rejection and let her walk away. Her view of passionate love was like that of Romeo and Juliet. "If I can't have you, I shall have no one and choose to die." If he truly loved her, how could Leonard just move on? MaryAnne had decided if they did not work out, she would spend the rest of her life as a single woman.

MaryAnne's perspective made no sense to Leonard. He was a passionate man who wanted to live, but not without love. Leonard loved life and wanted love in it. He would wait, work, and wile to win MaryAnne—if there was hope, but if she rejected him, he would accept her decision. MaryAnne would have to claim her desire.

Leonard welcomed the integration of his and her newly transformed selves. He was now more self-aware and she more self-advocating. Leonard knew he might not be comfortable constraining his big personality or butting up against her now vocal self, but he wanted her, and he was known for pushing himself beyond the comfort zone to achieve his goals. MaryAnne was proceeding cautiously.

The couple dove in, working together to renegotiate communication, partnership, and sex. Leonard yearned for MaryAnne to release her desire for him. He wanted her to experience passion and for him to experience her passion. There had been occasions throughout their marriage, but not with regularity, and he did not know how to unleash it. He learned to be more subtle in his flirtations and patient in her coming to him. Some gains were also made as MaryAnne continued to discover and voice her desires with him. They were willing to engage in transformation of desirability.

Affairs teach us a lot about our relationship, ourselves, and the power of eros. Eros prompts the physical manifestation of desire. Where one partner may be able to live without physical touch, the other may be dying on the vine. Physical intimacy is a way of knowing that is different than head or heart. Physical intimacy is not loving more; it is loving with more of you. Love-filled physical intimacy can be a co-feeling experience for the healing partner that they are safe and for the repairing partner to know that they are accepted again.

Physical intimacy, when it is passionate, can make a person feel desired, wanted, and alive. An affair has zest. Partners can tell when the other is not into it. Animals can have sex; humans can make love and be erotic. Partners can tell when sex is lovemaking or a raw, physical wanting. It is possible to have both in a healthy relationship. Most partners want it all—love and eroticism. Igniting or reigniting passion is not always easy, but there are ways.

Key Concepts

Marriages must not only be reliable, but desirable. Desire is wanting. Transformation of desirability is experiencing a mutually satisfying level of desire for each other. There will always be a difference in desire levels, but couples should seek a level where both can thrive.

- Thoughts that spark a desire for sex are erotic. Eroticism is normal.

- Erotic love is different than reliable love. Eroticism involves sexual wanting.
- A **desire gap** is where one partner desires more sex than the other.
  - The **high-desire** partner is the one who wants more
  - The **low-desire partner** is the one who wants less
  - A sex-starved marriage is where one partner desires more and the other doesn't care to make a change
  - Monogamy where one partner does not want sex and the other does is forced celibacy
- **Arousal** is not desire.
  - Sex without relationship is **instrumental**.
  - **Limerence** and **addiction** are not desire.
- Sexual desire should be expressed without coercion or violence.
- Arousal can spark desire.
- **Average Duration:** Transformation of desirability is ongoing as you gain experience and come to know more about yourself and your partner.
- **Goal:** Understand the value and importance of desirability in experiencing vibrancy and aliveness in yourself and your relationship.
- **Do:**
  - Explore what eroticism means to you and your partner
  - Communicate your needs
  - Strive for a mutually acceptable level of desire in your relationship
- **Don't:**
  - Force experiences you or partner do not want to have
  - Undervalue the importance of desire in a relationship
  - Overvalue the importance of desire in a relationship
  - Avoid a discussion
- **Actions for the healing partner:** Explore what level of desire you would like to experience in your relationship. Get in touch with what you find erotic. Communicate your needs to your partner.

- **Actions for the repairing partner:** Explore what level of desire you would like to experience in your relationship. Consider the difference between erotic desire and limerence or addiction. Get in touch with what you find erotic. Communicate your needs to your partner.

Chapter 22
Transformation of Sexuality

The challenge of transformation of sexuality
is to understand, explore, and express your sexuality.

Desire that sparks a drive for sexual expression is erotic. Erotic love can be nurtured, enjoyed, and visited on a regular basis. Exploring your sexual expression is part of your human birthright to pleasure. Your body can enjoy sex far beyond the years of its ability to procreate. The pleasure of sex is as natural as the pleasure of good food. Like food, an appetite for sex is best enjoyed within healthy limits. Too restricted is repression. Too much pursued is addiction. Understanding your and your partner's sexuality can help you find the way to your best expression, experience, and enjoyment of sex.

Sexual History and Self-Story

Each of us is genetically hard-wired with a desire for pleasure. Your natural desire is curbed or encouraged with life experience. Standards and expectations are defined, some are set by yourself, others are installed as default settings or goals by society. Old-school expectations where "good girls don't have sex" and "real men have it all the time" persist. Fortunately, that limited ideal of sexual expression is changing. Now is the time to heighten your awareness of your own default settings around sex.

Subtle and not-so-subtle influences shape your experience and expression of sexuality. You, as the healing or repairing partner, have a sexual history and narrative of those experiences that affect your current sexual relationship. Your understandings were influenced by temperament, family of origin, culture, religion, and trauma. An affair is trauma that can affect your sexual self-story.

As part of your journey through the map of affair repair and marriage transformation, you have learned to stay within your window of tolerance, allow space for your partner to have their own experience, and stay attuned. Use these skills to have a safe conversation about your sexual selves. Strive to be curious, compassionate, and nonjudgmental. Be your partner's best ally as they explore their history.

From the discovery phase, remember the importance of not responding rashly. You may learn things you didn't want but need to know. Stay well-grounded in truth telling and listening as you learned during crisis. Strive to bring the safe and stabilizing presence that was useful in dealing with affair PTS. Your best skills will come from the affair repair phase, in which you were able to have authentic affair repair talks within the window of tolerance. Use all these skills to remain open and nonjudgmental about your partner's sexual history.

Avoid negative labels like weird, perverted, naïve, whorish, or disgusting. Your reasoning is transformed now. The purpose of this sharing is understanding and uniting, not judging and dividing.

Continue the co-feeling and trustworthy actions of the establishing trust phase. Think positively and compassionately about your partner's experience. In marriage transformation phases, you can have a more nuanced understanding of what formed and motivates your partner sexually. New information, exchanged in a safe conversation, can forge greater intimacy and better sex.

Here are some beginning steps to guide your thinking and sharing about sexual history. If you find you would like to take this conversation deeper, check out a few books, podcasts, or meet with a professional sex therapist.

How to explore and process your sexual history.

1. Create a timeline of your chronological experience (history) of sex. Include on your timeline any experience such as indirect messages you picked up, chosen encounters, random exposures, or traumatic events that influenced your understanding of sex.

2. For each entry on your timeline, consider what self-story you accepted or wrote because of that encounter. What influenced those narratives?

3. How do your narratives influence your experience of sex with your partner? How have your experiences and narratives affected your coming back together in a sexual way?

4. Consider your sexual self-story before and after the affair. How has it changed?

5. What was your reaction to rejection before and after the affair? What meaning does "not tonight" hold?

6. What is your reaction now when sex is initiated? How do you initiate? How does it feel for you to initiate?

Reigniting Passion

The first question to ask yourself is *what do I want to experience sexually?* Some couples will want to bring back what they had. Others will want more, different, and/or better. Desire is fluid across and within couples. Expect times of high desire and periods of low. It is natural that when we begin to build a family, our high-energy erotic natures are curbed to protect and care for the family, then we have a second, adolescent-like surge when the children leave home. Periods of increased stress can reduce desire, whereas a vacation can unleash it.

Ask yourself other questions to explore the expression of sexuality. What are obstacles to experiencing and expressing the desire you want? Are you feeling any pain? Do you feel nothing? Is sex a chore? Are you feeling hounded versus wanted? Acknowledging, addressing, and creating new, deeper, and more exciting connections takes effort.

The Glass Case of Technology Story

Tonya and Brent finished washing the dishes after a long day. As they went upstairs, Tonya said she was tired, and Brent confessed he had had a stressful day. After Brent's affair, Tonya remained slightly defensive, a little insecure about her aging body, and feeling Brent should initiate sex. Brent had resigned himself to this marriage; he loved Tonya and accepted they would never be a sexual match. Years of a desire gap before his affair had led him to believe nothing would change. Their marriage had transformed into a reliable but not desirable relationship.

The two slid into bed, each on their side with a device in their hand. Each was trapped in their technology, encased within view. She was reading a novel and he channel surfing with the remote. An erotic passage in the novel aroused her. Barely perceptible, her breath quickened and body temperature rose. Like the main character, she imagined herself being taken by a man whose desire for her could not be quenched.

Beside her, Brent gave his attention blankly to the screen, pausing at the soft porn scene in an action film. He felt a slight stirring in his groin that quickly subsided. He fell asleep before the movie was over. After a time, Tonya turned off her tablet and wished him good night. Somewhere in the night, he awoke, turned off the TV, and fell back to sleep.

Both Tonya and Brent are like Sleeping Beauty waiting for Prince (or Princess) Charming to awaken them from the enclosed, sexually sleepy state within their glass case of technology. Perhaps one or both is harboring anger or holding a grudge. Maybe both are bored with themselves and the other. A history of rejection and ineffective communication may have created a canyon-sized desire gap. The fire is alive in each of them, but the flames have died to embers between. Tonya and Brent have work to do to achieve a transformation of sexuality.

Light Your Own Fire

Desire begins with a spark within you. Ask yourself, *if you weren't being hounded for sex, would you want it? If the answer is no, is that forever? If you never want sex again, revisit the concepts of eroticism, arousal, and forced celibacy discussed in the previous chapter on transformation of desirability. If the answer is yes, you would want sex, take ownership of* that spark and nurture that desire.

Sex may have gotten boring, and you may blame your partner. Perhaps you lost energy for creativity. Your own spark may not be strong enough to leap across the firebreak to join your partner's fading embers and light things up. Carlos let his affair partner spice up his sex life versus trying new things with Victoria. Having just started a small business, he had many valid reasons for not putting effort into their sex life. We can give ourselves a whole list of reasons not to have sex or a whole list of reasons *to* have sex. We can tell ourselves *things like "I am tired, stressed, or busy." Or we can tell ourselves "I want to try something new, feel close, or experience the thrill of sex."*

If you are a low-desire partner, take charge of your own sexuality. *Your first step in reigniting your sexual self is to address any medical issues that reduce performance and pleasure.* Pain, depression, anxiety, lethargy, stress, poor physical health, and medication can inhibit desire. Hormonal imbalance can greatly affect a woman's ability to physically experience pleasure. Erectile dysfunction (ED) begins in the brain when messages are sent to the nerves in the penis to relax, allowing blood to flow. Most often with medically based ED, blood is not engorging the penis. Other contributors to ED are cigarette smoking, diabetes, and high cholesterol. A doctor can help determine if the root of your challenge is physiological or psychological.

Once you have addressed any physiological problems, move forward to resolve any psychological challenges. Practice becoming more aware of when you are aroused. Meredith Chivers, Canadian sexologist and clinical psychologist, documented women's arousal beyond their awareness. Participants were shown images of various sexual activities, including heterosexual, homosexual, and animal. Women reported arousal congruent with their sexual orientation. In fact, measurements of vaginal blood flow showed female participants were aroused physically without them knowing it. Arousal can happen without awareness. If you desire to increase your desire, you might want to focus like a magnifying glass with the sun's rays to bring up the heat.

Men with low desire due to stress may need to productively prioritize self. Men who undertake their provider/protector role so seriously may subjugate their own desires to the point they forget that they even have desire. Men may bury themselves in work and socializing to relieve some stress, but they do not take care of their bodies. It is hard to get an erection when you are exhausted and cannot get the blood flowing. Low self-esteem may be dogging your psyche. Low self-esteem begins to resolve when problems get solved. If you are having trouble motivating yourself, a coach, personal trainer, or therapist can help. Action steps are the fastest way to feel better.

The quickest way to change how you feel is to *do* something about it. Nothing is more exciting than an excited partner. Do not have sex to please your partner if you are not in the mood. If you have little desire, listen to sexy music, try some saucy texting, or read erotic novels. What about that music, conversation, or reading stirred you? Often the imagination is far more powerful than porn. Where did you feel that stirring in your body? What did you do with that impulse of desire? Consider how comfortable you are or are not with your private thoughts about sex. Some people avoid them, others welcome and enjoy them. Address any obstacles you have when thinking about sex. If you are not in the mood, ask to be seduced. Splurge on sensual accessories for your own pleasure such as bath oils, scented creams, lingerie meant to arouse *you*—not them.

Some people just need the thought to remember they liked sex to light the fire. Some people need to be touched to be reminded they like sex, like two inert sticks rubbed together creating friction and heat that set the blaze. Practice, practice, practice. Most people take ten to fifteen minutes to climax. Get in touch with yourself, literally. If your partner is not in the mood for sex, masturbate where your partner can watch—if that is okay with you and your partner. Consider what it is like when you touch yourself, even if it is just putting lotion on your body or scrubbing down in a shower. Are you enjoying the experience or detaching as you "get the job done"? When you touch yourself sexually, what do you experience? When your partner touches you in a nonsexual way, what do you experience? What do you experience when your partner touches you sexually? Consider what turns you on and what turns you off. Become more aware of how you experience physical pleasure.

Often the person you were in your marriage pre-discovery was most likely not your best engaging, exciting, responsive, and sexual self. If you were involved with the affair, you most likely were not the radiant self you were with the affair partner than you are with your spouse. Your spouse was not getting your best energy. Try to bring that creativity now. Your healing partner may be slow to risk getting too close to you or they may feel as though they are competing with the affair partner. Use communication to bridge gaps with emotional safety, then take reasonable risks to connect physically. Your healing partner should be seeking and expecting fulfillment in this relationship as well as you. Holding back an openness to pleasure will only leave both of you unsatisfied.

Sexual Esteem Exercises

Sexual esteem exercises help you experience and explore your sexuality in an empowering, non-shaming way. **Masturbation** is an exercise that helps you understand your body and what works for you. Masturbation often drops off after we are married. Some people feel they should not take self-pleasure if they have a partner. If this is the case, consider mutual masturbation, which may be exciting.

Indirect requests are nonverbal cues or guidance as to what brings you pleasure. Practicing with indirect requests can build your sexual confidence and satisfaction. What worked before may no longer excite you. Bodies change. Routine becomes boring. Be bold, move your body or your partner's to positions you might prefer. Respond enthusiastically if it hits the spot.

Direct requests are verbal requests. Asking for a promotion at work is challenging but raises your self-esteem. You will raise your sexual self-esteem if you ask for what you want. You may not want to make direct requests for fear of rejection, looking silly, or being judged. Most lovers shrink at criticism but are happy for direction to please you better. A sentence is often heard as a criticism, whereas a word is heard as direction. Use one-word directions in the moment, such as *left*, *up*, *harder*, or *down*. After an affair, a repairing partner might not make a request for fear of triggering affair PTS and a barrage of questions. If affair PTS is triggered, be honest and process the trigger as you have learned in the earlier phases.

Light Each Other's Fire

Requesting Pleasure

Communicating your desires to your partner can be difficult if you have not done so in the past or are overcoming an erotic injury. As you think about what you want to communicate, plan to include appreciation and affirmation of what your partner does now that pleases you sexually.

Here are a few more guidelines to help you have a safe, honest, and productive conversation to request pleasure.

The first step is to have the talk. Hope is not a method. Hoping your partner will read between the lines, catch a hint, or magically intuit your sexual needs will not work. Have a conversation. The conversation should happen at a non-threatening, relaxed time. Do not attempt to have the talk when you are arguing, distracted, or stressed. A good time to have the talk is when your partner will not feel pressured to have sex. Consider lunchtime, a walk, or a commute. Start small. You can have several talks. Let the first talk be a seed that is planted just to get the conversation started. Avoid challenging your partner's opinions or attitudes.

Keep it safe. Establish with each other that there will be no labels or harsh language such as weird, slut, or wrong. Avoid language like horny or sex-obsessed, which might shame someone's desire. Equally, do not use words like frigid, impotent, or over the hill. Be clear on your motives for more sex, a better relationship, or different sexual experiences. Sharing your sexual desires can be very vulnerable. Be mindful and go slow. Just because you have let your desires be known does not mean your partner must satisfy, but sexual honesty will help your partner understand and respond.

Sharing your sexual desires with your partner should be a reliably safe experience. Be respectful, open, and vulnerable. Avoid idealizing or comparing your partner to others. Make a list of strengths. Seek esteem and affirmation beyond sex. Affirm your partner sexually and non-sexually. Discuss life stressors that are affecting your expression of desire. Examine cultural myths, religious influences, and social norms influencing your approach to sex. Evaluate the source and current state of your beliefs about masturbation, positions, oral, kink, and sex as you age.

Consider the desire gap. The high-desire spouse should focus on expressing what sex means to them and how they feel. The low-desire spouse should be focusing on taking responsibility for their own fire of desire. (This does not mean either partner should do things they do not want to, but if they are willing to stoke the embers, consider how this might be done.)

Go slow. Support your partner's insecurities. Avoid demands and pressures. Be honest and sure to include what you really like sexually. Get comfortable in communicating directly about which parts of you are most responsive. Explain how you like to be touched. Become aware of your reaction to communicating your needs and to your partner's responses to this communication. Explore with each other what is happening. Practice with a small touch. For example, take your partner's hand and begin to massage the palm, fingers, and up the arm. Ask, "Do you like this?" Let your partner respond, yes, no, or do it differently. Invite direction. Discuss with each other what it is like to hear yes, no, or some other direction. Learn to reach for information and deal with the pivots when things don't go as planned. You might also try gazing at each other for sixty seconds. What was it like to be that intimate? What did you experience? Were you able to be present or did you detach from the moment?

Be sexually honest. As you become more comfortable with your own sexuality, practice being comfortable sharing that with your partner. Sexual fantasies may include situations, objects, clothing, dialogues, and/or strangers. Some fantasies may remain just that, fantasies, which are imaginings that inspire desire but are not ones you choose to act upon. Some fantasies may be brought to life. Transforming sexuality in your marriage using mutually agreed-upon fantasies can make things feel exciting, titillating, and a little scary or uncomfortable, without triggering craving or compulsive behavior.

Set goals. Take small, reasonable, and achievable steps toward releasing any obstacles to desire. Be open to change. You may not want to start with a new position, video, or toy, but may want to change routine. Start easy like trying a new restaurant, new clothing, or exploring a new hobby or location together. Celebrate your wins. Sex should be an oasis, a source of energy, and a sacred experience between you and your partner.

Take the time to design the sex life you want. A regular erotic connection can help transform your marriage. Your bodies will begin to call out for each other, even though your minds remain distracted and busy. An erotic connection can be snuggling while watching a sexy R-rated movie, playing cards naked, or just snuggling skin to skin. Each of these non-intercourse examples builds intimacy, trust, and anticipation.

As time progresses, evaluate how far you have come, what is working, and what is not. You may set stretch goals, which might include intercourse for the first time working to be 100 percent emotionally present and turned on. You might agree upon something more adventurous, exciting, or new, such as a new position, technique, location, or toy.

Be Playful

Imagination and sexual tension heighten attraction. Esther Perel, a Belgian-American marriage and family therapist known for her work on human relationships, points to the heightened desire of an affair which is intensified by **distance**, **imagination**, and **creativity**. An affair partner is not always around. Imagination fills the empty space. Energy is devoted to creating an experience different from the reliable one already secured. (This does not mean the reliable one is not wanted, valued, or appreciated, but the desire has turned toward something new.) Desire is not all about touching. Invest time and energy into erotic date nights that capitalize on the tension of anticipation, imagination, and sexual energy. Remember erotic date nights do not always involve sex. They involve sexuality and desire, but not necessarily a climax.

A great way to rekindle your relationship is to bring back flirtation. Consciously flirt, even and especially with no demand for sex. Make eye contact. Likely it has been a while since you last looked into your partner's eyes with some smolder. The smolder need not be hot and intense or deep and romantic. Try kindness, laughter, appreciation, or just an open look with erotic availability.

Use body language to seduce, posture, or suggest. Don't sit across from each other at the table or on the sofa with your arms crossed.

Practice light, pithy, and/or sexual banter. Play with a gentle suggestive tone, praise your mate's physical appearance, or tease (but not critically or sarcastically). Remember, a hint or suggestion can be much more imaginative and sexier than a dirty joke or crude comment. Inuendo or suggestion is like a delicious secret only you two know. Make physical contact with each other throughout the day. Use it sparingly, like salt. Touch your partner's hand or their arm to emphasize a point. Run your finger down their cheek, stroke your thumb across their arm, or brush up against a leg. Play footsie under the table.

Try reviving your energy of a teenager in lust. As lusty as you are, penetration is still inappropriate for now. Try to talk each other in and out of restraint. Tell your partner you have been "revirginized" and you won't go all the way, then let the temptation begin. Enjoy heavy petting, then resist. Go around the bases, starting first with a kiss, second feeling the breasts, and third fondling the genitals. Decide somewhere along the way you have gone too far and backtrack a base or two.

Play a game of dry humping or outercourse (pants off, underwear on, but no penetration). Rubbing may continue until she climaxes. If she then masturbates him to orgasm or allows him to come on her stomach, you both win. The idea is to stoke the desire when it cannot be satiated. Be a penis and/or vagina tease when nothing can be done about it. Tell your partner what you are going to do to them. Be very specific. Tell them exactly how you are going to make them come. Then make them ask for it in very specific detail. Since you are teasing, you get to decide what you will do.

Exploring Nonmonogamy (NM)

You and your partner may decide your emotional or physical needs are not met within your current relationship. You might want to explore some form or another of consensual nonmonogamy (NM). Nelson's book, *The New Monogamy, Redefining Your Relationship After Infidelity*, is an excellent resource for people considering NM. NM is when partners open their relationship to others with *mutual informed consent*.

This brief section may or may not be for you. Many people have a knee-jerk reaction of a hard "no!" to the idea, which may conceal a hidden curiosity. When the concept of NM is introduced, many people assume you go from sleeping with one person to sleeping with any person anytime you want. This is not necessarily the case.

The idea of a new relationship configuration can be explored with definitions, limitations, and boundaries. Having an opportunity to consider other constellations of your relationship may improve the likelihood of honest commitment. If you decide to explore NM, terms and conditions of the relationship should be *carefully defined and explicitly discussed. Nothing should be left unsaid or implicitly understood.*

Several terms may be useful in your NM discussion. A **closed marriage** is traditionally understood as monogamy. A **semi-open relationship** falls on a continuum that may accept emotional but not sexual connections with others or sexual but not emotional. Porn may be acceptable or lap dances in Vegas, but not paid, in-person sexual encounters. Some couples may be okay with flirting and/or touching others, but only when they are both present. An **open marriage** allows for outside sexual relationships. These outside relationships may be defined to set comfortable boundaries. The couple may agree not to have sex with people mutually known or not with work colleagues. Sex with others may be limited to anything but penetration or must never involve fluid exchange. Things can be discussed case by case. Honesty and disclosure are foundational to a successful open marriage. It can be challenging to maintain the sense of being the primary partner when another enters the relationship. **Polyamory** involves love of more than one person. It is not a legal term like polygamy, which means being married to more than one person. Polyamory is different than an open marriage, as it involves emotional bonds. It is not based upon sex. Polyamorous people do not consider themselves swingers and have agreements among the partners honoring the emotional bonds. **Relational anarchy** establishes agreements based upon individual freedom, not expectation. Agreements can take multiple forms, are freely entered, and left with clear communication.

NM means both partners get a say on the decision regarding an extra-marital encounter. The central tenet is honesty. A NM relationship will require a strong sense of self to be able to communicate vulner-abilities, accept hard truths, and make decisions accordingly without needing approval from your partner.

Open marriages are not affair-proof. Affairs are seeded in decep-tion. Prevent accidental deception by avoiding assumptions or unclear communication. If you decide upon an open marriage, *explicitly* define your boundaries. Do you want to know if your partner has sex with another? Can you tolerate the answer? Are you strong enough to provide the honest answer? What are the needs and expectations in your relationship, and what boundaries do you draw as a couple to meet them? Can you have sex with others, but maintain emotional monogamy?

Monogamy agreements can be time limited. Would you like to have a time-limited experiment? You might open the relationship once, for a weekend per month, or for summer, then redefine. Honesty and trans-parency will be the bedrock of intimacy and trust with your spouse. *More* work will be required, not necessarily less, to open your relation-ship. Open marriages should not be used as an excuse to have outside sexual relationships and remain emotionally unattached or uncaring without open communication.

If you are considering NM, you may be concerned that the relation-ship will not survive if you change the rules. Communicate your fears and desires. Express yourself, do not demand. Be open and nonjudge-mental as your partner expresses themselves. Do not make commit-ments you do not intend to keep. Explore how you might maintain the emotional connection and sense of being the primary partner in an NM relationship. Jealousy and insecurity will arise; plan to address these feelings. A step to open the relationship in one way is not encour-agement to openness in all ways. A step that has been taken can be retraced with open communication. Always be clear and explicit; do not assume you are understood or that things are implicit.

Agreements must be upheld and can be withdrawn or renegotiated at any time. If you find an agreement is no longer working for you or is bringing unwanted consequences, it is time to clearly renegotiate. Do not punish your partner for doing what you previously agreed to but also do not accept future continuance of the behavior because it was previously agreed to. Boundaries can be renegotiated. Communicate and behave with integrity.

Key Concepts

Transformation of sexuality is the ongoing understanding, exploration, and expression of your sexuality with each other. Sexuality in your relationship is the physical expression of reliability and desirability.

- The pleasure of sex is your natural birthright.
- Explore your **sexual history** and **self-story**.
  - Your sexual history is the timeline of experiences.
  - Your self-story is the narrative (understandings) you formed around it.
    - Our narratives are shaped by our family and broader culture.
- The first step to reigniting passion is to decide what you *want* to experience.
- *Physical* and *psychological* factors contribute to sexual challenges. Address the physical first.
- **You** are responsible for lighting your own fire. Practice sexual esteem exercises which include:
  - Masturbation
  - **Indirect requests** which are nonverbal communications during intimacy
  - **Direct requests** which are clear, nonviolent communication of what you want
- Light each other's fire by making and responding to requests for pleasure.
  - Keep it safe emotionally and physically

- o Consider the desire gap and work together toward a mutually acceptable level
- o Go slow to support your partner's insecurities
- o Be sexually honest
- o Set goals
- o Keep things playful with **distance**, **imagination**, and **creativity.**
- Consider consensual nonmonogamy (NM) with *informed mutual consent* based upon clear communication of expectations and boundaries.
- **Average Duration:** Transformation of sexuality is ongoing as you gain experience and come to know more about yourself and your partner.
- **Goal:** Understand the value and importance of your sexuality as part of normal human existence and relationship.
- **Do:**
  - o Explore what you would like to experience sexually
  - o Understand your sexual history and self-story
  - o Take ownership of your own sexual spark
  - o Learn to light a fire with your partner
  - o Discuss NM if it is of interest to you or your partner (this does not mean you have to agree)
- **Don't:**
  - o Avoid exploring your sexuality
  - o Rush your learning curve or experiences
  - o Force experiences you or your partner does not want to have
  - o Shame each other for past experiences or desires
  - o Engage in NM if you do not want to
- **Actions for the healing partner:** Identify any challenges to sexual expression you would enjoy. Address those challenges medically first, then psychologically. Come to know your own body and integrate the experiences of your repairing partner. Bring your spark. Listen and be patient. Work to integrate to a mutually gratifying level of desire and expressed sexuality.

- **Actions for the repairing partner:** Consider any challenges to sexual expression with your partner. Address medical challenges first, then psychological. Listen and be patient with your partner. Identify what level of desire and sexual expression you need. Be sure to bring your own spark as you integrate your partner's wants and needs.

Chapter 23
Transformation to Antifragility

*The challenge of transformation to antifragility
is to gain confidence that your relationship
will strengthen in difficult times.*

Nassim Nicholas Taleb, PhD, risk analyst and mathematical statistician, writes about the predictability and unpredictability of bad things happening in life. Taleb looks at the mathematical probability of bad things happening to you, such as war or natural disaster. His book, *The Black Swan*, takes an in-depth look at the difficult-to-predict, out-of-the-blue, life-altering disasters that befall some people. In his follow-on book, *Antifragile*, Taleb discusses the concept of antifragility, which is a possible response to the black swan. Taleb explains that fragility breaks easily under negative experience. Antifragility is the opposite. Antifragility is not to be confused with resilience. Resilience is overcoming and bouncing back to the original state. Over time, something resilient, like a rubber band, loses its ability to spring back. *Being **antifragile** means becoming stronger than before a negative event.* Black swan or not, you have the opportunity to become antifragile in this transformative healing journey.

Attachment Survey Retake

Attachment strategies are not permanent attributes. Attachment strategies are learned in early childhood and are a way of seeking and maintaining a sense of safety. Attachment strategies can change in response to trauma and evolve as relationships become stronger. Strategies learned early on are often the default strategy under stress. The journey through the map of affair repair and marriage transformation has taught you a lot about your attachment strategies.

As individuals and as a couple, you have become aware of what strategy is being used at any given moment. You have learned new skills to support secure attachment as you repaired from the trauma. You learned to attune to your partner by staying in the window of tolerance and co-feeling experiences. You kept yourself and your partner safe and connected while authentically communicating. As you progress in your healing journey, you continue to make your relationship reliable and desirable, negotiating the gaps.

Retake the attachment survey you took in Chapter 6. Reflect upon any movement you have made as an individual and as a couple toward secure attachment. If you were previously securely attached, have you recovered that attachment? If you were not previously securely attached, how have you moved more toward secure attachment? What work yet needs to be done?

You may need more affair repair talks, more co-feeling, more data, more intimacy, or more time. One or both of you may benefit from individual therapy to help sort things out. It is okay to accept your preferred attachment strategy and your desired limit for intimacy. You and your partner may be more comfortable generally with avoidant strategies. Or it may be enough to understand one of you is more anxious than the other. Discuss as a transformed couple where you have come from, where you are, and where you want to be with your attachment and intimacy levels.

Explicit Agreements

Often when people find each other and decide to stay together, they assume they are on the same page. As time progresses, each person makes compromises for the other and falls into roles. Unless these compromises and roles are discussed, the other partner assumes there is no issue. These assumptions and roles become implicit agreements. **Implicit agreements** are not officially stated, clearly discussed, or agreed upon. They seem to be agreed upon because there is no direct challenge. **Explicit agreements** clear the air. Explicit agreements are officially stated, clearly discussed and negotiated. Transformed marriages work to make agreements as explicit as possible.

Consider the implicit understandings you had earlier in your relationship versus any explicit agreements you might like to make. Agreements might include finances, parenting, sharing chores, who makes entertainment plans, who initiates sex, where to spend holidays, and more. The implicit agreements you had before marriage transformation may or may not have served you. Some may have endured and should continue. Make as many understandings as you can explicit. Transformation involves enlightenment and change.

Laurent and Gail had a calm, but distant relationship. Gail had sat through many silent dinners thinking she was serving her relationship by not burdening Laurent with connection after a long day at work. Distance was a factor in normalcy that contributed to Laurent's decision to have an affair. He did not do the work to connect with his wife, and Gail never made it explicit she wanted it. In transformation to antifragility, the couple made their expectations and needs clear. Both wanted attention and both were expected to work for it. Each partner must make and address any requests for change. Just because a request is made does not mean it will be honored, but it must be explicitly discussed so there will be no misunderstandings. Your transformed relationship communication style no longer includes lie-inviting, passive-aggressive or conflict-avoidant lying. Be clear and honest in what you can and will do. Be respectful of your partner's choice to accept or not accept the situation. Transformed relationships do not manipulate, they collaborate.

Transformed Forgiveness

Transformed forgiveness includes forgiveness of self and other. Each partner is humbled in an affair. The pride of the healing partner is wounded and humbled by the blow of betrayal. "How could you do this to me?" asks the ego. If you are the healing partner, you did not deserve the pain but must accept it to forgive it. The pride of the repairing partner must acknowledge its guilt and humble itself enough to work toward, not demand or expect, forgiveness. "I can't take it back!" says the ego. If you are the repairing partner, it is healthy to understand and forgive yourself but to transform your relationship you will need work toward and accept your partner's forgiveness. Both partners will benefit from being humble to overcome wounded pride.

Infidelity is now part of your marital story. Transformed forgiveness may or may not come. Start simply with acceptance. You may have to choose acceptance daily or even moment to moment. Both of you feel the pain will never end. Accepting may be hard to do because it feels unfair. If you are the healing partner, you did not deserve this. If you are the repairing partner you wonder what it will take to move past this. The Buddhists advise reducing suffering by reducing resistance. When you resist reality, you lose every time. When you wish this hadn't happened and stay in the headspace that you didn't deserve this, you are stuck. It has happened and can't be undone. When you wish your partner would just move on and they can't, you are increasing your and their suffering. You can lean into the skills learned along the map of affair repair, move toward forgiveness if possible, or you can take a break. Either way, reduce suffering by reducing resistance to what is. When you can accept reality, you are able to dedicate your energy to moving forward—together or not.

Transformed forgiveness, if it comes, is a natural process that evolves with new understandings and change. The crisis intervention treatment in the early phases of the map of affair repair and marriage transformation helped keep things from getting worse and allowed for some time to take in new information. Over the course of affair repair talks and establishing trust, you gained honest insights and provided fresh experiences to shape your future. Moving forward for you is grounded in an evolution of the relationship and acknowledgment of personal growth. That's antifragile transformation.

Forgiveness takes real courage, not stupidity or blind faith. Thoughtless forgiveness can be cheap forgiveness that does not last. Forgiveness comes for those who are willing to confront their pain, accept the changes it brings, and make tough decisions. Some people prefer to stay safe by holding on to resentment and hatred. That is refusing forgiveness. Other partners may forgive without reinvesting their hearts. This is forgiveness from a safe place and a distance will remain which may be the best it will ever get.

Healing partners who choose to forgive a betrayal are not foolish but have decided to take reasonable risks based on demonstrated transformation. They aren't satisfied with being stuck with distance or in that negativity. They want to live, and they want to love. They refuse to let their future be controlled by someone else's hurtful actions or holding onto bitterness. Like Leonard, who sought MaryAnne's forgiveness, but would accept it if she could not, he was transformed in his seeking forgiveness. Leonard and others who are able to transform forgiveness accept the pain of what has happened, take bold steps to rebuild their lives, and free themselves from the trauma of the past. Transformed forgiveness is not easy and it does not happen for everyone. That is ok.

The Transformed Forgiveness Story

Antoni began repairing the hole he had punched in the wall three years ago. He had made the hole late at night, alone in the dark kitchen, just weeks after the discovery of Clair's affair. He let the destruction sit there in plain sight as a symbol of the wreckage, emptiness, and rage he then felt.

Now, as he repaired the wall, it meant something to see the plaster covering up the hole and to observe the ridges in the repair as he let it harden. It meant even more to smooth the repair over and apply paint. More than one coat was necessary.

Antoni felt good to see the hole disappear. He had kept his promise to himself not to repair the hole until the pain went away. It took three years. He thought it never would. Antoni and Clair transformed their relationship. You can still see the patch if you look at it in just the right light from the right angle. He likes it that way.

Other Relationships that Transform

As your marriage transforms, so will your relationships with your kids, extended family, friends, and community. Others may think differently of you, and you may think differently of them. Some will be inspired by who you two have become. Everyone's thoughts and behaviors will change over the course of the map of affair repair and marriage transformation as you as a couple move through the challenges. Early on, family members may have been allied openly or quietly. Friends may have tried to be neutral or take the path of least resistance, avoiding conflict not wanting to get overly involved. Some people you care about may have disappointed you.

If you have children, hopefully you were able to keep them out of things. Children are self-focused, needing peace and normalcy. Any triangulation of children against the partner who had the affair will ultimately be seen as manipulative. It is true the affair will be seen as a breach of trust and a threat to the safety of the family, which will make children naturally upset with the parent who cheated, but as things level out, any emotional manipulation will be understood as another type of parental failure. There is a saying about children, "They grow and then they know." As your children mature, they will have a more informed perspective on what your family went through. They will know intuitively, if not directly, the facts of what happened. Avoid triangulation or any involvement of children. As your marriage transforms, you can assure the children their lives are secure and you are okay. Much of the drama involves the child trying to balance their own safety in a family unit, the wounding of one parent and the fear the other will do it again. Assure the children you are transformed.

Healing and repairing partners may experience discomfort being around friends and family who know what you have been through. One or both partners may worry about judgment, exposure, second-guessing, invasive questions, or just being around another who knows your secret wounding or failing. Be supportive of each other as people are reintroduced to your inner circle. You may be very comfortable having your family or friends over for dinner again, but your partner may be experiencing some uneasiness. Have a healthy affair repair talk to address any fears or concerns. (Yes, this is repairing though you are in the marriage transformation phase. Part of marriage transformation is knowing when to use which skills. Phases can overlap.) Be patient and supportive but also strategize how the friend or family member might be welcomed. It may be that the reliability of patience and support is enough co-feeling and solidarity to make it easier for your partner to move forward.

Most friends will try to be supportive and ready to forgive everything in order to get back to happiness. Some friends may pull back, unable to forgive. Some friends will pull away and you will have to mourn their loss. You may need to reset boundaries on friends that were too involved in the map of affair repair and marriage transformation. This may be difficult as those friends may feel betrayed as they held your hand in your darkest hour. Those friends may have been dedicated to the idea of you leaving the relationship. Spend time with those friends who gave you support, truly care, and are now confused. Take time to explain your actions and decisions, but not too long. You do not owe these friends all the details, but thanking them and sharing with them your experience along the map of affair repair may help transform the relationship between you and them as well as your partner. Overall, healthy friends care but respect boundaries and are more concerned with their own lives than controlling yours. True friends will cheer when healthy love wins.

Extended family relationships may be the most difficult or easiest to transform. Family is loyal. Family loyalty usually begins and ends with the safety and happiness of the blood relative. If the blood relative rededicates to the relationship, the family will also. Some family members will welcome the repairing partner back but never forget. A distance may be felt. Sometimes the passage of time will take this away as the family regains trust and the relationship transforms.

Remember, your primary relationship is with your partner, not with the extended family. You and your partner should be a unified front in presenting yourself as a transformed couple. Strive for working, sustainable relationships with family members. If you had a very close relationship with your partner's family, you may venture a repair conversation. Repairing with your partner's family is not necessary; it is your option.

Before having the conversation, discuss it with your partner. If you agree, decide if the conversation should be held with both of you present or not. In the conversation, tell the family member how you feel and what you want. For example, if you are the repairing partner, you might say, "I know I hurt your daughter and therefore you and the family by my actions. I want you to know I regret the hurt I caused and hope we will be able to repair our relationship, just as she and I are doing. I realize that may take some time." Or if you are the healing partner, you might say, "I know you have allegiance to your daughter, and there may be some awkwardness for us, but I want you to know I hope we will be able to regain closeness in our relationship, just as she and I are doing. I love her and want our family, including you, to be close again."

Do not expect miracles! Some people will respond warmly and quickly to this communication; others will be hesitant or distant for their own reasons. This conversation is your opportunity to clear the air, not control it. Stay in the window of tolerance and work with the extended family members with whom you want to reconnect. Remember, as you did in the affair repair phase, work together; do not rush ahead of where the other person is.

In most cases, children, extended families, friends, and communities do not excommunicate the person who had the affair. Most people move on, some realign their allegiance, and a few will distance themselves from the problem. You may have lost your careers and/or community due to the affair. Career loss must be overcome practically and with time. You may have to get a new job or move to a new town if you are in a particularly unforgiving community. However, as is proven by nearly every political picadillo of the past, people's attention spans are short and they forget. Sometimes just sticking it out and demonstrating your healthy transformation will pull you through. Focus on the relationships that are close to you. Repair where or when you can. Regardless of how your relationships transform, your primary relationship is most important. If you are both happy and healthy, others will come along.

Key Concepts

Transformation to antifragility is complete when you know you have the relationship skills not only to overcome but *grow* from any challenge.

- **Antifragile** means problems *strengthen* your relationship.
- Reassess your attachment style. Compare how it was in normalcy to the current phase of marriage transformation. How did it evolve?

- **Implicit agreements** are understood but not clearly stated and can set a couple up for resentment and failure due to assumption.
- **Explicit agreements** are clearly stated and empower the couple to troubleshoot before problems occur.
- **Transformed forgiveness** includes self and your partner. Forgiveness, if it comes, deepens with new understandings and experiences. As your relationship continues to grow, trust and perspective may change, enabling more forgiveness.
- **Other relationships transform**, including those with your children, friends, family, and community. Most will follow your lead and celebrate your growth. Some will need tending; others will need to be left behind.
- **Average Duration:** Marriage transformation of antifragility is ongoing as you gain experience and come to know more about yourself and your partner. Continue to hone your skills in transforming challenges. With each transformation, you will become increasingly antifragile.
- **Goal:** Lean into challenges with confidence.
- **Do:**
  - Know you and your partner have done hard work
    - You can be antifragile
    - Your relationship can be antifragile
  - Continue to apply all skills learned to date
  - Make as many agreements as possible explicit
  - Welcome greater levels of forgiveness thanks to your deepening transformation to antifragility
  - Expect other relationships to transform
- **Don't:**
  - Revert to lesser ways of relating
  - Continue with implicit understandings
  - Stop growing
- **Actions for the healing partner:** Embrace your new transformation. You are antifragile, independent of the relationship, and because of that, you can build an antifragile relationship with

another. The past has occurred; you have transformed. The future is your friend now that you know you can not only handle it but make it better.

- **Actions for the repairing partner:** Embrace your new transformation. You are antifragile, independent of the relationship, and because of that can build an antifragile relationship with another. Regardless of complete forgiveness, a desire gap, or other challenge, you know you can overcome to create a relationship that is better, truer, and more satisfying.

Chapter 24
Transcendent Transformation

Transcendent transformation has happened when your relationship has become reliable, desirable, and antifragile.

Even a transformed marriage will have to transcend. To transcend means to rise above the unchangeable reality. You will have problems going forward. Some will be related to the affair. Things can be good between you; you are joking and happy, intimacy is happening, your partner has truly apologized, and both have recommitted. Then suddenly, something happens in the brain, and you are triggered. The beautiful moment you were just enjoying is ruined. Perhaps it is a random thought or comment. Or it could be that the anniversary of discovery is approaching. You might find yourself at the place where the affair took place or encounter people who knew about the affair. Sometimes just the turning color of leaves not only announces the fall season but memories of the difficult time in your marriage. You may want to keep the uncomfortable feelings to yourself, not wanting to ruin the moment, and that may be best. But you do not have to go alone. You can transcend together.

It is okay to share your pain in a productive way. You now have the skills. Your partner can transcend with you. If you decide, share the melancholic mix of happiness and sadness. Your goal is not to bring sadness, anger, or even apology. Your goal is to transcend the pain that is resurfacing from an old wound, with the help of your partner. Now you know how to address the pain, so the healing will happen faster. You have many communication tools in your toolbox. You are **transcendent transformed partners.** You know your marriage has transformed when it is reliable, desirable, antifragile, and capable of transcendence.

Through the map of affair repair and marriage transformation, you have become aware of what is happening within you and/or your partner. You can choose the appropriate response with the best tool. Over time you will master the process, such that you may hardly need it for long. Compathy, or co-feeling—as described in the establishing trust phase, where one partner feels in their own body the pain of their partner—always has the potential for deeper connection and healing. In the transcendent transformed marriage, this co-feeling is mastered and accessed appropriately, not abused or manipulated. It is a mutual, free-will gift offered not only in moments of affair PTS, but in any pain, loneliness, need, or hurt for either partner. Compathy can also be a deeper experience of joy.

Transcendent transformed marriages have an expanded view of self. Though you maintain personal boundaries while having a connection, you can experience a sense of feeling the shared self. You can feel sad and trust your partner to be honest as an individual and present in the shared self. You can tolerate it if your partner's feelings do not match but accept the shared space of mutual respect and caring.

Transcendent transformed marriages have an element of stoicism. Some things may not change, but your reaction to them can. Your reaction is capable and virtuous. That does not mean accommodating or sucking it up. You can be honest and virtuous in leaving a relationship if you cannot inspire the change you need. Transcendent transformed marriages are not their past. People are not their trauma. Trauma is something that has happened to people. People can transform and transcend trauma.

The Transcendent Transformed Marriage Story

MaryAnne and Leonard were planning their future together after three years of separation. A relationship for Leonard that did not last and a dating experience for MaryAnne that tapped something new in her helped them each discover more of what they really wanted. At this time of their lives, they each were financially secure, independent, and complete within themselves. There was no need, only want had brought them back together.

The couple had done their work on the map of affair repair and marriage transformation. The couple was open and transparent with each other, willing to have difficult conversations, knowing a lack of authenticity would hurt them in the long run.

Leonard would like to sell his home and move in with MaryAnne. His thought was to begin living life together as soon as possible since they had recommitted to being together forever. MaryAnne affirmed she was committed to forever but would like to go slowly. MaryAnne welcomed Leonard when he came to stay. She pointed out her home did not have the living space that would better accommodate the habits of two people. MaryAnne had gotten used to peace and quiet.

MaryAnne had found the voice she muffled in normalcy. She was strong enough to say she was unwilling to lose the freedom she had discovered during their separation but was not yet practiced at claiming it and feeling secure in relationship with him.

Though Leonard would like to get on with forever and find their forever home, he suggested they put their house hunting on hold, so as not to pressure MaryAnne. Leonard realized his pushing didn't help and was transformed for the long run. He was never giving up on winning MaryAnne back.

MaryAnne was enjoying the process of house hunting, carefully evaluating each option for their future. She was moving things forward, and the slow, careful process gave her time to get used to the permanence of the idea. She began to trust their transformed marriage at a safe pace and was patient so that their future home really would be their dream home.

Leonard jumped to action. MaryAnne planned. Both were committed. Their transformation was an exercise in negotiating boundaries, respecting each other's needs, and affirming love for one another. MaryAnne was practicing communicating clearly and balancing Leonard's big energy. She appreciated his newly demonstrated patient love. Leonard was learning to remain curious and open to MaryAnne versus skipping to the end goal. From the way she smiled at him, with sparkling bright eyes I had not seen before, I could see Leonard's patient sacrifice would pay off.

Couples embark on the map of affair repair and marriage transformation for many reasons. The trauma of discovery sends people rushing for normalcy whether it is for the sake of the kids or for themselves. Over the course of the healing journey, partners discover more about themselves and each other. No two journeys are alike. MaryAnne and Leonard came back together post-divorce. **I have found that the most potent ingredient for reviving a marriage has been the love of one or both partners.** Often, it is the undying love of one partner that bridges the couple through the horrifying gap. The love gives them the strength to go on, to fight, to endure the painful process, and it is the love that is resurrected in the partnership, though it may have been dead and missing from its tomb. Leonard had it right; he was going to pursue until MaryAnne said it was over. Fortunately, MaryAnne gave her heart's desire a well-protected, thoughtful shot at what it really wanted. Each transformed so that their relationship was now reliable, desirable, and antifragile.

The Golden Repair

There is a Japanese art known as Kintsukuroi, which means "golden repair." Kintsukuroi is the craft of repairing broken pottery with lacquer mixed with powdered gold, silver, or platinum. Instead of repairing the pottery so that the crack becomes invisible, a bit of gold is added to the glue so that the cracks may be seen as fine golden lines. Things repaired in this way are far more treasured than unbroken ones. For some couples, nothing but an affair could have broken them. Now, along the map of affair repair and marriage transformation, those cracks have been repaired with love's gold. Your marriage is more treasured than it ever was before.

When I met Ellie and Aaron, Ellie was caught in limerence, thinking only of leaving. Nonetheless, we embarked on the journey on the map of affair repair and marriage transformation. There were dark, scary times of no hope other than knowing what to do, as outlined here in this book. Like a broken leg, hidden in a cast, the healing process was nearly invisible. The couple moved from pain and ambivalence to trust and hope. Ellie was tired of the pain of being ignored she experienced in normalcy. She had stepped out of the marriage and wasn't sure she wanted to come back. Aaron resisted his natural anger and attack response. He focused only on the changes necessary to encourage Ellie to try again for the thousandth time. He proved to her there was a reason to trust. He had changed, and because of that, she gave him hope that his changes would make the difference. Ellie and Aaron transformed and transcended. Together they made their relationship reliable and desirable. The friendship and intimacy that first brought them together had grown even deeper. They still take bubble baths together to this day.

About the Author

Amanda Deverich, LMFT, is an author, presenter, therapist supervisor and trainer, practice owner, and relationship repair expert. For more than a decade she has been helping couples overcome an affair and transform their marriages.

Amanda became interested in helping couples work through an affair when she witnessed a miracle. One partner had given up on the marriage while another was clinging in pain. Amanda did not know what would happen, but she knew what to do—and the outcome was her inspiration.

This is Amanda's guidebook of hard-won lessons so you don't have to face this crisis in the dark.

A widow who raised two daughters on her own, Amanda brings both professional wisdom and lived resilience to her work. She is also a TEDx speaker and author of *Motivate and Move On*.

You can learn more about Amanda at www.AffairRepair.com.

www.ingramcontent.com/pod-product-compliance
Lightning Source LLC
Chambersburg PA
CBHW071630140626
46555CB00022B/2033